Designs
on Truth

Gregory G. Colomb

Designs on Truth
The Poetics *of* the Augustan Mock-Epic

The Pennsylvania State University Press
University Park, Pennsylvania

Quotations from the *Twickenham Edition of the Poems of Alexander Pope* are by permission of Methuen & Co.

Library of Congress Cataloging-in-Publication Data

Colomb, Gregory G.
    Designs on truth : the poetics of the Augustan mock-epic / Gregory G. Colomb.
        p.   cm.
    Includes bibliographical references and index.
    ISBN 0-271-00805-9 (alk. paper)
    1. English poetry—18th century—History and criticism. 2. Mock-heroic literature—History and criticism. 3. Epic poetry, English— History and criticism. 4. English poetry—Roman influences. 5. Rhetoric—1500–1800. 6. Poetics. I. Title.
PR559.M63C6   1992
821'.0320905—dc20
                                                                                               91–19151
                                                                                                               CIP

Copyright © 1992 The Pennsylvania State University
All rights reserved
Printed in the United States of America

It is the policy of the Pennsylvania State University Press to use acid-free paper for the first printing of all clothbound books. Publications on uncoated stock satisfy the minimum requirements of American National Standard for Information Sciences—Permanence of Paper for Printed Library Materials, ANSI Z39.48–1984.

For Sandra

Contents

List of Abbreviations	ix
Preface	xi
Acknowledgments	xxi
A Note on the Text of *The Dispensary*	xxiii
1 Introduction: Moralizing the Song	1

Part I: Figures of the City

Prologue	33
2 Naming Names	35
3 "*Dullness* by Its Proper Name"	59
4 Urban Gravitation	79
5 Ranging Afield	95

Part II: The Figure in the Portrait

Prologue	119
6 From Caricature to Portraiture	129
7 "Dishonourable Confederacies"	145
8 A Taxonomy of Dunces	163
9 A Succession of Monarchs	183
Epilogue	207
Bibliography	209
Index	219

List of Abbreviations

Corr.   Pope, Alexander. 1956. *The Correspondence of Alexander Pope.* 5 vols. George Sherburn, ed. Oxford: The Clarendon Press.

DNB   *Dictionary of National Biography.* 1885–1900. 63 vols. Leslie Stephen and Sidney Lee, eds. London.

E-C   Pope, Alexander. 1882. *The Works of Alexander Pope.* Whitwell Elwin and William John Courthope, eds. London.

Essay   Locke, John. 1706. *An Essay Concerning Humane Understanding, In Four Books, The Fifth Edition, with Large Additions.* Rpt. 1972. John W. Yolton, ed. New York: Dutton.

HO   Ellis, Frank H. 1963. "Garth's Harveian Oration." *Journal of the History of Medicine* 18:8–19.

POAS   *Poems on Affairs of State: Augustan Satirical Verse, 1660–1714.* 1963–75. 7 vols. George deF. Lord, gen. ed. New Haven: Yale University Press.

TE   *The Twickenham Edition of the Poems of Alexander Pope.* London and New Haven: Methuen and Yale University Press. Volume I: *Pastoral Poetry and An Essay on Criticism.* 1961. E. Audra and Aubrey Williams, eds. Volume II: *The Rape of the Lock and Other Poems.* 1940. Geoffrey Tillotson, ed. Volume IIIi: *An Essay on Man.* 1950. Maynard Mack, ed. Volume IIIii: *Epistles to Several Persons (Moral Essays).* 1951. F. W. Bateson, ed. Volume IV: *Imitations of Horace with an Epistle to Dr. Arbuthnot and The Epilogue to the Satires.* 2d ed. 1953. John Butt, ed. Volume V: *The Dunciad.* 1943. James Sutherland, ed. Volume VI: *Minor Poems.* 1964. Norman Ault and John Butt, eds. Volume VII–VIII: *The Iliad of Homer.* 1967. Maynard Mack, ed. Volume IX–X: *The Odyssey of Homer.* 1967. Maynard Mack, ed.

Preface

Pope's workmanship is here [in The Dunciad*] even more than usually minute... and if we would do him full justice, we must give to understanding his work something of the pains which he spent on producing it.*
—William John Courthope

In the last year of the seventeenth century an unpublished physician named Samuel Garth created a poetic form that, refined by the most accomplished poetic craftsman of the eighteenth century, became the paradigmatic genre of high Augustan poetry. This book tells the story of that genre. It is not a story of influence, although one strand follows the many, largely unexplored ties between Garth and his young friend Alexander Pope. Nor is it a genetic story, although it will trace the well-known role of Dryden, Boileau, and Tassoni as models for the mock-epic, as well as the equally important but unrecognized role of less canonical political poetry of the Restoration. This is a study of the poetics of the Augustan mock-epic. These poems—Pope's several *Dunciad*s, *The Rape of the Lock,* Garth's *Dispensary,* Dryden's *MacFlecknoe,* and such peripheral works as Swift's *Battle of the Books*—are usually grouped with the widely assorted varieties of mock-heroics, especially mock-heroic satire. In fact, they constitute a well-defined genre, with a coherent poetics, only the smallest part of which is manifested in the mock-heroic style by which the genre is usually defined. That poetics gives the genre a substantial relation to epic, but this is above all a genre made for and by early modern England.

This story is not a simple one, for it is first and foremost a story of details, of what Augustans called "particulars." It demands a level and a kind of historical attention—the "pains" Courthope speaks of—that few readers have been willing to give. Not that particulars tell the whole story of the mock-epic. The standard account of the mock-epic has emphasized its ties to the heroic tradition as perpetuated through Christian humanism. That account explains the mock-epic in terms of a balance between, on the one hand, the traditional form of the epic, with its well-regulated ideals, its enduring values, and its clear-cut class structure, and, on the other hand, the messy, undifferentiated mass of particulars that defines modern urban life and that forces the poet into such "low" forms. Now told with emphasis on the traditional, intertextual aspects we discuss so well, this over-simple story has its attractions. But as I will show, that and all the stories about these poems are motivated by their undeniable, difficult, massive particularity.

Not the first to raise the issue of particulars in the mock-epic, I am concerned equally with the historical criticism made necessary by those particulars and with the poetics that must underlie it. What historical scholarship the mock-epic has enjoyed has too little shaped our understanding of the *poetics* of the works whose background it studies. The traditional historicism of eighteenth-century studies is, however, not alone in its neglect of poetics. It stands on a par with the "new" historicism whose influence in eighteenth-century studies has been chiefly felt in the study of the novel. While the new historicists do not relegate particulars to the background, neither do they give them much detailed analysis, preferring to work with larger, more abstract thematic patterns. New historicism or old, we lack a historical, materialist poetics to rival the ahistorical, trope-centered poetics of the new criticism and its structuralist and semiotic siblings.

In this study I conjoin historical scholarship to poetic theory. Through a semiotic analysis of the genre, I formulate a poetics to replace the modernist poetics that has been the norm in most studies of Augustan poetry. Focusing chiefly on forms of representation, I return historical particulars to the central role the poets had always given them, and look to understand *how* they are made poetic. This historical and materialist poetics redefines the notion of particulars, treating *poetic* particulars (words, images, figures) as parts of an intricate web connecting the social facts of persons and places with the "prosaic" particulars of history. Doing so, it shows how the poems themselves subvert any easy distinction between history and poetry. This often philosophical genre grounds itself in a reconsideration of reference (fact) and value in representation, especially in the judgments embodied and evoked by the poems' representations. It presents an important opportunity to those who seek a truly historical poetics, for such a materialist poetics was the special project of the mock-epic and is a defining feature of works we think of as prototypically Augustan.

Preface

My interest in the mock-epic began as a fascination with *The Dunciad*. It became a study of the genre when I learned to understand *The Dispensary* and recognized its formative role. Contrary to the standard story, which takes *The Rape of the Lock* as the generic model and *The Dunciad* as a divergent, mutant form, the generic model was in fact established by *The Dispensary*, was diverged from (though only slightly) by *The Rape of the Lock*, and was then confirmed by each succeeding *Dunciad*. In addition to this dissatisfaction with the standard accounts were two others. The first concerns the polemics in the poems. In thinking and writing about *The Dunciad*, I found myself moved to utter sentences that were not my own, sentences grounded in beliefs I do not hold and do not much like. Puzzling about this, I noticed how many other readers had been moved to utter Pope's and Garth's pieties, even when they were obviously self-serving propaganda. The second, related dissatisfaction concerns the role of pieties in accounts of the poetics of the mock-epic. I found that those critics whose works had most taught me to read *The Dunciad* looked past the particulars that increasingly seemed to me the poem's chief interest. Though it sounds too much like sloganeering, I might now say that the real figures about and for whom the poem was written had been pushed off center stage to be replaced by metaphors and other honorific terms of modernist criticism.[1] In the last few years, something like this complaint has begun to appear in the best studies of Pope.[2] Two studies take the complaint as a starting point, David Morris (1984) using it to define Pope's style, and Laura Brown (1985) turning the complaint into a litany.[3]

When I began this study (more than ten years ago, before I became involved in a major project in text linguistics and writing pedagogy), the language for talking about the myriad details in these poems was overcharged with modernist aesthetics—with the language of transformation and metaphor, of myth and mythic "lands of larger values," of simple and absolute distinctions between history and poetry, all legacies

---

1. See R. Cohen (1977, 101–4).

2. As early as 1976, Donald Siebert ridiculed the "School of Deep Intent," but reached the surprising conclusion that *The Dunciad* is "more good fun than anything else." A more convincing account of the comic element is found in Jones (1968); Morris shows how that comic element is contained and controlled by the poem's larger purposes (276–78).

3. Brown's list, though selective, approaches the present: "Readers of Pope's work must prove that the poetry is imagistically rich [Spacks, 1971], that it is intellectually coherent [White, 1970], that it represents a complex subjectivity [Griffin, 1978], that it is humane [Edwards, 1963], visionary [W. Jackson, 1983] and passionate [Shankman, 1983]" (2).

of the poetics of the middle of this century.[4] The influence of midcentury poetics was heightened by the continuing authority of the "high humanist" reading, a reading intended chiefly to rehabilitate Augustan poetry after its abuse at the hands of the Victorians.[5] In the course of "restor[ing] Dryden and Pope as classics of poetry *for Matthew Arnold*" (R. Cohen, 1977, 104), the high humanist reading prosecuted a historical criticism that pushed historical particulars into the background and promoted "literary" and "poetic" particulars to the position of foreground or "figure." Its methods were principally tropological, sublimating the cruel and particular pleasures of the mock-epic's literary pillory into emblems and metaphors of eternal truth.

That high humanist reading and its mid-century poetics has withstood significant revisions, the challenge of new formalisms, and even the influence of the new historicism. As I came to know and admire such works as Pat Rogers's *Grub Street* (1972) and Howard Erskine-Hill's *Social Milieu of Alexander Pope* (1975), works that finally put the poems' figures on center stage, it was clear that even here was the influence of a poetics that distrusted particulars. Although figures and their haunts held center stage in these studies, the studies themselves avoided poetics and were cast deep into categories—history and biography, "ecology" and "milieu"—that mid-century poetics had banished to the background.

Now that we have discovered a "new" eighteenth century, history promises to be less a matter of background (Nussbaum and Brown, 1987). Even so, there are few direct challenges to the poetics of the midcentury, as though poetics were inherently doomed to arrive at the midcentury's ahistorical results. There are even more than a few who continue to endorse it. For example, in his 1978 study of Pope (subtitled *The Poet in the Poems*), Dustin Griffin nods to Rogers for "provid[ing] rich documentation about the *reality* of Grub Street" and then blames him for "fail[ing] to give enough emphasis to Pope's transforming imagination" (264n). David Morris shows admirable impatience with such language in his 1984 study *Alexander Pope: The Genius of*

---

4. Though much influenced by the "new criticism," eighteenth-century studies was too interested in such "background" matters as history and biography. By laying earlier errors at the door of new criticism (as in Griffin, xiv), we miss the more lasting effect of the general mid-century poetic.

5. "We deny that Pope was, in Arnold's sense, the high priest of an age of prose and reason.... [Pope] serves as a useful corrective to a too narrow idea of poetry" (Edwards, 1971, 303–4). Also see Clifford (1965) and Miller (1972).

Sense, but at times defers to mid-century poetics and its transformations—in a work also cast as a species of biography. Even Leopold Damrosch's often superb 1987 study, which recognizes that "these poems stubbornly insist on the world from which they grew" (215), defers to mid-century poetics in centering on *The Imaginative World of Alexander Pope*. I do not mean to question such studies: I only note that, with respect to poetics, the legacy of the success of mid-century poetics has been chiefly avoidance and silence.[6]

My study presents a new, historical poetics of the Augustan mock-epic. I follow three primary lines of argument. First, I characterize the genre of mock-heroic poems in the line running from *MacFlecknoe* to *The Dunciad*, locating that genre with respect to the broader line of the mock-heroic and with respect to other forms of Augustan satire. Because the mock-epic presented the standards it sought to preserve and enforce in stories of tradition and cultural inheritance, the poems are dominated by legacies of all sorts, chiefly the legacy memorialized in the epic. And yet no high Augustan poems are so modern—so tied to contemporary events, so full of the things of modernity, so technically innovative, so self-consciously novel. This duality has usually been described in terms of some unspecified balance between ideal and real, traditional and modern, view and object of view. My argument will show how "balance" is the wrong image for the myriad of compromises, translations, misreadings, and other adjustments that compose the mock-epic's confrontation between the epic and the modern. The mock-epic poet does deploy a system of values that he depicts as deriving from the classical past, but no mock-epic adopts traditional values wholesale,[7] and every mock-epic puts them in service of propaganda. They are supported in the poems less by tradition than by some of the more innovative aspects of the genre's poetics. The question is not how the mock-epic poet can balance the ancient ideal and modern reality, but how he can forge a version of the modern mind and culture whose allegiance to the ancient does not belie itself as so much self-indulgent or self-interested nostalgia.

In the second and most sustained line of argument I describe the poetics of the Augustan mock-epic, especially the role of particulars. I begin the argument with the semiotic pairing that eighteenth-century

---

6. For a productive kind of avoidance, see Fabricant (1982), Pollak (1985), and Brown.

7. For the complexity of eighteenth-century attitudes toward the classical inheritance, see Weinbrot (1978). Although Weinbrot has led some to abandon the term *Augustan*, I use it with all appropriate caveats.

critics inherited from the Renaissance, the correlation between the form of representation (the "Poetical relation")[8] and its effects on readers (the moral instruction), and examine both in terms of a larger cultural semiotic that encompasses many discourses and social practices. The poetical relation of the mock-epic is chiefly description, depiction. It centers on a form of depiction—partly caricature, partly the taxonomy of natural philosophy—that shapes all the poem's major designs, including even its narrative form. The effects that mock-epic aims for, which only the most interested account could think of as moral instruction, have two related poles. One is personal and particular. The mock-epic's personal satire punishes its victims, ostensibly to make them examples to deter others but actually to make them outcasts in the polite societies the poets seek to reform. The other pole is particular, but also general. Mock-epic gives a new twist to the old analogy between medicine and satire, "curing" individual victims but also diagnosing the social mechanism of the disease. It identifies and isolates its individual persons in terms of a wealth of particulars arrayed in a diagnostic network of metonymic (and causal) relations. These figures are represented as a point of focus in a field of view, a configuration that mimics an emergent Newtonian cosmology, where a universe of causal mechanism is ordered by a first cause that gives it "design," at once intention and structure.[9] (Duncery embraces the world of mechanism but is blind to its design; modern criticism embraces that world's design but has been blind to its mechanism.) In a sentence, the mock-epic is a portrait gallery, placing its victims on a poetic pillory that, as it punishes, displays the poet's diagnosis of their disruptions of the social order.

The pillory is, of course, an instrument of meaning. The mock-epic's poetic pillory attempts to take control over the good sense—and so the behavior—of the citizenry by taking control of its language. Mock-epic is fascinated by language, its powers of social control, and its frightening—and thrilling—malleability. Mock-epic engages the manipulative powers of poetry in an effort to fix language, to make it a stable instrument for passing judgment on affairs of state. The effort was in some respects doomed, since it was cut off from the social forces that drive language change; but it also succeeded in the way that all propagandis-

---

8. Garth, "Preface" to *The Dispensary,* [A5v].

9. For *design* as order, see Battestin (1974); for *design* as intention, see Erwin (1985). As order, design conjoins aesthetics, theology, and epistemology. As intention, design conjoins desires and their fulfillment, with plans and plots the exemplars of intentionality.

tic, official histories succeed when they become canonical and so silence other voices.

The pillory is also an instrument of law and social domination. The third line of argument concerns politics and ideology. The mock-epic has a complex relation to law—because it presumes to remedy the failings of the law and because it is so concerned with questions of lawful establishment. Each poem's particular concern with electoral politics, literary politics, medical politics, the politics of the community of Catholic families, even sexual politics is part of a larger polemic on the rights and duties of establishment. Since mock-epic holds the conservative view that social order rests on individuals, this explanation of the relationship between civic duty and the public interest is ultimately directed at persons, at private duty and private interests. In the poems, duties and interests are bridged chiefly in myths such as Pope's story of a natural aristocracy of poetry. And yet the establishment served by these stories was finally just the establishment of the professional, its ideology a product of an economic organization defined increasingly in terms of professions and trades. In the mock-epic, this ideology is expressed in the genre's exploration of "professional" interest and affiliation as the motive force of social action, building that exploration into the most basic structures of the genre. This exploration shapes the point-field structures of the poems' settings, there functioning as the lines of force that order the Newtonian fields. In the portraits, interest and affiliation prove to be definitive of the individual person, the one sure sign of identity and identification. In spite of its ties to tradition and of its stand with aristocracy and wit and against the sober professionals of the City, the mock-epic strikes a notably bourgeois pose.

This book is arrayed in two parts, organized by topics: one part focuses on places and one on persons. With my emphasis on poetics and on generic continuities, I do not attempt a comprehensive account of these poems. I will show little interest in tracking down epic sources of this or that mock-epic detail. I will not, unfortunately, have much to say about how mock-epic changes when it becomes a poem about a woman. I will not address any number of differences among the poems—how *The Dispensary* is the most Lucretian mock-epic; how the *Dunciad*s are the most personal; how *The New Dunciad* is the most abstract and emblematic; how *The Battle of the Books* is the least complex.

As genres go, the Augustan mock-epic has precious few instances. Those poems I isolate as mock-epic are normally folded into the mock-heroic, which is more a literary mode than a genre.[10] I take the genre as a nodal and exemplary point in the general sweep of the mock-heroic—exemplary because it most complexly realizes the mock-heroic mode; because it is the most inclusive of Augustan mock-forms, and the most doggedly particular; because (next only to the novel) it most successfully forges the uneasy alliance with low forms that is one crucial determinant of Augustan literature; because (along with the novel) it struggles to create a coherent concept of fiction. Always a lightning rod for judgments of what is high and low in the period, the mock-epic poses some of the most pressing questions now facing the study of Augustan poetry.

Because the mock-epic is such a narrow genre, almost a nonce genre, it tests our concept of what a genre is. Augustan poets and critics spoke of genre in rationalist, Aristotelian terms that correlated genres to cultural systems relatively external to literature. Augustan poets reacted to genre as something constricting yet unavoidable—and so as a ground of self-conscious variation, something to be exploited and then exploded.[11] A self-consciously innovative genre such as the mock-epic presented an insoluble puzzle for rationalist critics, its mysteries best captured by Richard Owen Cambridge's distinction between the true mock-epic, which he thought must systematically invert each feature of the epic (a genre with one member, his *Scribleriad*), and poems like *The Rape of the Lock* or *The Dunciad*, which he thought no more than adventitious vehicles for satire (*Scribleriad*, v–vii). Critics from Cambridge to John E. Sitter have struggled with the problem, and what we now say about mock-epic is largely shaped by our failure to come to terms with such rationalist, essentialist distinctions.[12] Since Joseph Warton's 1756 attempt to assess Pope's career, critics have taken *The Rape of the Lock* as "the perfection of the mock-epic" and have read not only

---

10. Augustan writers had no consistent terminology for mock-epic. In the seventeenth century, mock-epic was an aspect of burlesque. Pope called *The Rape of the Lock* "An Heroi-comical Poem"; in the "Postscript" to the *Odyssey* he used the term *mock-epic*; and *The Dunciad* called itself a "little epic." Twentieth-century critics have been no more consistent. For a helpful survey of the mock-heroic, see Rothstein (21–29).

11. Doody gives a useful overview of Augustan "generic self-consciousness" (57–83).

12. The conjunction of two modal genres, satire and mock-heroic, is at best a first description of mock-epic. Satire is characterized at the level of a global speech act, to blame. Since *blame* might or might not take a particular object, satire might or might not be particular. Mock-heroic is characterized at the level of style: its style (discourse) is "higher" than its "substance" (story) (for discourse and story, see Chatman [1978]). A mock-heroic might or might not mock the epic, just as it might or might not mock its subject. These are questions of interpretation, not to be decided on the basis of any formal description.

The Dunciad but all other mock-epics accordingly. This, I argue, has been a mistake. When we try to explain *The Dunciad* so that it fits categories constructed around the solitary instance of *The Rape of the Lock*, we misjudge both poems.

So I here focus on two poems, Garth's long unread *Dispensary* and Pope's *Dunciad*, poems that come closest to exemplifying the model of the mock-epic. The influences of Garth's forgotten poem on Pope's masterpiece are extensive, essential, and largely unrecognized. Garth has been routinely credited with giving Pope stylistic hints, and Pope did borrow lines, figures, and prosodic patterns.[13] But the important relationship lies deeper. *The Dispensary* set the form of the Augustan mock-epic, and in doing so established patterns of poetic representation that would have significance for much late Augustan satiric poetry. *The Dispensary* is especially useful for understanding these patterns of representation because it has virtually no mid-century readings.[14] If we can learn to see the depth of kinship between *The Dispensary* and those mock-epics still alive in our regard, we can learn much about them and about ourselves. I leave to posterity the question whether *The Dispensary* can become again a work of intrinsic interest. If my attention to *The Dispensary* causes a reader or two to share my interest, let that be lagniappe for both of us.

Finally, like the critics of the last half century, I too hope to explain the double—or multiple—vision of the mock-epic, of the mock-form, and of high Augustan poetry generally. But I see no need to assume that the doubleness of the genre must contain or control the multiplicity of its discourses. Nor do I see a need to apologize for or avoid the topical, personal, particular side of that doubleness. I say with them, Pope "serves as a useful corrective to a too narrow idea of poetry." Only the narrowness I have in mind is not Matthew Arnold's. If we would understand the Augustan mock-epics, it is time to ask again those hard questions about particulars that had been asked by the nineteenth-century critics—the very questions that had been asked by Dr. Johnson and by the dunces. We cannot ask them in quite the same way, of course, for the dunces' questions prejudice the case. I want to ask them in a way that continues and transforms the mid-century endeavor: "What is desperately needed today is inquiry that deals neither with origins nor effects, but with artifice" (Mack, 1951, 85). We need today to study artifice, but

---

13. See Cook (127–32).

14. For a helpful account of *The Dispensary* and its circumstances, see Sena (1986) and the references cited therein. The poem has received a small share of scattered commentary, usefully collected in Cook.

we need to understand that to study artifice requires that we study origins and effects,[15] and that we study them in light of all that we now know about the nature of meaning and the texts we use to create it, poetic and otherwise.

---

15. Poetics explains the correlation between marks on a page or sounds in the air and their effects—what they mean (*and do*) to some community of readers. That correlation constitutes texts, and its description constitutes poetics. (For a general explanation, see Colomb [1986]; for a standard technical account, see Eco [1979].) Origins, too, play a role, since contemporary readers are, by and large, responsive to matters of intentionality, of original context, of literary and social affiliations.

Acknowledgments

All books gather debts, but I have been more fortunate than most in the number and generosity of those who have helped me. The genesis of the project I owe to a suggestion by Stuart Baker, but it developed under the guidance of Marty Battestin and Ralph Cohen, to both of whom I owe more than I can say. Their critical differences made me grow to meet their divergent expectations, while the humanity and decency they shared set an example I can only hope to live up to. The manuscript was saved, not quite from the fire as Swift is said to have saved *The Dunciad,* but from the claims of other interests, by Bill Veeder, whose extraordinarily careful reading and detailed advice rekindled the project for me. The manuscript was also read in various stages by others, to all of whom I give my thanks: Beth Ash, Wayne Booth, Jim Chandler, Leopold Damrosch, Irvin Ehrenpreis, William Frost, Roger Lund, Tom Mitchell, Austin Quigley, Richard Strier, Pat Rogers, and John Wallace. Especially helpful was the advice of an anonymous reader for Penn State Press. My editor, Philip Winsor, played his role to perfection, as did my copyeditor, Andrew Lewis. I was also helped by two graduate assistants, Paul Peppis and especially Gwen Flynn, whose sleuthing abilities were a godsend at a time when other obligations threatened to overwhelm me.

Throughout this project, I had the benefit of friends and colleagues generous with their time and ideas. Early on, my understanding of the literature was improved and broadened by Frans De Bruyn, Roger Lund, Doug Patey, Jim Slevin, John Stevenson, Harold Weber, David Wheeler, and other students at the University of Virginia whose weekly meetings kept us all reading and thinking. My understanding of *The Dispensary* was significantly advanced by Steve Ackerman, whose 1979 article may be said to have opened a serious reconsideration of the poem. My view of literary criticism was substantially shaped by the amazing goings-on associated with The University of Virginia's "Theory Club," which we organized at a time when *New Literary History* was still new and *Critical Inquiry* not yet the second major journal for theory, and I am thankful to all who participated. Later, my colleagues at the University of Chicago were consistently helpful, especially Tom Mitchell and Jim

Chandler, both of whom gave early criticism and support. Other early help came from the 1980 Summer Fellows at the William Andrews Clark Library. The graduate students at Chicago were also a constant source of challenge and stimulation, especially those in my seminars, the Scriblerians and Form and Mock-Form. Among them, Tim Erwin's work on the concept of design in Augustan literature did much to advance my understanding and inspired my title.

I am grateful for fellowship and other support to the William Andrews Clark Library, the University of Virginia, and the University of Chicago. I found kind and professional assistance at the William Andrews Clark Library, the Folger Shakespeare Library, the Henry Huntington Library, the Newberry Library, the library of the National Institutes of Health, the Regenstein and Crerar Libraries of the University of Chicago, and the libraries of the University of Virginia, UCLA, the Illinois Institute of Technology, the National Judicial College, the Georgia Institute of Technology, and Emory University. I was also aided by the electronic database services of the University of Illinois and the University of California at Berkeley.

Most of all, I am every day thankful that this book was composed amid the occasionally chaotic but always loving activities of a growing family.

A Note on the Text of *The Dispensary*

There is at present no widely available modern edition of the several revisions of *The Dispensary*. In order to have the benefit of Garth's final revisions, I have, unless otherwise noted, taken all quotations of *The Dispensary* from the 1725 Dublin edition, which is imperfect but is available in a 1975 reprint (Jo Allen Bradham, ed.; Scholars' Facsimiles & Reprints). The text of the 1725 Dublin edition is substantially identical to that of the 1714 London edition (Garth's last revision); it also includes *A Compleat Key to the Dispensary* and lists all lines removed from earlier versions. Frank Ellis has produced an excellent edition of Garth's first corrected text (1699), including helpful notes and a record of the text of subsequent editions. This edition is available in volume six of the Yale *Poems on Affairs of State* (1970). All quotations from the 1699 text are from Ellis's edition, and are noted as "1699." Some larger libraries will have Wilhelm Josef Leicht's 1905 edition of the 1714 text (with notes and apparatus in German); my quotations differ from Leicht's text only occasionally. Though often incorrect, Chalmers's 1810 edition in *The Works of the English Poets* will serve those who cannot find one of the better texts.

Introduction: Moralizing the Song

1

For the moral (as Bossu observes) is the first business of the [epic] poet, as being the groundwork of his instruction. This being formed, he contrives such a design, or fable, as may be most suitable to the moral; after this he begins to think of the persons whom he is to employ in carrying on his design; and gives them the manners which are most proper to their several characters. The thoughts and words are the last parts, which give beauty and colouring to the piece.
—Dryden, "A Parallel of Poetry and Painting" (1695)

Take out of any old Poem, History-books, Romance, or Legend, (for instance Geffry of Monmouth or Don Belianis of Greece) those Parts of Story which afford most scope for long Descriptions....

For the Moral and Allegory. These you may Extract out of the Fable afterwards at your Leisure; Be sure you strain them sufficiently.
—Pope, A Receit to make an Epick Poem (1713)

What kind of epic is mock-epic? Mock-epic is surely something like epic, but how like? Is the *mock* in mock-epic like that when the class clown mocks teacher? Or like that when vigilantes make a mockery of justice? Or like that in mock turtle soup? None of these seems quite right, since mock-epic is not burlesque, nor a base degradation, nor a humble yet exact imitation. The mock-epic does have strong and abiding ties to the epic. One tie runs, with systematic inversion, to a central theme of this study. Epic represented the great actions of heroic figures on whom depends the well-being of civilization and the state. Mock-epic represents not actions but the personal and collective desires that the poets believed were the motive forces of their unheroic social antagonists. Those representations are a major expression of a conservative ideology that opposed the increasing effort to legitimate self-interest as a natural and so morally neutral social force mediated chiefly through economic relations. Unable to deny the force of self-interest, the poets represented it conjoined in the narrative with inevitable and reprehensible consequences—for civilization and the state. But that tie is one of many, not only to epic but to a number of Augustan genres.

The mock-epic is often said to occupy the place among Augustan genres that in better times would have been occupied by the epic, but that view oversimplifies. Granted that genres as self-conscious as mock-epic tend to arise in response to perceived lacunae in the generic repertoire. Granted also that the mock-epic calls attention to the absence of respectable Augustan epic and, in Richard Blackmore, the interminable presence of unrespectable epic.[1] Although mock-epic's place is defined by that absent epic, the mock-epic does not stand in the stead of the epic, a shadow—whether grotesque or exquisite—of its great original. What more nearly stands in stead of the Augustan epic are the great translations and, later, the novel. The genres whose role the mock-epic most directly adopts are panegyric, elegy, and the other forms of "official" poetry of contemporary civil affairs. The most immediate precursor to the mock-epic, *MacFlecknoe,* is explicitly a mock-panegyric, its succession "fable" more indebted to panegyric than to epic.[2] Questions of succession and, more generally, of establishment had come to dominate panegyric and its kin, driven as they were by the tumult of seventeenth-century politics. By the end of the century, however, those forms had been too much used to serve too many political interests, and had fallen into disrepute as the work of hacks. Then the mock-epic, by way of Dryden's example, stepped into that breach, to continue as the poetry of succession and establishment—and as the poetry of hacks.

Although mock-epic fills the role of panegyric and related occasional forms, it looks (at least at first) like nothing so much as epic, and it contrives to include a satiric medley of poetic kinds. We have learned to expect such complex generic interrelations, so that generic innovation now seems a staple of Augustan poetics.[3] What lends unity to such

---

1. Sitter, focusing on Blackmore, argues that *The Dunciad* is an anti-epic (55–65). Though he is right to be suspicious of the traditional account, Sitter's solution isolates *The Dunciad* from the genre to which it belongs.
2. See Garrison (1975). For succession in satire, see Seidel (1979).
3. See Cohen (1974) and Doody (57–83).

mixed forms is the varied contributions of the parts to a common, overriding end. In the epic, the unity of means and end was achieved by the fable. Augustan critics knew that the fable was the most important feature, its "soul" the relation between narrative form and didactic end. That relation is also key to the mock-epic, as Augustan narrative forms moved from epic's preceptual fables to, on the one hand, the progressive narrative of the novel and, on the other, the conservative narrative of mock-epic.[4] The end products may differ—not least in that the novel was a new beginning and the mock-epic an end—but much was shared: the ever-increasing domestication of literary forms; the emphasis on the particulars of the here and now; the influence of popular, often journalistic literary forms. In the novel, these changes produced such travesties of neoclassical doctrine as comic epics and stories told in the letters of servant girls. In the mock-epic, they produced *The Dunciad.*

In this study of the poetics of particularity in the mock-epic, we will be concerned chiefly with those aspects of the mock-epic which are, at first glance, least tied to the epic. But since mock-epic's ties to epic come first, in Augustan minds as well as ours, they will be addressed first, in terms of the fable, which collects those matters of overall design that Augustan critics and poets universally agreed were the "soul" of the epic.

In that regard, there is a sense in which mock-epic "mocks" its eponymous form by turning traditional epic doctrine on its head, drastically attenuating the role of action in the fable, and lodging the "soul" of the form elsewhere. But that change is not as sweeping as it might seem. One striking feature of neoclassical accounts of epic—which is to say, of narrative generally—is how action is subordinated to argument or precept. In the mock-epic, action serves argument, but both are in turn subordinated to judgment, to description.[5] Mock-epic follows Pope's ironic "Receipt" for epic: "Take ... those Parts of Story which afford

---

4. See McKeon (1987, 218–37), although McKeon has virtually nothing to say about mock-epic. Watt (1957) gives a formal account of the development of the novel. Paulson (1967) presents a preliminary account of the relationship between particularity in satire and the emergent novel. But if, as Lukács notes, "the epic ... is empirical at its deepest, most decisive, all-determining transcendental base" (1971, 46), then the emergence of the mock-epic (or of the novel) presents a question less of the rise of than the form of its empiricism.

5. Sitter recognizes that "[t]he *Dunciad* is primarily a descriptive poem," but he sees the description in *The Dunciad* as "dealing with the emblematic manifestations of an abstraction" (80). Though this is true of the machinery, Sitter would give all the persons in the poem the abstract status of the machines: "The descriptions of Cibber seated complacently in the midst of adulation, of Jacob 'emulating' Curll, of Benson 'propt' on Milton's name, and of Opera 'upheld' by singing peers are all actually iconographic portraits" (77).

most scope for long Descriptions." In that catchall category, Description, neoclassical doctrine lumped such things as settings, "thoughts and words," and other aspects of "colouring," which were, as Dryden says, "the last parts." How they came to be the first parts in mock-epic narrative is the story of this chapter.

Precept and Example, Allegory and Action

When in 1699 Garth turned to poetry to judge and punish the enemies of the Royal College of Physicians, he could draw on a number of models. Epic connections were easy to find. His mock-heroic framework he borrowed almost whole from Boileau. His mock-heroic style he found in Dryden. And for modern epic he looked to Milton and Cowley, not to mention Dryden's Virgil. For his kind of particularized poetry, connections were equally available. Garth found an important example in Denham's *Cooper's Hill* (1642, 1655), and he had gone to school on Dryden's works, not only *MacFlecknoe* but also the political satire. The most pertinent examples, though, he found in the voluminous corpus of "Poems on Affairs of State," long consigned to the baleful category, 'subliterary' (see *POAS*). There Garth found particulars galore, and a variety of techniques for dealing with them. He found one genre, the "Advice to a Painter" poem, which provided models for his satiric portraiture and which, in Marvell's *Last Instructions to a Painter* (1667, 1689), included at least one fully literary precursor to the mock-epic.

If Garth was aided by his models, he was only hampered by those who sought to explain and prescribe the task before him. Critics of the epic were no help. Epic was "a feign'd or devis'd Story of an *Illustrious Action*, related in Verse in an *Allegorical, Probable, Delightful,* and *Admirable* manner, to cultivate the Mind with Instructions of Virtue."[6] This union of action and moral was accomplished by the fable, which characteristically mixed aspects of formal, structural design with aspects of didactic, intentional design. For the premier neoclassical critic of the epic, René Le Bossu, the fable was "un discours invente pour former les moeurs par des instructions deguisees sous les allegories d'une action" (*Traité*, 21). Le Bossu and most of his English followers saw epic fable largely in terms of the traditional genre exemplified by

---

6. Blackmore, "Preface" to *Prince Arthur* (1695; Spingarn, III.235).

Aesop's tales. More sophisticated critics used allegorical readings of the classical epics[7] to distinguish fables "raised altogether upon brutes and vegetables" from those "in which the actors are passions, virtues, vices": "Some of the ancient critics will have it that the *Iliad* and *Odyssey* of Homer are fables of this nature, and that the several names of the gods and heroes are nothing else but the affections of the mind in a visible shape and character" (*Spectator* 183).

Although there was disagreement about details, almost everyone accepted a version of Le Bossu's simple formula: the fable allegorically united an Action (defined in Aristotelian terms) with a Moral. John Dennis's attack on Blackmore's *Prince Arthur* includes a good, if somewhat dogmatic, summary:

> That the Design of him who writes an Epick Poem, is to give Moral Instructions to Mankind. That there are but two Ways of giving Moral instruction, Precept and Example, or, in other words, Action; that Historical Actions were too particular to give general Instructions, and consequently, that the Action, which is the Subject of an Epick Poem, must be general; that is, feign'd, or, in other words, a Fable; a Fable compounded of Truth and Fiction; the Truth disguis'd and convey'd by the Fiction. (I.57)

Dennis, however, is characteristically willing to push the logic of his position, collapsing the epic fable into argument itself.

> That the Action is only fram'd for the Instruction; and that it is design'd for a proof of the Moral; that every part of that Action ought to be a gradual Progress in the proof; and that consequently all the Parts of it ought to be as dependant one of another, as the Propositions are of a Syllogism;... That an Epick Poet is to drive on his Action, which is but urging his Argument; and that he is still to have an eye to the end of his Action, and to make hast to that which is the conclusion of his Argument. (I.57–58)

In its emphasis on argument and fiction, epic theory was consonant with the poetic inherited from the Renaissance: "Restoration critics... are bound firmly to the earlier by their concern with poetry's moral

---

7. For a modern account of allegory in epic, see Murrin (1969).

function and by the central shared assumption that its sensuous vividness and imaginative freedom make poetry the best moral teacher—better than philosophy because it furnishes examples rather than precepts and better than history because its examples are feigned rather than true" (Youngren, 1968, 160). Renaissance critics had been little concerned with generality and particularity but very much concerned with the value of poetry as a form of writing relative to history and philosophy, with emphasis on poetry's "sharp, sensuously vivid examples (or images or pictures)," which are not "tied to the messy (because fallen) world of fact" (Youngren, 1982, 267). Aristotle had placed philosophy above poetry (whose value was its resemblance to philosophy). Humanists had preferred history on the ground that its examples teach "with much greater grace efficacie, and speede" because "examples be the very formes of our deedes, and accompanied with all circumstances." The poets preferred poetry. Sidney's *Apology for Poetry,* for example, repeats the argument of the advantages of examples over precepts, but finds that the representations in poetry have subtle advantages, based (and this is Aristotle's point) in the poet's creative control and "imaginative freedom" from fact. Although it has become *de rigueur* to repeat Sidney's affirmation of the fictiveness of poetry as though that were his final word (the poet, he says, "nothing affirmeth"), for Sidney as for Restoration critics, the many powers of poetry are consequent to its one great end, to move that it might instruct.[8]

Their question was not our question—What is the true nature of the poetic utterance?—but a question we hardly ever ask: Is poetry the best form of moral instruction? This poetic rests on the issue of the *effects* of kinds of representations. It left a clear program for the poet:

> The author who invented a fable... would understand that his fiction should contain general truths rather than specific references to individual persons and events in his own times. If he wished to moralize about contemporary affairs and yet to write a piece of literature that would be as permanent and universal as a good fable should be, he would first be obliged to generalize topical history; that is, to see in the local incidents the general rules they typified. Then he had to find his fable, usually in his-

---

8. Although Youngren (1982) has suggested otherwise, Pope and his colleagues continued to use the language of precept and example, specifically in response to questions of the efficacy of their poems. The terms became less central, but the discourse of precept and example (as, for example, in Addison's account of Chevy Chase in *Spectator* 70) continued right through Dr. Johnson's several famous dissertations on generality.

tory books, although no source was barred and a pure invention was quite permissible; and finally—the true test of his art—he must work up his fable with all the expertise at his command. The reader, but only if he wished, would reverse the process, going from particulars to generals to particulars again. (Wallace, 1974, 185–86)

How then did Garth manage to circumvent such longstanding authority? By dint of his unique circumstances: Garth was no poet and need not be responsible to the tradition as one with more serious poetic ambitions might. He was free, not so much to do as he pleased, as to open the path that his poetic examples high and low had mapped out. That path, which leads to a highly particularized satiric form of instruction and polemic, might make one wonder whether it makes sense to speak of a mock-epic fable at all. By all accounts, the epic fable is general and fictional, its theme the destiny of an entire community. Its action "must be General Action; something in which all might be equally concern'd" (Dennis, I.56),[9] a necessity grounded in the logic of argument: "From a Particular Action, a General Precept could not be deduced." This seems to drive a wedge between epic and mock-epic fables (Dennis thought it did). If nothing else, the pother over the action, or lack of it, in *The Dunciad* should give us pause. Critics who have accepted these formulas have variously blamed or excused *The Dunciad* because its Action lacks action, lacks unity of action, has activity but no real action, is anti-action, and other variations on this theme—all with such unsatisfying results that we can only wonder about the original assumption.

Herein lies the chief challenge of Augustan satirists, who though committed to "General Precepts" were above all else (as so many have complained) satirists of the particular. Here also is the "soul" of the mock-epic, whose fable bears a strong, if caricatured resemblance to the epic fable, but with the fictional and the actual damnably mixed—not, as Dennis recommended, to "make his Action credible" (I.56), but with a boldfaced openness that seems to make the mixture the point of the story. Pope said as much in the Scriblerian "receit" for *The Dunciad*:

First, taking things from their original, he considereth the Causes creative of such authors, namely *Dulness* and *Poverty*.... This

---

9. Dennis, like twentieth-century critics of the mock-epic, sees this fictionality as dominating all actualities brought into the poem: "[T]hose Poetical Persons, to which Particular names are assign'd, remain at the bottom Universal and Allegorical" (I.58).

truth he wrapp'd in an *Allegory* (as the constitution of Epic poetry requires) and feigns, that one of these Goddesses had taken up her abode with the other, and that they jointly inspir'd all such writers and such works.... The great power of these Goddesses acting in alliance... was to be exemplified in some *one, great* and *remarkable* action... or in other words, the Action of the Dunciad is the Removal of the Imperial seat of Dulness from the City to the polite world....

A *Person* must be fix'd upon to support this action.... He finds his name to be *Tibbald*, and he becomes of course the Hero of the poem....

As for the *Characters*, the publick hath already acknowledged how justly they are drawn: the manners are so depicted, and the sentiments so peculiar to those to whom applied, that surely to transfer them to any other, or wiser, personages, wou'd be exceeding difficult. (TE, V.50–51)

The Allegory and the Machinary are fictional, but the Persons and their Characters are not. (How else could the public acknowledge "how justly," or unjustly, "they are drawn"?) Moreover, it was obviously "such authors," the actual Persons and their Characters, not the Moral or the Action, that came first. Pope's slyly Scriblerian account suspends itself in the contradictory logic of the genre. That suspension, not any emphasis on Pope as a maker of fictions, is the point of Pope's even slier remark on the occasion of Theobald's displacement by Cibber, "the *Poem was not made for these Authors, but these Authors for the Poem*" (TE, V.205).

Though only Pope had the genius to make his characters actually seem made for his poem, the complex logic that made this possible was the work of one Samuel Garth. In the last year of the seventeenth century Garth at once responded to and circumvented the traditional program for topical poetry. The issue remained the same: Which forms of representation best advanced poetry's moral instruction? Garth's response—mock-epic—adapted a mock-heroic fable to a form of representation whose immediate object was not a precept but some actual state of affairs. The result is a poem with actual persons and a story at least partially fictional. But how fictional? What of the Action, where the feigned Allegory and the actual Persons meet? As we shall see first in the case of *The Dispensary* and then of *The Rape of the Lock* and *The Dunciad*, in this configuration are, as the good Scriblerus puts it, "*Mysteries* or ἀπόρρητα" and so "more... than meets the ear" (B IV.4n).

Action

The Action in epic centers on the action of its hero, who merits our attention because he has, as we now say, "seen action" in combat. As Pope has Sarpedon say, "Why boast.... Unless great Acts superior Merit prove[?]" In mock-epic, matters are disposed otherwise. In Garth's story, for example, the action is a squabble in a controversial outpatient clinic established for the care of the poor: "The description of the Battel is grounded upon a Feud that happen'd in the *Dispensary* betwixt a Member of the *College* with his Retinue, and some of the Servants that attended there to dispense the Medicines; and is so far real, tho' the Poetical Relation be fictitious" ([A5v]–[A6r]). The poem has its battle, but the battle is only a minor episode and only tangentially involves the "heroes" of the poem. Our interest is far less in the battle than in its fictitious "Poetical Relation." Much the same puzzle dogs *The Dunciad.* It has no battle at all, substituting instead the spectacle of heroic games. Recapitulating the civilizing moment of the funeral games by which Homer begins to move beyond the individualistic, antisocial heroic code, this action in the streets is also rather tangential, a mere collection of episodes that do not involve the hero, who doesn't have much of anything to do in the poem. It has left critics to damn or excuse the poem on grounds that seem, somehow, unhappily beside the point. Here too, the action disquietingly involves a fictitious relation: "that alleged action of the 'Dunciad' is not a recognized fact, like that of the 'Lutrin,' the 'Rape of the Lock,' and the 'Secchia Rapita,' but only an inference which Pope chose to found on the real actions of the various persons whom he satirises" (E-C, IV.21).

It is no accident that critics have gravitated toward fiction to cope with what seemed the excessive particulars of the mock-epic, for fiction lies at the heart of the genre's designs. But the fiction in the mock-epic seems not to be well served by any of our usual ways of talking about it. After all, fiction is now synonymous with that other late Augustan branch of the epic, the novel. Like the mock-epic poets, early novelists struggled to come to terms with the fiction in their genre by forging an accommodation between traditional narrative and new forms with new social agendas.[10] Their struggles were no less difficult than those of the mock-epic poets, but they are harder for us to see because our own literary experience is dominated by the genre created in that struggle, as

---

10. See Watt, Davis (1983), and McKeon. Also see Richetti (1969).

is our idea of fiction. Moreover, early novelists were less tied than the poets to traditional forms. Of the novelists, only Fielding and perhaps Sterne felt any very powerful need to accommodate their fictions to neoclassical theories of epic narrative—and they came rather late in the game. But the mock-epic poet could not avoid this critical authority. Not only did he have to forge a new form for his fiction, he had to do so in a way that seemed responsive to the tradition of the epic, casting the plot in terms of canonical epic actions, battles, games, journeys.

Naturally enough, the neophyte Garth felt most constrained to maintain a conventional epic surface and so to tell—or seem to tell—a story of a battle. Garth systematically mimics as many epic conventions as he can manage, and does so by parodying episodes in earlier epics.[11] Moreover, his focus on the battle makes it much easier to cast his story as "some *one, great* and *remarkable* action." By concentrating on the action inside the Dispensary, Garth can tell a story with canonical epic matter arranged in a canonical plot, moving steadily from the first construction of the Dispensary to the scuffle that occasioned the poem.

Concentrating on the action inside the Dispensary also furthers the poem's thematic design. Garth's ostensible subject is a "civil war between two factions within the College itself" (*POAS,* V.60). The action is intramural and narrow, but the story of the Dispensary project is, as many readers would know, a long one that involves many issues and many players. Garth finds the causes of the disease outside the College proper, in those raised above their station when in 1687 James II forced the College to enlarge its membership as part of his effort to fill Parliament and other political institutions with his supporters. These outsiders brought with them all the wrong associations and the wrong interests. As Charles Goodall (Stentor in the poem) charged in an official College publication of 1684, "[W]e have to deal with a sort of men not of Academical, but Mechanick education; who being either actually engaged in the late Rebellion, or bred up in some mean and contemptible trades, were never taught the duty they owe to God or to their Sovereign, to their Native Country or the Laws thereof" (*Royal College,* A3v–A4r). Even so, by 1699 the factionalism within the College was old news. What was new was that a paper and political battle had become violent: "[T]his Difference... did not break out to Fury and Excess, till the Time of Erecting the *Dispensary.*" The "Fury and Excess" of a basement scuffle is barely violence, but such is the stuff of mock-epic. How

---

11. For Garth's use of models, see Cook (63–73, 78–80).

ever minor the incident itself, a new factor had been introduced, one that Garth would use to give new bite to the bad old joke about physicians and apothecaries as homicides.

The violence, then, serves as a center within the center, the focus of Garth's focus on the battle. Throughout the poem, we see the battle in terms of the principals' persistent movement toward violence and away from any commitment, or even the pretense of a commitment, to saving lives. As Garth recounts the episodes leading up to the battle, the story becomes one of awakening desire (for power, prestige, wealth) and anxiety (lest they be lost). These corrupt practitioners, who are shown to be specialists chiefly in preying on the desires and anxieties of their patients, find themselves caught up by their own. Once Sloth is disturbed by the College's renewed industry, the stage is set for Envy and Discord to do their work. Giving the agency in the story over to the machinery, Garth makes the action chiefly psychological, chiefly a matter of desire and obligation.

Each major episode—Horoscope's and Mirmillo's nights of decision, the Apothecaries' "great consult" in Apothecaries Hall, the Apothecaries Physicians' extended debate at Mirmillo's house, the Collegiate Physicians' brief one before the battle—details an inexorable psychological progress to violence, a progress in which passion and interest, the twin poles of early modern social theory,[12] become the driving force of a mob. The only reservations to slow this progress stem from the cowardice, never the good sense, of these civilian warriors. No one in the poem is able to resist the heroic lure of violence, as Garth renews the Virgilian conflict between *pietas* and *furor* and shows us the militaristic ethos of the epic not only wanting, but inimical to civil life. With the couplet added in 1714 to the account of the heroic exploits of the College's military leader, Stentor-Goodall,[13] Garth made palpable what had always been his chief concern: this is a battle in which none can engage with honor.

> On *Stentor*'s Crest the useful Chrystal breaks,
> And tears of *Amber* gutter'd down his Cheeks.
> (V.315–16)

---

12. See Hirshman (1977).
13. Goodall was an assiduous controversialist who in fact as in the poem lived up to his name. Homer's "Stentor the strong, endu'd with Brazen Lungs" is used by Juno to rouse the Trojans to action: "Her Speech new Fury to their Hearts convey'd" (Pope, *Iliad,* 5.978, 986).

Fortune knew it would come to this,

> Both Sides shall conquer, and yet Both shall fall;
> The Mortar now, and then the Urinal.
> (IV.338–39)[14]

and Health is shamed that it has,

> Enough th' Atchievement of your Arms you've shown,
> You seek a Triumph you shou'd blush to own.
> (VI.13–14)

It is easy enough to see the blame here, even the blame cautiously meted out to Garth's fellow Collegians. By the end, Health will say it out loud. But there is more at stake than blame and punishment. As much as it is a bravura propaganda piece, by far the most effective of the College's entries in the controversy, *The Dispensary* is also, in its stand for civil obedience and social stability, a well-reasoned defense of Garth's interests, those of his College, and more generally those of his class. At the center of that defense is a warning—a warning for his fellow physicians, both loyal and not, that if they wish to keep their place, they had better know their place and its demands on them; and a warning for his countrymen at large, that the demands of place have just as strong a claim on them. The College does not face this disorder alone.

A similarly disposed fable grounds Pope's mock-epics. Especially in its expanded version, the action in *The Rape of the Lock* also seems a steady progress from the inception of the Baron's scheme to the battle.[15] Yet, as was the case in *The Dispensary,* the battle of *The Rape of the Lock* gave Pope a subject whose over-narrow focus became one of the more explicit concerns of the poem. How and why Arabella and Lord Petre might be led to fetishize her ringlets of hair—and then to think of them as her lock—is among the errors the poem explores; however, we err in thinking that Arabella is simply guilty of "the logical fallacy of metonymy" (Krieger, 303). It is true that all hairs are not the same and that hairs are not hymen, but they are each boundaries of Arabella's person. Belinda-Arabella may overvalue her lock: indeed she attends so assiduously to the accoutrements of her person that she

---

14. The 1725 Dublin edition misprints "fail" for "fall" in IV.338.
15. For an account of the action in the two versions of *The Rape of the Lock,* see Morris (85–90) and J. Jackson (1950).

neglects the person inside, leaving herself defenseless against the "Earthly Lover lurking at her Heart" (III.144). But to violate her lock is to violate her person, and both she and the Baron know it.

The battle in the poem arises because Belinda-Arabella is an absolutist. She holds a view of personal integrity that requires her to be untouched by human hand or heart, a view that leads only to the sylphs' airy immunity from penetration. For Belinda any penetration is total violation. Release the lock and all is lost. Thus in a poem that explores how social rituals enclose and contain desire and its aggression, how our rituals give us games in which to exercise aggression within the bounds of the ombre table, how they give us ringlets as objects of desire, Belinda thinks that all victories over man are the same, in ombre or in love, and that all objects of desire are also the same—hair or hymen, honor or brocade. Thus the battle is anticlimax. The lock lost, all is lost, and Belinda has no further bounds to contain her passion. The battle only manifests her already lost lock and composure. Unbounded desire, like the heroic lure of violence, destroys all social good: "And Chiefs contend 'till all the Prize is lost!" (V.108).

The equally narrow focus of *The Dunciad* is by now familiar fare. Pope focuses his poem on those who devalue literature, but he ranges it through those who devalue economic, political, social, and spiritual life. Dulness "conglob'd" (B IV.79) brings them together to take their share in Pope's "public punishment" (TE, V.14). Massing her dunces, Dulness also displays the "fact" that underlies Pope's warning. England is overrun with dunces: there are more of them than meet the eye, and they are engaged in a mysterious "progress." Although the poem has no battle, as though the mock-epic focus on a battle has narrowed to nonexistence, there are epic games and plenty of activity, each book after the first featuring something like a parade, each parade testifying to the fact that the dunces are everywhere. We see this fact again when, in the almost cinematic final gesture, Pope slowly widens his focus (and generalizes his language) to give us the benefit of the distant sight and to speak with the foreknowledge and wisdom of an Anchises. In that perspective, Pope adopts the stance that was Dryden's and Garth's before him, in many ways *the* stance of the Augustan satirist. He is the quick-sighted, sharp-tongued advance guard of his society with the poet's power to speak the future because he can remember the past and see in small signs the true (inner, disguised) character of the present.

These brief accounts of these mock-epic fables are centered (as such accounts typically are) on the poets' thematic designs and didactic intent. Although they will have to be supported in the remainder of this study, they can, I hope, stand as first formulations. But as answers to our question of poetics—the role of fiction in the fables—they are incomplete. The kind of strongly thematic account I have given says (to use a Gricean distinction) very much more about what the poet does *by* focusing his poem on the violence or the lock or literature than about what he does *in* focusing his poem (the question of poetics). These accounts speak more to our reading of the work and its didactic aims than to its poetic structure—which is all well and good unless we forget that there is no direct route from statements about didactic or thematic force to statements about poetic structure.

The *thematic force* of an utterance (its ultimate point, if you will) is in no sense a part of the *text* uttered. When, for example, Pope reuses his (and others') lines, transplanting them from one work to another, their sense will differ, even differ radically, under the pressure of changing circumstances (genre, context, pretext, pragmatic goals, etc.) (R. Cohen, 1977). This is the lesson of J. L. Austin's (1962) analysis of the *illocutionary force* of sentence utterances. Austin finds two sources of sentence meaning in addition to "locutionary" (grammatical, textual) structure: (1) the *illocutionary force* of an sentence (what we mean *by* saying the utterance—to warn, to promise, and so on: analogous to my 'thematic force') and (2) the *perlocutionary force* of an utterance (the effect we mean to bring about—alerting someone, obligating oneself, and so on: loosely analogous to didactic intent). Austin demonstrates that illocutionary and perlocutionary force are grounded in a system of meaning not directly tied to the grammar (text) of the utterance itself. The relationship between illocutionary force and textual structure is loose and highly complex: think of the different things we might do with a simple declarative sentence such as "I didn't realize that the bull was so dangerous," things like convey information, offer an explanation, give a warning, ask a question, make an excuse. And the relationship between perlocutionary force and locutionary structure is even looser: think of the number of things we might say to keep a child from being frightened of the bull.

This distinction between the force and the structure of an utterance holds in both directions. Just as thematic force is not built into poetic structure, so poetic structure does not follow from thematic force. Thus there is no warrant for moving from statements about thematic force *directly* to claims about poetic structure, though critics interested in the didactic aspects of poems do so all the time. One prominent example is Aubrey Williams's effort to ground his oft-repeated conclusion with a three-step argument borrowed from Maynard Mack: (1) the text of *The Dunciad* speaks explicitly of persons and places ("It can be granted that Pope is using local, personal material" [52]); (2) *The Dunciad* speaks generally of values ("but it must be admitted at the same time that such material becomes the bridge by which we cross to a land of larger values" [52]); therefore, (3) *The Dunciad* is full of metaphors and is, as a whole, one great metaphor. Though there is much insight in Williams's claim (and, as we shall see, there is a sense in which he is right), Williams has no argument to bridge the space between his observations about explicit meaning and thematic force and his conclusion about poetic structure. It does not follow that because Pope's thematic concerns are not explicitly represented in his statements, those statements are perforce figural. If we are to say something about the design of the fable, we must take care to distinguish between—and thereby relate—the design of the poem and the designs of its author.

Figures and Fictions

By concentrating on actions and battles we see mock-epic chiefly through its ties with epic. If, however, we concentrate on satire, and look on mock-epic's fables as representations of a body of historical facts, then our questions about fiction become more complex. We find, for example, that Garth's rejection of violence is accomplished by something of an act of violence, in the sense that we have relatively clear standards for when a representation "does violence" to its object. These widely shared standards are obviously violated in *The Dispensary,* as in the other poems. However appropriate Garth's story to his thematic and polemical concerns, the fact remains that there was never any violence, official or otherwise, on the part of the College (though Garth and his colleagues almost certainly felt moved to violence, and Garth probably heard some loose talk about violence). There were no armies, no battles worthy of the name, no councils of war, certainly no apparitions or magical journeys. All these are part of the "Poetical Relation" which is, as Garth says, "fictitious." They are, an Augustan would say, merely part of the "poetic license."

We could say poetic license, if that were any kind of explanation. When Garth invokes poetic license ("tho' the Poetical Relation be fictitious"), he is protecting himself, making excuses. Only the relation is fictitious (and then only partly so). The "ground" is not: "The description of the Battel is grounded upon a[n actual] Feud... and is so far real." Garth is clear enough that the point of the relation is not to make fictions but to make judgments. So, too, does Scriblerus make excuses. He tries to head off the inevitable attacks by focusing on the presumed Moral ("the Causes creative of such authors, namely *Dulness* and *Poverty*") and by attributing the poem's fictions to that Moral: "This truth he wrapped in an *Allegory* (as the constitution of Epic poesy requires)" (TE, V.50). Doing so, Scriblerus asks us to judge by a truth rather less interesting and less dangerous to the poet than the "ground" of Pope's "poetical relation," the actualities out of which he built his poem. Such excuses would be unnecessary were accuracy of representation not central both to the constitution of these poems and to their audiences' judgments of them. So we can't just say poetic license.

The problem arises because poetic license was understood chiefly as a matter of style, rhetoric. In his "Apology for Heroic Poetry and Poetic Licence" of 1677, Dryden defended the poet's right "of speaking things in verse which are beyond the severity of prose": "This, as to what regards the thought or imagination of a poet, consists in fiction: but then those thoughts must be expressed; and here arise two other branches of it: for if this licence be included in a single word, it admits of tropes; if in a sentence or proposition, of figures; both of which are of a much larger extent, and more forcibly to be used in verse than prose" (Ker, I.188–89).

This license grounds the mock-heroic in the relationship between word and idea (or thing)—not fiction, but rhetoric: the mock-heroic is distinguished by a high style and low subjects, and finds the material of its characteristic ridicule in the disjunction between the ethical, social, and economic associations of the style and those of the subjects. This rationale developed as English writers began to differentiate between the low burlesque (which Boileau and Dryden had censured) and the high burlesque of Boileau's *Le Lutrin* and Tassoni's *La Secchia Rapita*. This is Dryden:

> The *Secchia Rapita* is an Italian poem, of the Varronian kind. 'Tis written in the stanza of eight, which is their measure for heroic verse. The words are stately, the numbers smooth, the turn both of thoughts and words is happy. The first six lines of the stanza seem majestical and severe; but the two last turn all into a pleasant ridicule. Boileau, if I am not much deceiv'd, has model'd from hence his famous *Lutrin*.... He writes it in the French heroic verse, and calls it an heroic poem; his subject is trivial, but his

verse is noble.... And, as Virgil in his *Fourth Georgic*, of the Bees, perpetually raises the lowness of his subject by the loftiness of his words, and ennobles it by comparisons drawn from empires, and from monarchs.[16]

Dryden's account gives exclusive attention to rhetoric because it occurs in a discussion of versification in satire. But this focus on rhetoric had its effect on the standard view of the mock-heroic. Dennis defended Butler's octosyllabic line and strange rhymes against Dryden's preference for the larger compass of Tassoni and Boileau, which in turn prompted Peter Motteux's notably early attempt to distinguish explicitly between the two kinds of burlesque solely in terms of their rhetorical features. "The distinguishing mark" of burlesque, Motteux writes, is a "disproportion between the style in which we speak of a thing and its true *Idea*, as when low and mean expressions are us'd to represent the greatest Events, as in *Scarron's Virgil-Travesty*, or great and lofty terms to describe common things, as in *Boileau's Lutrin*, which (by the way) he hath call'd an Heroic Poem, and *Tassone's Secchia Rapita*."[17]

Finally, to make a long story short, by 1726 Pope had fully consolidated this largely rhetorical thinking into his ideas about the mock-epic and its relation to other kinds:

> I believe, now I am upon this Head, it will be found a just observation, that the *low actions of life* cannot be put into a figurative style without being ridiculous, but *things natural* can. Metaphors raise the latter into Dignity, as we see in the *Georgicks*; but throw the former into Ridicule, as in the *Lutrin*. ... The use of pompous expression for low actions or thoughts is the *true Sublime of Don Quixote*. How far unfit it is for Epic Poetry, appears in its being the perfection of the Mock-Epic. ("Postscript," *Odyssey*)

These passages epitomize a long and full critical dialogue, and the rationale they present remains the basis of most of our own discussion of the mock-heroic. For the Augustans as for us, the key to analyzing the

---

16. "Discourse concerning the Original and Progress of Satire" (1693; Ker, II.319).

17. *Gentleman's Journal*, (January 1692/3, 26–27). See Bond (1932, 32–33). A note on chronology: Dennis and Motteux can respond in January 1693 to Dryden's "Discourse" of 1693 because the "Discourse" hit the stands as early as October 1692.

mock-epic is the relationship between the poem's structure of representation and the judgments conveyed by that representation. That structure of representation Augustan critics typically describe in terms of a particular kind of language being used to represent a particular kind of object, with the result that the talk of style and subject guides them to the purely rhetorical aspects of the matter. Even though the poet's license includes his fable or fiction, critics consistently avoided the question of the mock-epic fable in favor of its rhetoric—unless, of course, those critics were also the victims of the representation.

I take it that what we see here is avoidance and not neglect. In other situations, Augustan critics exhibit a keen interest in larger questions of forms of representation—Dryden's analysis of the "Aristotelian" unities in "Of Dramatic Poesy" and Theobald's sophisticated defense of poetic justice in the *Censor* (no. 36, 12 January 1717) are just two of many examples. But because its satire is personal, the mock-epic raises the question of the relationship between the fable and its object of representation in its most intractable form, as a question about the relationship between poet and victim. The traditional Renaissance account had nothing to say on the matter. Indeed, it hindered further discussion by saturating all the relevant vocabulary. Not surprisingly, the issue was almost always raised by the poets' victims and enemies (who had the traditional story to tell) and was almost always avoided by the poets (who had no coherent story to offer in return).

The traditional account of feigned examples can be made to work for the mock-epic fable only by forcing it into an epic straitjacket. But there are always those who are willing to do just that. Aside from Dennis, whose injury and irascibility prejudice his case, Richard Owen Cambridge is perhaps the earliest example of a critic whose conception of the systematic relations among genres forces him to rationalize the mock-epic fully: "A Mock-Heroic poem should, in as many respects as possible, imitate the True Heroic. The more particulars it copies from them, the more perfect it will be. By the same rule it should admit as few things as possible, which are not of the cast and color of the ancient Heroic poems. The more of these it admits, the more imperfect will it be" (*Scribleriad,* v). Of course, in that case "the *Lutrin, Dispensary, Rape of the Lock,* and *Dunciad...* [do] not come up to the true Idea of a Mock-Heroic poem" (vii). Put so baldly, this seems just silly. But Cambridge's aprioristic conception of the genre is not so far from the position argued, often with great ingenuity, by our own mid-century critics. The difference is that Cambridge was sure that "nobody believes that the primary Design of either of these Poets was to write a Mock-Heroic":

> *Boileau* being struck with the absurd Disputes of certain contending Ecclesiasticks, resolv'd to make them the subject of his ridicule; and *afterwards* pitched upon the imitation of the Heroic as a vehicle for his Satire. The comic humor of *Garth,* was strongly excited by the factious divisions in his own profession, and would probably have vented itself in prose, but that the admir'd performance of *Boileau* invited his imitation. And *Pope* wrote his first essay of this kind to put an end, by ridicule, to a quarrel between two families; and his second from a just indignation against his libellers, and not from any form'd design to write a true Mock-Heroic Poem. (vii)

A less rationalist account can be found in the semiotics of poetic license. According to Dryden, poetic license has three "branches," which fall into two distinct kinds. That branch which relates to "the thought or imagination of a poet, consists in fiction." The other two branches arise when "those thoughts must be expressed": "if this licence be included in a single word, it admits of tropes; if in a sentence or proposition, of figures." This is standard deviationist theory of poetic language, and it gives Dryden a continuity among the three branches of poetic license. The differences among them lie only in the ground of the deviation. The one significant distinction is that between deviations based on thought or imagination and those based on words or propositions. Fiction falls into the domain of ideas, rhetoric in the domain of expression.

For Dryden, as for nearly all his contemporaries, the truth of any discourse consists in an appropriate expression of an idea or complex of ideas that accurately represents an object or state of affairs. Hence the two kinds of poetic license: that concerning expression and that concerning ideas. Dryden's defense of expressive license, rhetoric, allows the poet great latitude because the ideas were there to guarantee truth and ensure reliable communication. In a history, for example, writers might be held to a "literal belief" in what is said, but rhetoric reserves a wide domain in poetry, in which readers know enough to be "pleased with the image, without being cozened by the fiction" (Ker, I.185).

When it came to ideas, however, there was far less room to maneuver. Here Dryden defends only a small, specialized set of fanciful ideas: those "authorized by Scripture," whose truth is guaranteed, and those "founded on popular belief," whose fictionality is presumably too well known for any thinking reader to be "cozened." This leaves only a very narrow margin for fiction, but then Dryden's criticism had always moved within that narrow margin.[18] How narrow can best be seen in an example from a more popular forum, Peter Motteux's chatty book reviews and "News of Learning" in the *Gentleman's Journal*. Reacting to the news that there was evidence "that *Eneas* never went into Italy" and closely following Dryden's line of argument, Motteux concludes, "If this be true, the *Eneis* of *Virgil* is a Fiction much exceeding what we call Poetical Licence."[19] That historical study could in this way threaten Virgil's status as a poet is testimony to how little license the poet was thought to have at the level of ideas.

What, then, does this logic imply for those cases in which the fiction consists in a fable that is not a "feigned example" and cannot be explained away by recourse to imaginary creatures or popular belief, a case such as *MacFlecknoe*? Its poetic license must be a matter of expression. Given the obvious liberties of a work like *MacFlecknoe*, neither Dryden's integrity nor his good sense can survive the assumption that the license is a matter of ideas. As Motteux put it, the mock-heroic lives on "disproportion between the style in which we speak of a thing and its true *Idea*," but I know of no argument, nor can I see how an Augustan could make a coherent argument, that the poet has any license to maintain a disproportion between ideas and the shared world of experience. Such is the province of fools, madmen, and liars.

If those fables which refer to the actual world must be explained in terms of an expressive license, then it seems that such fables must be something very much like figures. It's hard to say such fables simply are figures, though speaking loosely we say such things all the time: *The Oxford Dictionary of English Literature*, for example, calls allegory "a figurative narrative or description, conveying a veiled moral meaning; an extended metaphor, or a sustained personification." There is, however, a difference between a figurative narrative and a figurative description, a difference that Dryden took the trouble to preserve because to lump them together is to confuse what Augustan critics and language philosophers most wanted to distinguish—words, ideas, and things. Spenser

---

18. Five years before the "Apology," pressured by objections against *The Conquest of Granada*, Dryden gave his most vigorous defense of fiction: "I boldly answer him, that an heroic poet is not tied to a bare representation of what is true, or exceeding probable; but that he may let himself loose to visionary objects, and to representation of such things as depending not on sense, and therefore not to be comprehended by knowledge, may give him a freer scope for imagination" (Ker, I.153). But in the end, Dryden defends only "those gods and spirits, and those enthusiastic parts of poetry" which, he is willing to concede, are "not to be comprehended by knowledge." The defense is grounded on the old standby, popular belief.

19. Motteux saves Virgil by resorting to popular belief; Dryden uses almost exactly the same terms in his "Dedication to the Aeneis" (Ker, II.172).

may have thought of his allegory as a continued metaphor, and loosely speaking he was right. But no careful Augustan could rest with that account. Strictly speaking, only words and atomic propositions can be figures, and all figures are parasitic on a corresponding literal utterance. The notion of license in "expressive license" is unintelligible without some prior notion of a corresponding literal expression, and yet it's unlikely that the Augustan notion of the literal could survive any attempt to extend it to cover complex signs like fables. This leaves us a double bind. The referential fables of the mock-epic must, it seems, be figural expressions; but they are figures without counterparts in the all-or-nothing world of the literal. That paradox explains why the question was for the Augustans central yet unspoken and for us central and so variously and extensively answered.

That paradox begets another. Because the mock-epic fable must be a figure, it becomes something of an extended description—not a continued metaphor but a literalized one. Narrative serves description, and *The Dunciad* is a picture of Dulness, a group picture since Dulness is only her massed minions. Augustan poets habitually used narrative to enliven description, from Pope's expansion of Donne's adjectives into stories in his "versifications" to Gay's ability to capture stories in a single adjective ("The sudden turn may stretch the swelling vein, / Thy cracking joint unhinge, the ankle sprain" [*Trivia*, I.37]). In the mock-epic, the fable is little more than an organizing principle: prescribed and canonical, and so rich in its network of cultural knowledge; lively and affective, and so better able to enforce its example; but chiefly a device on which to hang the poem's many descriptions. As in the preceptual fable, the sign relationship in the mock-epic's fable is from whole to whole: the whole of the poem stands for the whole of a state of affairs.[20] In that organizing principle—the literalized metaphor—are the "rules of relationship that account for coherence in speech and nature," rules that are thought to be the foundation of truth (M. Cohen, 25). Just as the preceptual fable subordinated narrative to (preceptual) argument, so the referential fable subordinates narrative to (descriptive) argument. While the mock-epic does narrate, that rhetorical action serves another, more dominant one—to describe, to speak the truth.

No mock-epic offers its readers the pleasures of narrative, as the responses to the poems clearly show. The lack of action in *The Dunciad* is

---

20. Fielding's novelistic formulation of the epic fable also postulates a sign relationship between the whole of his plot (whose organizing principle is poetic justice) and the whole of God's providence; see Battestin (141–63).

notorious. Although it is a poem of progress, Dulness accomplishes nothing in *The Dunciad*: she only recognizes, ratifies, and celebrates what is already accomplished by the dunces. The action is all in the description of the prophetic *"Pisgah-sight"* of the ending. Although the action in *The Dispensary* records an inexorable progress to violence, its narrative is only an occasion for a series of descriptions and portraits, its battle a fraction of a canto. In *The Rape of the Lock,* the battle and especially the game of ombre give a greater sense of action; but the poem is a series of descriptive set pieces, frozen moments that accrue to a portrait-apotheosis of Belinda-Arabella. In mock-epic, action serves description.

Literalizing Figures

By understanding "poetic license," we grasp the explanatory force of Garth's "apology," which tells the story of all mock-epics: "The Description of the Battel is grounded upon a Feud that happen'd in the *Dispensary*... and is so far real; tho' the Poetical Relation be fictitious." Garth's fictitious relation makes his fable an allegory by building a story out of literalized metaphors.[21] He makes the long-standing "battle" for power between the various unlicensed practitioners and the College into a fictionally actual battle between well-known Apothecaries Physicians and well-known Collegiate Physicians. Literalizing conventional metaphors for social and political strife, Garth takes the leading figures in that strife and makes them warriors, their political struggles a physical combat of sorts. The literalizations, then, supply the rationale that generates the Action, which is the major locus of the poem's fictionality.[22]

The life of that fiction can hardly be said to stem from the metaphors themselves, which are as tired as they are common. From the first, the language of the larger quarrel between the College and the Apothecar-

---

21. For an extended account of literalized metaphors as the basis of Augustan narrative, see Colomb (1978). McKeon discusses *Pilgrim's Progress* as a literalized allegory.

22. The exception is Canto VI, which records Celsus's underworld journey to the shade of Harvey. In part, this journey returns Garth to the scientific and philosophic concerns that dominate Canto I, before the literalized action begins. This fantastic voyage also brings the poem back to reality and out of the literalization: its traditional epic allegory and narrative structure carry the reader forward to Harvey's closing speech (VI.305–83), which returns the metaphors to their proper use.

ies' Company was highly conventionalized, and it very soon developed that both sides were using largely the same vocabulary, and charging each other with what looked to be the same offenses. Among the most widely shared areas of this conventional language were a group of metaphors of warfare, which were first used by Collegiate writers to describe the assaults on their privileges, but which soon became common property.[23] These metaphors were used not only to conduct the quarrel, but also to report, comment on, and analyze its progress. They dominate Garth's account of the quarrel in his 1697 *Harveian Oration*: "England suffers more by Quacks than distempers." These are "Homicides" who "invade this City" as a "Troop of Cheats [that] wounds not with Weapons, but with a certain more destructive Theriac Medicine; they ... kill not with Bullets but with Pills as fatal" (13). Such descriptions are figural, but as part of the standard technique of College record keepers, journalists, and controversialists, the metaphors in them had become almost technical language, long since emptied of any figural force.

Turn now from the argument of the *Harveian Oration* to the story of *The Dispensary*. This is the speech of "Keen *Colocynthis*," the most irascible of the College's enemies:

> Sound but to Arms, the Foe shall soon confess
> Our Force encreases, as our Funds grow less;
> . . . .
> We'll raise our num'rous Cohorts and oppose
> The feeble Forces of our pigmy Foes;
> Legions of Quacks shall join us on the Place,
> From Great *Kirleus* down to *Doctor Case*.
> . . . .
> Arm therefore gallant Friends, 'tis Honour's Call,
> Or let us boldly Fight, or bravely Fall.
> (III.250–69)

Here, within the story, the "Troop of Cheats" are about to take up weapons. The talk of warfare is literal, its proper, "original" use: Colocynthis

---

23. Civil strife and violence were very sensitive issues at the turn of the century. Talk of actual battles would have been a very serious matter—a fact that Garth exploits in his poem. But these metaphors of battle are also grounded in the basic cultural metaphor, argument is war (see Lakoff and Turner, 1989). Their use to describe political contests, especially the Dispensary quarrel, was widespread and growing (see Colomb, 1978). Garth's poem and the response to it made talk of "the Blood-Thirsty Hussars of *Parnassus*" (Ayloffe, 1707) even more common.

has no use for euphemism. His opponents in the debate would cut words off from their origins in sense, and so fail to understand what they say. Worse still, they fail to understand what they do. Like the physicians who, in Colocynthis's scornful phrase, "out o' Consultation scarce can kill" (III.228), they have used words to absent themselves from the consequences of their actions. Garth's models for Colocynthis are Achilles and Milton's "furious king," Moloch (*PL,* VI.357). He is a primitive who argues against hypocrisy and for what he sees as the basic self-knowledge that keeps language in touch with sense. Indeed, his point is won only when Mirmillo agrees to understand this language as Colocynthis does. After Mirmillo boasts, "By this Right Arm what mighty Numbers fell,"

> With Pen in Hand I push'd to that Degree,
> I scarce had left a Wretch to give a Fee.
> Some fell by *Laudanum,* and some by *Steel,*
> And Death in Ambush lay in ev'ry Pill.
> (IV.56–65)

he gives in to "Honour" (passion) and changes both his mind and his language:

> Physicians, if they're wise shou'd never think
> Of any Arms but such as Pen and Ink:
> But th' Enemy, at their Expense, shall find,
> When Honour calls, I'll scorn to stay behind.
> (IV.74–77)

He is congratulated by Askaris, who marks the change with a pun on *list*:

> Each word, Sir, you impart
> Has something killing in it, like your Art.
> . . . .
> Fate smiles on your attempts, and when you list,
> In vain the Cowards fly, or Brave resist.
> Then let us Arm, we need not fear success,
> No Labours are too hard for Hercules.
> Our military Ensigns we'll display;
> Conquest pursues, where Courage leads the Way.
> (IV.80–99)

This debate foregrounds the linguistic manipulations that underlie the narrative. Any knowledgeable reader will recognize the metaphors as the conventional language of the controversy; although technically figural, their proper, normal use is metaphoric. Recognizing the literalization for what it is, the reader will see that Colocynthis is making mistakes and that Garth is making fictions. But it then becomes hard to distinguish between figure and ground. The literal use carries all the creative surprise of the figural, while the figural use asserts the normative, conventional claims of the literal. And so, in the face of those mistakes and fictions, the tired propriety of the metaphors is challenged. By reestablishing the literal sense of this language, Garth renews its force as metaphor. By invoking its origins in the senses, he makes it once again a true measure of value and a viable tool of moral argument. Of course, Garth does not think he can simply reestablish any origins, erase the linguistic history of the dispute, and new mint old words. Quite the contrary. Garth embraces the meanings impressed on these words by their history of abuse, filling his poem with references, direct and indirect, to that history and those abuses. He wants his reader to stand at the edge between figure and ground—not uncertain, but aware and discriminating in the face of complexity.

For Garth, to make this language a tool of moral argument is to make us able to say who is to blame. No longer will "[t]he killing of numbers of patients [be] so trite a piece of Raillery, that it ought not to make the least impression either upon the Reader, or on the Person 'tis apply'd to" ([A6r]). Garth expects us to be impressed by what it means to see this conflict as a battle, what it means that we have accepted the language of warfare as the standard language for social conflict. These automatized perceptions and forms of understanding are, as the saying goes, "made strange," and so are themselves made objects of perception and understanding. The shock at the violence in *The Dispensary* is not to be found in the literalized version. No reader will take very seriously the prospect that the apothecaries themselves will take up arms, that the pills will become bullets, the pens swords. The shock comes when we recognize the original truth of the metaphors that have been literalized into the story. By reinvigorating the metaphors and reconnecting them to the horrific reality of early modern warfare, Garth makes readers recognize what they should already have known but what the controversy had overshadowed—that the fellows of these two corporate bodies, the Society of Apothecaries and the College of Physicians, are between them responsible for the lives of all their fellows. We are made to see the *justice* in calling a careless, greedy, ignorant, or incompetent physician or apothecary a killer.

So too would Pope build the action in his mock-epics out of literalized metaphors whose force the poems would renew. Though Pope's admirers seem not to know it, there is precious little wit in calling a bad writer dull or a dunce—in Cibber's memorable phrase, "so trite a Repetition." Cibber is right that we might have expected from Pope "something more spirited," and he is right that so little wit can make but little impression. Of course Cibber, dull and much pained, gets only half the story: "What, am I only to be dull, and dull still, and again, and for ever?" (*A Letter,* 27). The Action in *The Dunciad* is grounded in the truth that the dunces are dunces. But the thrill Pope feels and creates when he says as much

> Out with it, *Dunciad*! let the secret pass,
> That Secret to each Fool, that he's an Ass.
> (*Arbuthnot,* 79–80)

comes not from knowing the "Secret" (that all already know) but from the danger that comes from saying it aloud of these persons (Pope here refers to King George) and in such exquisite detail. The wit, the "spirit" in this name-calling is not in the names but in their poetical relation. That relation becomes spirited when we recognize the original truth and the chilling consequences of the names that have been literalized into a story.[24]

By reinvigorating the tired language of literary controversy, Pope makes readers recognize what its trite repetitions had overshadowed: that poets hold in their pens the responsibility for the cultural values and the intellectual vigor of all their fellows. That task is in important ways more difficult for Pope. Garth's literalization and the language it renews stand in defense of an institution whose buildings, grounds, procedures, and persons are made the stuff of his poem; and behind Garth's charge of homicide lay tangible, literal victims. Pope's literalization is less firmly grounded: there is no College of Poets for him to defend.[25] The institution Pope defends—literature—is not so well defined, although Pope does make its buildings, grounds, procedures, and persons the stuff of his poem. Pope reaches toward defining that institution by

---

24. These are largely literalized metaphors, although *dull* is not. However, Pope's interest in Dulness and *dullness* focuses on its metaphoric senses and synonyms: weighty, slow, obtuse, foggy, misty, soporific, etc.

25. The College of Physicians does not, however, give Garth's literalization quite the solidity it might seem. The College's stewardship of the physical health of the nation now looks to be as much of a myth as Pope's stewardship of the cultural health of the nation. The bleak fact of late seventeenth-century medical practice was that at its best it was usually no more beneficial than doing nothing at all, and only the most incompetent care could be worse than indifferent.

making *The Dunciad* a poem of education, thus giving substance to the claim of literature's central responsibility. Even so, the real victims—"*Art* after *Art* goes out" (B IV.640)—still seem less solidly realized. Nonetheless, in Pope as in Garth, we are asked to see the justice and be impressed by the horror of calling a careless, or greedy, or ignorant, or incompetent poet a dunce.

There is still a difference in the action of *The Dunciad*. The action that results from Garth's literalized metaphors is, not accidentally, of the canonical form. As John Sitter reminds us, "For the Augustan humanist the greatness of the epic and the epic hero lay in the fact that the 'one, great, and remarkable action' performed in such works might be regarded as a broadly political accomplishment affecting an entire society (or, in the rather troublesome case of *Paradise Lost*, as an action concerning all of mankind). In this scheme of things, active males won the decisive battles (for better or worse) and founded countries" (59). Garth's action is a programmatic reflection (inverted, of course) of this canonical epic matter. Pope's is not. Sitter thinks that Pope engages in a studied avoidance of the canonical epic action by means of a studied parody of Blackmore's heterodox theories of the epic, and that this makes *The Dunciad* not a mock-epic but an anti-epic. Perhaps so, but the question of the militaristic cast of the epic—its action, its hero, its ethic—was far more complicated.

Garth's literalized metaphors give him the story of a battle, but his story engages a sustained questioning of the ethos of the militaristic epic. Garth does not reject it outright: he praises both William and Anne for their state militarism.[26] Yet he sharply differentiates between what is appropriate state action, the province of the head of state, and what is appropriate for the citizen. Garth stresses that his is a poem about civil affairs, and is in that sense domestic. His hero/villains are not active males who win decisive battles, but passive, anxious males who are prodded into action by machines (i.e., their desires) that visit them on sleepless nights. Even after they are set in motion, these heroes would rather talk than act, and they fight not as the first in battle but as the instigators of a mob. More than a century later, the irrelevance and the dangers of the heroic ethos in the mass warfare of a mass culture would be given monumental expression in Tolstoy's epic novel: "The ancients have left us model heroic poems in which the heroes furnish the whole interest of the story, and we are still unable to accustom ourselves to the fact that for our epoch histories of that kind are meaningless" (*War and*

---

26. See Sena (1986, 62–64).

Peace, X.19). Here, in the last year before the eighteenth century, Garth would stand precisely at the cusp of this change, willing to entertain a vestigial heroism for the likes of a William or an Anne, but denying its relevance in all other spheres. In this first mock-epic, action is mob violence, civil war, and the proper course is to submit oneself to others. This, not any simple endorsement of the significant, brutal action of the classical epic, reflects Augustan humanist thinking. Think of Dryden's heroic dramas, with their series of increasingly domesticated figures; of Swift's *Battle of the Books,* whose action is marred by the taint of civil war; of *Paradise Lost,* in which the proper, albeit unchosen course for each of the major persons is not to act; of *Paradise Regained,* where that lesson is reaffirmed.

Most interesting is the case of *The Rape of the Lock,* whose battle of the sexes fully conjoins domestic and epic action. As in *The Dispensary,* the action focuses on civil violence, now in its most plainly domestic sphere. Pope explores the limits of civilization in the *Rape,* just as Garth does in *The Dispensary.* Among the wild swings of mood in *The Rape of the Lock*—from desire, to anticipation, to exaltation, to gloom, to fury—the one constant is anxiety. Anxiety is the fixed point as Pope explores the need for and the fragility of those social rituals by which we seek to contain desire and resolve conflict. The action of *The Rape of the Lock* records the process by which desire, first and foremost the Baron's but also Belinda's, breaks out into violence that, however small, threatens a chaos that only an external force can return to order. There is not so much difference between this and Garth's study of how heroic ardor, fed by desire, is a menace to the social order. If in the *Rape* Clarissa's "Moral," which is by no means definitive, or the apotheosis of the lock seem unsatisfactory resolutions to the conflict, they are hardly more so than Harvey's dully bureaucratic solution at the end of *The Dispensary* or Pope's apocalyptic one at the close of *The Dunciad.* What our dissatisfaction shows us is that the poets had no idea how to cope with the subject to which the mock-epic was drawn.

Thus if *The Dunciad* does not in any obvious way return to the militarism of the epic, it thereby completes the logic of the mock-epic. Dunces "war with Words alone" (B IV.178), and the violence they do is to those words, to the culture those words inscribe, and to the Word man's words must serve. Although Courthope complains that "the alleged action of the 'Dunciad' is not a recognized fact... but only an inference which Pope chose to found on the real actions of the various persons whom he satirises" (E-C, IV.21), the real action whose figural description is literalized into the Action of the poem is just as much a fact as is the action that underlies *The Rape of the Lock* and *The Dispensary.* The action by which the dunces wage war with words, bring the Smithfield Muses to the ear of kings, and thereby establish the state of Dulness is that they write and publish. The relation between that action and the Action of *The Dunciad* is identical to the relation between Arabella losing her lock and the battle of the sexes or between a scuffle among servants and the battle of the Dispensary. Indeed, in the *Dunciad*s the relation is more compelling, for Pope's effort to rehabilitate a language of judgment through poetic representation is itself another episode in the war with words. In the *Dunciad*s Pope makes the action that is the poem and the action in response to the poem as much a part of the Action of the poem as the events the poem depicts.

Although Garth's is the mock-epic original and among the more systematic Augustan uses of literalized metaphor, the technique is antecedent to Garth. Literalized metaphor is a common feature in Augustan satire, especially in narrative satire. Milton's war in heaven provides an early, almost mock-heroic example, though one grounded on a very different rationale.[27] Swift's *Tale of a Tub,* which was published in 1704 but written largely before 1699, uses literalized metaphors as extensively and in many of the same ways (see Quinlan). Literalized metaphor is the key to the design of the fables in almost all mock-heroic satire, before and after Garth—from the dimensional literalizations of Boileau's pulpits to Shadwell's kingdom in *MacFlecknoe,* Swift's battle in the *Battle of the Books,* Pope's battle of the sexes in the *Rape of the Lock,* Walpole's burden in Fielding's *Vernoniad,* and the dunces' delivery of the Smithfield Muses in *The Dunciad.* In each case the work presents an argument about some real situation, event, or persons. In each case, the work also tells a story in which the actors are those persons who are the objects of the argument, but the events and situation are fictional—in a special sense. Taken purely as story, the narration of the events is simply fictional. The Apothecaries did not storm the College; Arabella Fermor did not fell Lord Petre; the dunces held no Fleet-Ditch Olympiad. But taken as argument, these can very well be seen as appropriate, fair, truthful descriptions—figurative to be sure—of the actual events and situations. There is nothing whatever remarkable about these figures—the Apothecaries attacked the College, Arabella declared war when Lord Petre attacked her, the dunces deal in filth—not, that is,

---

27. Milton's literalization in *Paradise Lost* would be justified in Dryden's terms by Scripture: "For immaterial substances, we are authorized by Scripture in the description: and herein the text accommodates itself to vulgar apprehension, in giving angels the likeness of beautiful young men" (Ker, I.187).

until they are literalized and made into a story. Then the affective powers of narrative give life to the figures and give the force of conviction to the descriptions.

As befits a mock-epic, in *The Dispensary*, in *The Rape of the Lock*, in the *Dunciad*s, the story (Action) is designed to serve the argument (Moral), and their relationship (Fable) is allegorical. But theirs is not the simple unidirectional relationship of either the true allegory or the feigned example. Unlike the feigned example, which avoids "specific references to individual persons and events in [the poet's] own times" (Wallace, 1974, 286), the Action of the referential mock-epic fable is composed almost entirely of persons, places, and objects of the poet's world. Its tenuous fictionality must contend with the weight of all those actualities gravitating powerfully toward the here and now. Unlike the traditional allegory, which "required a symbolic mode of utterance which split [the] audience into the few who understood the code and the many who contented themselves with poetic surfaces," the referential fable dwells obsessively with the "poetic surfaces"—which is to say, with actuality itself. Not only does it work "within the assumptions" of its audience (Murrin, 173), it works within their shared experience. The poet has no secret code, only the moral good sense to know the right. His description deals in the particulars of the knowledge that all competent readers share; it is a mode of utterance that splits the poet's audience into the few who have virtue and the many who content themselves with the way things are.

In the mock-epic, story and argument are conjoined in an uneasy but powerful alliance. While the story, properly understood, makes the argument, the argument, properly understood, returns us to the story. Seeing the justice in calling a bad doctor or apothecary a killer or a bad writer or editor a dunce makes us see the truth of the story and, most important, the true nature of its Persons. In such a referential fable, we dwell on the Action as much as the Moral, and both Action and Moral dwell in the world of experience. The point is not to teach the Moral, but to apply it in the poem. In this sense these stories are fictions; and in this sense its fables are figures. And in this way, we can be "pleased with the image, without being cozened by the fiction."

Part One

Figures of the City

Prologue

"Speak, Goddess! Since 'tis Thou that best can'st tell"
—The Dispensary

Epics begin *in medias res*, it was said, because "[t]his Method both shortens the Action, and exceedingly entertains the Reader." The pleasure this arrangement affords is partly the pleasure of precipitate excitement, "of being immediately plunged into the Depth of the Action." It is also the pleasure of a slowly emergent *ordonnance*, of finding order in what had seemed "Wilderness" and of being led by one who can see design where we cannot (Trapp, 1744, II.9–10n). Mock-epics begin *in mediam civitatem*. We are immediately plunged into the middle of a city and placed among its citizenry, faced with streets, ditches, buildings, stalls, carriages, chairs, and all the plentiful furniture of urban life, whose good order is precisely the issue at hand. This method does not shorten the action, but does supplement it, giving the reader a perspective from which to comprehend and to judge it. The method entertains, not least because the city—teeming, growing but not yet overgrown, old, new, elegant, vulgar, and most of all commercial, thriving London—is an urban wilderness that fascinates our poets and their readers. This method entertains also because in this bustle the *ordonnance* of the city and its citizens will emerge slowly and under the guidance of one whose sight and art are able to find and display the design in its mazy dance.

The obligatory first parts of the epic behind them, both Garth in *The Dispensary* and Pope in *The Dunciad* place us immediately in the city and among its citizens. Though awash in particulars, we are expected to judge the order in what we find, to judge the state of the commonweal. Like his epic counterpart, the mock-epic poet expects to give laws to his fellow citizens. His is first and foremost a battle of judgment, and his chief battleground is not the city in which he sees action but the language by which he portrays it. Understanding that language is an instrument of social and moral control, the mock-epic poet strives to take control of his language, and that labor is Herculean. It ranges the poet against what seems an army of language abusers, an army that draws its strength from the inexorable forces of social change. It thus plunges the poet—and with him his reader—into a superfluity of detail. Though a Pope might sometimes wish to stand apart and above the battle and to sweep away the detritus of a decaying culture and the "insects" who produce it, he cannot be rid of them. For among their products is his language.

The mock-epic poet's plan of battle rests on the designing powers of his verse, but his ordnance in that battle is particulars. As much as he is obsessed with inheritance, with preserving the usable past, he is also obsessed with the details of the present. Both obsessions strain the knowledge and tolerance of readers, but the obsession with particulars is the hardest to take. For some readers and some mock-epics, it can overwhelm and deaden the poem. The poets knew the dangers, of course, and as they indulge their obsession they also use it, making our experience of superfluity an occasion of just the sort of judgment that can break through obsession to a more capacious understanding. If the excess of particulars does not overwhelm the poetry for us, that is because particulars are made the means by which the poet gains control over his—our—language. If the effort to take control over our language does not sour the poetry for us, that is because the appeal of *ordonnance* is powerful. In the mock-epic things are so arranged that, if we are willing to become the kind of "initiated" reader the poem demands, our knowledge and the poet's judgment are the same. In mock-epic as in epic, *ordonnance* becomes law.

The questions of the mock-epic are the questions of truth. Who can tell? Who can see the truth of the wild creation of modern civilization, and who has the power—both the ability and the right—to say it? These are Samuel Garth's questions in the first lines of the first mock-epic, questions that only deepen as the genre develops. The aims of the mock-epic, however, are first and last polemical, more akin to the truth of propaganda than the truth of science. In Part I, I will show how the mock-epic found a language that could be an instrument of its truth. The goals of this truth telling are deeply ideological, to reform the conceptual repertoire of the nation. Its tools are, on the one hand, the facts of modern life, all those teeming particulars that London affords, and, on the other hand, the *ordonnance* that only poetry can achieve. Together, they comprise the mock-epic's designs on truth.

Naming Names

2

All I shall say for my Self on this Score is this, if I appear to anyone like a Counterfeit, even for the sake of that chiefly, ought I to be constru'd a true Man, who is the Counterfeit's example, his Original, and that which he Imploys his Industry, and Pains to Imitate, & Copy. Is it, therefore my fault, if ye Cheat, by his Wits and endeavours, makes himself so like me, that consequently I cannot avoid resembling him? ... 'tis only y^r experience, must distinguish betwixt them to wch I willingly submit myself.

—*Rochester,* Dr. Bendo's Bill

For a genre that gives such large place to description, the mock-epic displays a significant anxiety about language. Prototypically enmeshed in controversy, especially those controversies that have a long paper trail, the genre lived in and by propaganda. It was fostered by circumstances in which social change, and so language change, seemed most to present its cutting edge. Even when a mock-epic does accept the new, it sees only continuity in change—as, for example, Garth embraces the new science but portrays it as the result of the College's established tradition of inquiry. The mock-epic's implied author stands as a bulwark against change, but with his weapons battered and abused. So his first task was to repair that language, to new hone its satiric edge. His mission was a sacred one, for the mock-epic poet was driven by a new and powerful attitude that saw language change as a moral issue, as the product of moral and social corruption. In the mock-epic, language change is a sure sign of social and political disease.[1]

---

1. Isolated comments linking language change to moral and social corruption began to appear near the end of the sixteenth century. In the last quarter of the seventeenth century that

Key to this mission is to restore the truth-telling power of names, both proper and "general" names. Pope acknowledges as much when he announces the most striking of *The Dunciad*'s technical innovations. Explaining that the *Variorum* notes "bestow a word or two upon each" of his persons, Pope adds, "[T]is only as a paper pinn'd upon the breast to mark the Enormities for which they suffer'd" (TE, V.9). Pope's mark upon the breast perfectly exemplifies the name-calling task of mock-epic satire: to correlate a judgment, picture, or characterization ("bestow a word or two") with a name or referring expression ("a paper pinned upon the breast"). This is not the simple name-calling of invective, with its characteristically more violent badge: "I mean to hang, and Gibbet up thy Name."[2] Where invective punishes by smearing the proper name with all the epithets that might be made to stick, mock-epic is concerned to give its persons a very specific name, one that bespeaks the poet's judgment of their character.

The mark upon the breast also answers Pope's hope to make his judgment stick. Pope guarded against misapplication with proper names and identifying notes, a move he likens to the most unmistakable of ostensive references, "a paper pinned upon the breast." But he saw a greater danger to the significance of the badge: that his judgment—and especially the values underlying it—might become unpinned. As, of course, they quickly did, first when the dunces accepted and then reinterpreted Pope's mark and later when it began to seem that the only blamable party in *The Dunciad* was Pope himself.

The story of the Augustan mock-epic is in many ways the story of a search for a firm ground from which to call names and establish the stability of its judgments. Because this was such a rearguard action, its most natural polemical resources lay in the continued appeal of an honored past. But the resources of the honored past were too much museum pieces, while the poems' victims had ready access to the social and linguistic vitality of the forces driving change. So the mock-epic poets sought to use both. The most notable of those efforts is Pope's *Variorum* apparatus in the *Dunciad*s, in which he appropriates one of the institutions by which literary meaning is preserved but which he fills with the life and the language of the streets. But Pope's reach for sta-

---

attitude came to dominate thinking about language, and by the end of the century it was a powerful commonplace (see J. Williams, forthcoming). For "the breakdown of language" as "a decline of culture," see Price (205–8). For an early mention of this concern, see Jack (25–30); for the most complete discussion of the Augustan literary concern over linguistic change, see Hatfield (1968).

2. Oldham, "Upon a Printer," *Works* (1710), 144.

bility in the notes only completes the logic of a far more pervasive design, whose ground is the knowledge and experience of readers and whose goal is to stabilize a language of judgment.

In pursuit of that design, the mock-epic gives special prominence to the names of persons and of places. True to its contrarian character, the mock-epic uses the personal names convention says it ought to avoid, and avoids the place names it might as well use. It banishes proper place names to notes and margins, only to replace them with extended descriptions. These periphrastic place names emphasize large views and wholistic judgments, all in the interest of protecting those judgments against the kinds of linguistic and social change that make the genre possible, and in the poets' view necessary. In this periphrastic emphasis on wholes and large views, the mock-epic can encompass and judge a vast range of particulars, mapping them as a network of knowledge and values grounded in experience. Garth, building on his models in Dryden and Boileau, complicated and revived the simple pattern of mock-heroic reversal. Although Pope would be the great master of this reversal, playing endless variations on its pace, rhythm, suspense, pathos, and bathos, Garth is the one who first understood how to play the mock-epic game of multiplied particulars and unifying values without the easy, fully authorized stance that Dryden assumes when he names "*Nonsense,* absolute" (*MacFlecknoe,* 6). Garth first understood how essential it would be that mock-epic throw its readers back onto their own ethical resources and their own experience of the world by throwing them back into the poetic design, in which truth, proper judgment, is a matter of wholes, not parts.

Knowledge as the Foundation of Belief

Like Pope's *Variorum* notes, the mock-epic's settings bestow on their places considerably more than "a word or two" as they turn from names to specifying properties. *The Dispensary's* first place, the Old Bailey, is identified in virtue of the objects and the events it houses and the persons who frequent it. In the same way, *The Dunciad* identifies Bedlam not by name but by the places, objects, persons, and events proximate to it. Normally writers name those things or concepts that readers are likely to know, to expect, or to assume; periphrastic explanations and depictions are reserved for things or concepts likely to be unknown, unfamiliar, or surprising. FSP has amply confirmed this principle. So will the intuitions of most of my readers when they realize that the previous sentence should have read: This principle has been amply confirmed by the theory of information structure in sentences, known as Functional Sentence Perspective or FSP. This norm of communication—one names what is familiar, explains or depicts what is not—is egregiously violated by the periphrases in mock-epic settings. They take forever to identify the most familiar places, leaving those who do not rush through them to wonder just how familiar these places really are. That is, by violating so basic a norm of communication they shift the issue from identification to identity, from location to evaluation.

The shift from identification to identity also underlies what is usually thought of as the prototypical Augustan periphrasis, that found in natural description (Tillotson, 76–77):

> When Thomson speaks of the sportsmen with 'gun' and 'spaniel' who
>> Distress the Feathery, or the Footed *Game*
>
> he is not merely decorating his poem but differentiating the game that is hit while it flies from the game that is hit while it runs.... Pope uses 'scaly breed' for fish because he has been speaking of game birds, and particularly of the partridge with its 'shining plumes' and 'breast that flames with gold', and is now changing to another kind of game, one with a different covering (scales instead of feathers) but one, otherwise, splendidly the same:
>> The silver eel, in *shining* volumes roll'd,
>> The yellow carp, in *scales* bedropp'd with *gold.*

In both kinds of periphrasis, the poet sacrifices directness for the "precision of meaning" that comes from detail—in the natural descriptions, fleecy, finny, feathery, footed, scaly; in the mock-epics, angry Justice, little villains, great villains, Folly's throne, brazen and brainless brothers.

The two kinds share a semiotic structure: each is a scientific technique whose ground is the reader's knowledge and whose aim is discrimination, precise measures of relation and distinction. But they serve different poetic functions. The brief periphrases of natural description merely replicate the biological taxonomies that explain the natural order. The extended periphrases of mock-epic descriptions create new social taxonomies intended to explain human disorder, supplementing the failed discourse of "human science."[3] Mock-epic periphrasis stands in stead of the name, which it banishes to footnotes and keys—where the given name can ensure correct identification but leave the work of identity to the periphrastic name that displaces it.

Periphrastic names displaced given names because the poets distrusted the truth-telling powers of their language. Augustan thinking about language exhibits a pervasive concern—and fascination—with what seemed an excess of significance. Language theory followed the Port-Royal masters in distrusting usage: "The difference between the truth of things and the truth of usage is that, in the latter, there are accessory ideas associated with the principal idea of a word."[4] Recalling the traditional distinction between the philosopher's "bare representation" and the poet's sensuous and vivid examples, Dryden emphasized "the representation of such things as depending not on sense, and therefore not to be comprehended by knowledge" (Ker, I.153). In this way, Dryden could embrace a correspondence theory whose "principal idea" is referential, but focus on "accessory ideas" that opened the way for "cognitive content beyond ... perception" or reference.[5] In the cognitive excess of accessory ideas, the poet whose aim is truth found important resources focused on all those matters of attitude, value, and judgment which had always been reserved as the poet's special province (Ker, I.153).

The danger in accessory ideas lies in their changeability. Because they are grounded in use, not reference, they are subject to decay—from conscious manipulation or other vagaries of use. Locke noted that "common use, by a Tacit consent, appropriates certain sounds to certain *ideas* in all languages" (*Essay*, 3.2.7).[6] When Dryden argues that his elevated language is derived from the conversation of "the gentlemen of the court" (Ker, I.176), the accessory ideas that mark elevation are derived from use, from the social position of the speakers. When Addison

3. Richetti notes that Locke too used volubility as a defense "against the distancing or distorting effects of language" (1983, 58–59).

4. Quoted in M. Cohen (36).

5. Land (1974, 35). Murray Cohen adds that this "drift away from the strongest claims language can make to be isomorphic to reality" shifted attention to "the rules of relationship that account for coherence in speech and nature" (25). Ralph Cohen argues that the ever-increasing syntactic complexity and interrelation of the "Augustan mode" reflects "an increasing awareness of the unresolvably complicated world of men and nature" (1967, 32).

6. The first modern linguist to examine carefully the role of value in language was V. N. Volosinov: "No utterance can be put together without value judgment. Every utterance is above all an *evaluative orientation*" (1973, 105). See Halliday on *characteristic collocation* (1961, 275–76).

warns that "a Poet should take particular Care to guard himself against idiomatic Ways of Speaking," he registers the equal power of low associations (note the revulsion in the anatomic detail): "[I]t often happens that the obvious Phrases, and those which are used in ordinary Conversation, become too familiar to the Ear, and contract a Kind of Meanness, by passing through the Mouths of the Vulgar" (*Spectator* 285). Dr. Johnson also weighs in, complaining of Shakespeare's use of *dun* because it is "now seldom heard but in the stable": "Words become low by the occasions to which they are applied or the general character of them who use them;... they are in time debased by vulgar mouths and can no longer be heard without the involuntary recollection of unpleasing images" (*Rambler* 168).

If words are subject to such involuntary excess of significance, then language is a dangerously malleable instrument of truth. Any correspondence theory requires that in understanding a "singular term" or name of an object "one must think of that object *in a particular way*," and that "every competent user of the language who understands the utterance will think of the object in the same way."[7] But when Augustan poets surveyed the names they must use to describe the world about them, they found that competent users of the language just did not "think of the object in the same way." It seemed to them that most users of the language thought of the objects in question in precisely the wrong way. Language changes as the world changes, and the mock-epic's rearguard action could no more prevent one than the other. The poets' response to this change was to rename—and, in the process, to be sure to call a dunce a dunce. The essential project of the mock-epic is finally name-calling, renaming its objects so that it can recharacterize its world by restructuring its public language.

In this renaming project, periphrastic names offered essential resources. Best understood is the much-discussed tie to the epic tradition. In their fund of classical reference, periphrastic names gave the mock-epic setting a Virgilian scope and an established hierarchy of value that has seemed to twentieth-century critics always ready to judge the debased Augustan reality. But the classical frame had to be applied, and in the application had already become a tarnished glory. Virgilian periphrasis had been as useful to Blackmore as to Garth, and "Blackmore's endless line" (*Dunciad,* A I.72) had already eked out a monumental bar-

---

7. Evans (1982, 16). Though this account describes Frege's truth-functional theory of language as articulated in "On Sense and Meaning" in 1892, the point holds as well for Augustan correspondence theories.

rier to any sure value in the Virgilian association. It is wrong to suppose that it could be a decisive value judgment for the poet to juxtapose the contemporary persons and the great classical ideal when those very persons had already done the juxtaposing many times over. So the poets undertook to give that ideal, the classical associations themselves, a stable ground and sure foundation.

The more basic resources of periphrastic names are their specifying properties. Periphrastic names designate their objects so that we recognize them already embedded in a *network* of associations specified in the name itself. The periphrastic name selects, perhaps even creates those associated ideas that are the foundation of the truth of usage and that govern valuation. Doing so, it brings to the object in question a larger body of judgments arrayed in a network whose interrelations are specified in the design of the verse. This network can be thought to speak more surely of values because of its interrelatedness, because the network has some of the features of a self-regulating (and thus self-correcting) system. Some objects may be mistakenly judged—indeed, that's why they have a place in the poem. But that mistake (presumably) cannot be universal: *all* objects cannot be misvalued. The interrelated force of the whole will be expected to tend toward uniformity, and so toward the truth the poet would enforce.

The poetic procedure produces its truth by exactly reversing the process by which particular names and ideas were thought to become general. Augustan semantic theory was in all cases founded on "particular names," which were taken as the most specific, individuating instance of language and the bedrock of all reliable meaning.[8] The language of predication, composed of so-called general words, was a derivative language, parasitic on the truth of particular names. It was therefore one remove from its foundations and correspondingly uncertain (*Essay*, 3.3.11). Locke argued that general names and general ideas, though a function of experience, are nevertheless our ideas, and ours alone (*Essay* 3.2.4–5). This is so because the abstraction of general ideas is finally just a matter of creating classes by reducing information, by subtracting particulars from those complex ideas gained from experience of particular existents (3.3.6). In general names resides the classificatory powers of language—the powers most essential to the satirist, powers our best

---

8. Locke, *Essay*, 3.1.2–3. Although I take Locke as my example, the features of Augustan semantics that bear on the names in satire were shared by Dryden and by almost all language theorists and philosophers (see Land, 1986). I might, for instance, use examples from Pope's friend, the philosopher George Berkeley, whose views Pope knew and understood, at least on the basic issues.

contemporary semantics takes as primitive but that Augustan semantics grounded in the prior referential tie between idea and immediate experience, the tie captured in particular names.

By reversing the process by which general names are created, the mock-epic setting seeks to rehabilitate a general, predicative truth. Each opening setting centers on a general place name, "Place," "Dome," "walls," "gates." From that general name the poet works back to the particular idea by adding circumstantial detail. As the details collect, the depiction grows to a spark of recognition. When the depiction and the reader's knowledge engage, the particular idea that the depiction builds stands in unstable juxtaposition with the reader's own particular idea. The reader is faced with an act of judgment, a competition between two ideas that, at the moment of identification, stand impossibly together for the same object. Both ideas are representations and both are grounded in experience (for an Augustan, in the senses). The depicted idea represents the object by the collection of particulars the poem selects; the known/remembered idea represents the object by the collection of particulars memory selects. In the interplay of poetic and mnemonic selection lies the struggle to fix values and to shape judgment. And in this interplay is a return to experience, to the putative original of all knowledge, value, or meaning.

Particulars, the details of experience, are the poet's most reliable tools in the struggle to fix the values of his treasured, endangered inheritance and to enforce his judgments against those who endanger it.[9] The mock-epic poet knows from bitter experience that words will serve any master, however corrupting, and that he dare not take for granted the accessory ideas of value (their "full significance and worth"), no matter how carefully "self-conscious" his practice (A. Williams, 53). The mock-epic poet also knows, and his twentieth-century readers have preferred to forget, that, however much the resources of his inheritance might enrich his poem, that heritage nevertheless could not find a purchase to stand on its own. Only *within* such battles as Swift contrives in his mock-epic, or as we retell in our histories, do the ancients so securely retain their hold on Parnassus and so resoundingly drag the moderns through the dirt. Only when the poet can find or create some stable ground of shared knowledge and experience from which to draw particulars to serve as specifying, value-fixing properties can the epic in mock-epic be achieved.

---

9. Youngren has noted the importance of detail (and openings) in his early essay on generality in Augustan poetry (1968, 209).

The rich particulars of London's topography have long been known to have valuative associations.[10] There are few essentials to add to Courthope's 1882 analysis of the thematic role of London's topography in *The Dunciad* (E-C, IV.23–27), although Aubrey Williams has ably enlarged our sense of how those matters further the poem's larger designs (9–41). In his introduction to *The Rape of the Lock*, Geoffrey Tillotson made the point that "the scene of the epics is empty desert beside the milieu of the *Rape of the Lock*, its close-packed London" (TE, II.118). Pat Rogers's *Grub Street* has shown how such thematic use of topography is a characteristic mark of a variety of Scriblerian work.[11]

With respect to the more general pattern of particulars in the mock-epic, topography is only one of many sources of value-fixing properties. "The epic is thing-less," adds Tillotson, "beside Pope's poem with its close-packed material objects" (TE, II.118–19). What topography shares with the other sources of particulars is this: topography brings language ever closer to its foundations in the senses. The stench of Fleet Ditch or of Moorfields, the squalor of Rag-Fair or Grub Street, the hypersensuality of Covent Garden and Drury, the coal dust of the East End—all speak eloquently to those who know them. In this sense, the oft-lamented scatology of these poems is in fact a foundation of their argument of values: there can be no mistaking how we value one who carries on his face the "brown dishonors" of a Curl or the "amber tears" of a Stentor.

Such moments of unmistakable evaluation cannot, however, remain isolated. In that case, the poet really is, as his detractors like to think, only slinging dirt. What lends legitimacy to the valuation of individual particulars is their place in the design of the whole.[12] Only because Stentor's "Tears of *Amber*" reflect Garth's diagnosis of the College's disease can they carry the burden of fixing the blame on his fellow Collegians.[13] In the matter of values, no one detail, however pungent, can be decisive. The locus of true and reliable valuation is the whole,

---

10. For discussion of London in eighteenth-century literature, see Rogers (1972) and Byrd (1978). Hunter notes a more direct relationship: since meaning (knowledge) is additive and progressive, "experience and education were equated with the conquest of space" (1975, 150).

11. A useful early source is William Henry Irving's *John Gay's London* (1928).

12. See Rothstein's important account of Augustan "positional poetry" (49–68). Rothstein's view, which emphasizes the metonymic qualities of the verse, is in many ways similar to what I argue here.

13. Garth added Stentor's tears ("On *Stentor's* Crest the useful Chrystal breaks, / And Tears of *Amber* gutter'd down his Cheeks" [V.315–16]) in 1714. Ellis laments the addition as a debasement of the poem, but in fact it only completes the logic of the poem's representations.

which, in the case of the settings, is realized by the reader as something like an annotated map.

In poetry relationship is all, and poetry has the power to contrive—and to enforce—a truth that might escape a less crafted form. Since poetry is a "dense" medium (Goodman, 252–53) in which all is interrelated and every detail counts, its wholes constitute the kind of self-regulating system that can stabilize valuations. These wholes might have some one overarching design, such as Fielding creates in *Tom Jones*; but they might not, and in most Augustan poetry they do not.[14] What is necessary (and sufficient) is that the design of the whole leave no part isolated, that each part enter into some network of interrelations and that all these networks be themselves related. In the mock-epic, no term is singular.

Waiting for Closure

The mock-epic setting calls on its reader to identify its places by fixing them within a network of related knowledge. Much of that knowledge is literary, much is classical, but most is local and particular—and not always explicitly specified by the poem. In mapping a system of values against which to measure its objects, the poem begins with places because they offer a ground of shared experience and value that can be assumed to carry the authority to compel belief. Then, as the narrative unfolds, the values mapped in the settings can, by the same process of valuation by association, be transferred to the main items in the story—the persons and their actions.

Readers can be led to judgment by these periphrastic settings because poems are linear. Texts come to us in a linear stream (though not normally one word at a time), and they come to us with traces of that linearity built into *all* their formal structures. The experience of reading is the experience of waiting, anticipating, remembering, reconsidering—the experience of time. Such delay is important to most of the figures we think of as characteristically Augustan: the ever-present zeugma ("Dost sometimes counsel take—and sometimes Tea"), the wonderfully mixed lists ("Puffs, Patches, Powders, Bibles, Billet-Doux"), chiasmas and other forms of couplet design, the many forms

---

14. See R. Cohen (1967) and Hughes (1977).

of ellipsis—all are figures of combination, of delayed and extended comprehension.

The role of time and expectation in the mock-epic has been understood in substantially the same way since the poems were first studied. The story goes something like this: the inversion of values that defines mock-heroic develops over time and in a standard sequence. Recognizing the epic frame, readers begin to expect the uplifting pleasures of the epic. When they learn that, in this poem, manner and matter are at odds—"small things are compared with great"—readers experience a deflation of values, what Williams calls "epic breakdown" (54). The story of epic breakdown underlies Dryden's praise of Tassoni for suspending the epic pretense before breaking into mock-heroic: "The first six lines of the stanza seem majestical and severe; but the two last turn all into a pleasant ridicule" (Ker, II.319). Boileau's practice was much the same:

> Je chante les combats et ce Prelat terrible,
> Qui, par ses long travaux, et sa force invincible,
> Dans une illustre Eglise exerçant son grand coeur,
> Fit placer à la fin un Lutrin dans le Choeur.
> (*Lutrin*, I.1–4)

In his own mock-heroic, Dryden not only sustained the delay more fully, but also integrated the collapse of the suspended epic sense more successfully into the thematic structure of his poem:

> All human things are subject to decay,
> And when Fate summons, Monarchs must obey.
> This *Flecknoe* found, who, like *Augustus*, young
> Was call'd to Empire, and had govern'd long;
> In Prose and Verse, was own'd, without dispute,
> Through all the Realms of *Nonsense*, absolute.
> (*MacFlecknoe*, 1–6)

The story of epic breakdown is, however, far too simple. It requires us to think that the mock-heroic inversion defeats our expectation, or at least desire, for the promised epic sense. It also requires a reader always ready to be surprised, a perpetual naïf. Such readers have to be as willing as critics to confine themselves to local moments, local effects. But it is a rare reader who does not know what is coming, who can simply enact and reenact an epic elevation subject to breakdown. Even in the opening lines from Boileau and Dryden, few readers would not know what to expect from these mock-heroics. At the same time, there is something like a turn or breakdown in those lines. What we need, then, is an account of the mock-heroic turn or breakdown that does not require the impossible: readers who have neither knowledge nor experience of the larger wholes—both social and poetic—within which those lines function.

Mock-forms need readers who understand that at some level their expectations will be defeated. Since this understanding is itself an expectation that will be met, these genres always have the character of meta-genres in which readers entertain expectations that they do not seriously hold. This is one particularly useful way of thinking about the Augustan "double perspectives" that critics find so attractive. But this explanation would seem to give the lie to any account of a suspended epic sense or epic breakdown. Once I learn the game and am firmly in the grip of the meta-expectation of the mock-form, then it will *never* be true that "the last two lines turn all into a pleasant ridicule." "All" will *already* be a pleasant ridicule, and the two last lines only enact a denouement of exposure that confirms and displays my pleasure in the ridicule.

The reader in the grip of the meta-expectation of the mock-heroic has no need to wait since the deflation is already figured (often explicitly so) in the whole. Epic breakdown reenacts at the most local level the ceremony of poetic justice, openly displaying what was already figured in every aspect of the poem or passage. Poetic justice is a figure of wholes, its ceremony giving us the satisfactions of the open return of those values we had held through the trials of the plot—or, here, through the trials of the suspended epic sense. Thus poetic justice is also a figure of excess, its ceremony only supplemental testimony to what was always there. With each new instance of epic breakdown, the reader experiences both the satisfaction of seeing the victims stand still for their degradation and the satisfaction of seeing the world whole, a satisfaction that lies at the heart of so much Augustan literature, however fragmentary, disordered, particolored. This is also a satisfaction of Pope's vatic, apocalyptic ending to *The Dunciad*, which ought only to horrify but actually thrills. Seeing the world whole may be worth almost any price, perhaps even universal darkness.

In mock-epic at its best, however, the deflation that we know will come will often surprise, coming in unpredictable ways or failing to come when we most expect it. Moreover, in the mock-epic, deflation is only one aspect of a more general disruption of values—the mock-epic effect is as likely to be *in*flation as deflation. Although the mock-epic will in general satisfy our meta-expectation of a doubled perspective, the reader who comes to the mock-epic expecting only a consistent double perspective will be sure to lose the way. Mock-epic frustrates the reader's desire for easy coherence, the impulse to rush to closure, even as it grounds its judgments on the reader's ability to make coherence. The good reader will be ever wary—and so must be persuaded or chastised into withholding judgment until all the facts are in. But in addition to patience, this process—what we might call a suspension of belief—requires of the reader at once a degree of knowledge and a degree of innocence that no one can simply, simultaneously possess. Since *all* the major accounts of the mock-heroic report some such experience, readers must come by this mix by means of an artifice. One such artifice is the object of the first setting in the first mock-epic.

A Starting Point: The Opening of The Dispensary

The Dispensary opens in the conventional way: the Muse is invoked, the topics announced, the reader warned, and the future predicted. Then the poem launches into an extended, stage-setting periphrasis, which serves the expectation-generating functions of all beginnings. It calls up the body of knowledge (and values) that readers are to bring to bear as they construct the relations that will constitute the poem's coherence and judgments. Moreover, this first periphrasis in the first mock-epic bears a double burden of first things. Since it cannot rely on generic expectations as can texts of a more familiar kind, Garth's opening must serve as something of an object lesson, teaching readers what it will mean to read a mock-epic, what kinds of judgments they will be called on to make, and what aids and obstacles the mock-epic will present—most of all, teaching them that the task of constructing relations warrants care and time.

The opening periphrasis in *The Dispensary* sets the scene of the impending battle:

> Not far from that most celebrated Place,
> Where angry Justice shews her awful Face;
> Where little Villains must submit to Fate,
> That great Ones may enjoy the World in State;

> There stands a Dome, Majestick to the Sight,
> And sumptuous Arches bear its oval Height;
> A golden Globe plac'd high with artful Skill,
> Seems, to the distant Sight, a gilded Pill:
> This Pile was, by the Pious Patron's Aim,
> Rais'd for a Use as Noble as its Frame:
>
> (I.7–16)

The first concern of this setting is, it seems, physical location. The battle that the poem will celebrate had occurred in the Dispensary itself, the outpatient clinic located in the basement of the College of Physicians in Warwick Lane. So the poem begins by presenting two buildings—the College and the Sessions House of the Old Bailey, whose yard was just the other side of the city wall. Neither is named, and the not-far-from topos locates the less familiar structure, the College, in terms of the more familiar one, the Old Bailey. Like any good guidebook and every contemporary Londoner (Rogers, 1972, 5), the poem uses well-known landmarks, fixing its locations by means of the proximity of the two structures and the notoriety of Old Bailey. And, like all good mock-heroics, the poem uses periphrasis to open the way for an initial exercise in epic elevation.

In these and the very similar lines that open the second half of *The Dispensary* (IV.1–16), Garth follows Dryden's example in *MacFlecknoe*. Dryden too had used mock-heroic periphrasis to make location a means of evaluation.

> Close to the Walls which fair *Augusta* bind
> (The fair *Augusta* much to fears inclin'd)
> An ancient fabrick rais'd t'inform the sight,
> There stood of yore, and *Barbican* it hight:
> A Watchtower once; but now, so Fate ordains,
> Of all the Pile an empty name remains.
>
> (64–69)

Garth closely imitates Dryden's lines, even punning within the allusions,[15] but only to highlight key differences. One difference is that

---

15. Dryden's locative phrase uses the periphrastic construction, determiner + noun + restrictive clause ("The walls which fair *Augusta* bind" rather than "the City Wall"), making the periphrasis an opportunity to raise additional topics. Garth uses the same structure, adding a second restrictive clause appositive to the first. Less direct relationships can be seen in "de-

Dryden saved his setting for the middle of his poem, well after its system of mock-heroic values had been established. Garth's lines have the greater burden of setting values as well as location. Another difference lies in how the two settings use the reader's knowledge of the place in question. Both speak of known places, but Garth imparts to his description a more insistent, almost ostensive referential force: where Dryden uses the neutral demonstrative *the* ("the walls," "the fair Augusta," "the sight," "the pile"), Garth in key instances reverts to selective demonstratives ("that most celebrated Place," "This Pile," "that great Design")—not "the most celebrated place" but that one, there, now.

The grammatical difference highlights another difference. Garth's account is far less economical, as though these places, there and now, were being introduced to us for the first time. Where Dryden informs us quickly and easily, getting right down to the point, Garth displays an odd reticence, withholding as much as he can for as long as he can. Where Dryden uses two lines for his locative prepositional phrase, Garth uses four; where Dryden uses four lines to describe his pile, characterize its purpose, name it, and delineate its fate, Garth uses eight only to describe and characterize the purpose of his. Although Dryden does indulge himself in the mock-heroic suspension and delay that he praised in Tassoni, his periphrasis is quick enough not to leave the reader in doubt:

> An ancient fabrick rais'd t'inform the sight,
> There stood yore, and *Barbican* it hight.
> (66–67)

Most important, Dryden's setting names what it designates. Barbican is "an empty name" because "the Pile" can no longer inform Augusta of the dangers without the walls and has succumbed to the same power that dooms Flecknoe: "All human things are subject to decay" (1). However empty, the name still designates the place unequivocally and is, for the knowledgeable reader, full. It is charged with the Virgilian associations of Dryden's mock-heroic and with the associations of the "brothelhouses" and the "Nursery" that rise out of Barbican's ruins. Yet Garth,

cline" and "propagation" (*Dispensary*, I.17–18), which pick up Dryden's bawdy joke of brothels rising and a nursery erecting its head out of a ruined tower. More complex is Garth's use of Dryden's allusion to Cowley's *Davideis*: compare *Dispensary*, I.21–27; *MacFlecknoe*, 70–78; and *Davideis*, I.244. For the "suburban" character of this location, see Rogers (1972, 66–70).

whose place and pile are there now and whose deictic constructions insist on their there-now-ness, just will not name names. And to make sure we don't miss what he's up to, Garth uses the allusion to Dryden to emphasize names twice over. First, he repeats Dryden's sight-hight rhyme just where a name ought to be (and again in the next couplet, "plac'd high... distant sight")—although Garth substitutes epic elevation (height) for naming (hight). Second, the name Garth avoids is the same one Dryden had not used: the Old Bailey takes its name from the London Wall (*bailie:* a wall enclosing a fortress or castle). Thus, Garth strings his reader along, greatly extending the suspension and delay that he found in Dryden, withholding the information we need to get a sure fix on the story, and especially withholding names.

In Garth's periphrasis, there is even a hitch in identifying the locale, as the reader must wait for the second line and a glance to Garth's footnote to fix the referent of "that most celebrated Place." The hitch here has to do with what the poem finds in the "Place / Where angry Justice shews her awful Face." Though the law court is a natural home of Justice and the Old Bailey was widely known as "Justice Hall" or "the Justice House," this particular Justice displays an anger that is, in the impartial confines of the court of law, most unseemly.[16] That anger will, in the course of the poem, center one strand of the major satiric theme—the uncivil dangers of passion. Moreover, this Justice conspicuously lacks the blindfold that exemplifies her dispassionate impartiality.[17] By 1699, Justice's blindfold had become a key feature in the conventional iconography, and Justice without her blindfold was an emblem of *interested* judgment.[18] Although Justice might properly dis-

---

16. Then, as now, the normative discourse of adjudication systematically excludes all talk of passion or self-interest on the part of the adjudicators: indeed, the English legal tradition provides elaborate mechanisms for ensuring dispassionate impartiality. As the legal scholar Robert Cover used to say, "Procedure is the blindfold of Justice" (Curtis and Resnik, 1987, 1728). Curtis and Resnik identify a minor tradition of an "angry" or "maimed" Justice, but those depictions were used to signify abuses of justice by judges who served inappropriate interests, either their own or the sovereign's.

17. In 1699 the Old Bailey presented a plain front: "It standeth backwards, so that it hath no Front towards the Street" (Strype, *Survey,* III.281). The present Old Bailey (a new structure, the second since 1699) has at its top a statute of Justice without a blindfold. But it does so, its brochures proclaim, in defiance of convention, because Justice was originally not blindfolded and because her "maidenly form" is supposed to guarantee her impartiality, thus rendering the blindfold redundant. See Simmonds (1977) and Curtis and Resnik (1987).

18. Justice's blindfold first appeared in Sebastian Brant's *Ship of Fools* (1494), where it mocks the ignorance and dishonesty of the courts. The blindfold has a similar significance in the *Bambergensis Constitutio Criminalis* (1510). Early in the sixteenth century the blindfold came to be an emblem of Justice's impartiality, specifically "impartiality between great and

play her anger in the appropriate circumstances, those are not the circumstances of the court. Looking for a place with an *angry* Justice, we might just as well turn to the three prisons (Newgate, Ludgate, and the Fleet) that surrounded the College. Garth's description suits them as well or better than the Old Bailey, since prisons are places where "little Villains" do "submit to Fate" and so are places where Justice is properly angry, properly "shews her awful Face."

Garth's delay and our uncertainty are, more than the locations, the ultimate point of the setting. It makes sense to use the Old Bailey as a landmark. It even makes some sense to center the Old Bailey on an angry Justice. But once we understand *why* the Old Bailey is an apt landmark for the College, both institutions suffer an epic breakdown. The sense of the whole comes only as an aspect of a complex act of judgment that first correlates the depiction with our knowledge of its referent, and then must resolve the dissonance between what the depiction designates and the way the depiction characterizes it. The question of names is foregrounded by every aspect of the opening lines, whose "ancient Leagues" (I.2), "celebrated Place" (I.7), "Dome" (I.11), and "Pious Patron" (I.15) offer small tests of the reader's judgment—tests in which, as we shall see, very good readers have been wrong. Whatever Garth's limitations in versification, these lines are highly crafted to impart an insistent and disquieting forward movement to the verse—the very movement Dryden had called the chief pleasure of the mock-heroic.

Take a small example, the noun phrase that syntactically dominates the Old Bailey couplets, *that most celebrated Place.* The most informative word in this uninformative phrase is *celebrated,* which narrows slightly the field of possible places. The place begins to be more surely designated only with the restrictive where-clauses ("Where angry Justice shews her awful Face; / Where little Villains must submit to Fate, / That great Ones may enjoy the World in State"). But as those clauses narrow the field of reference, they also narrow—one might say overturn—the relatively rich and positively valued semantic potential of *celebrated.* Now *celebrated* takes the neutrally valued and very new

---

small" (Simmonds, 1977, 1164). By the end of the sixteenth century, Ripa presents the blindfold as a standard feature of the iconography: "She is blindfolded, for nothing but pure reason, not the often misleading evidence of the senses, should be used in making judgments" (120 n.16). For Justice without a blindfold see a late advice-to-a-painter poem attributed to Nahum Tate: "The blackest traitors here [in the City] a refuge find, / For City painters ne'er draw justice blind" ("Old England" [1682, 1685]; *POAS*).

sense of "well-known."[19] Displaced by the particularizing restrictive clauses, the unrealized heroic semantic potential casts a shadow over the place celebrated only by rogues and villains, shifting *celebrated* uncomfortably close to *notorious*.[20] Ultimately, though, the sense that Garth most has in mind is not new at all. The dissonance is resolved by the literal meaning of the word's Latin root, *celebrare*, to frequent. In this world, a place of judgment like the Old Bailey is best portrayed as much-frequented—not unlike that other scene of high drama that Garth uses to locate another of the poem's places:

> Not far from that frequented Theatre,
> Where wand'ring Punks each Night at Five repair;
> Where Purple Emperors in Buskins tread,
> And rule imaginary Worlds for Bread.
>
> (IV.1–4)[21]

In the first noun phrase of his first setting, Garth has his reader enact, however briefly, the double-take that is the temporal manifestation of the celebrated double perspective of high Augustan poetry. Only here, it is not yet the honored past against which the present is measured, but the values still alive in the language. The reversal of *celebrated* is complete only after two other revisions, of *Justice* and *awful*. A heroic, aweful Justice might move those who had no better guide to their actions, just as Garth's satiric "Poison" might move "some of our Disaffected Members into a Sense of their Duty" ([A5r]).[22] But once the reader comes to understand the next couplet, with its villains small and great,

---

19. The first adjectival use of this sense cited in the *OED* is Boyle, 1665–69: "Those Celebrated Ladies taught their Children to Sway those Rulers of the World." The *OED* cites a verbal use as early as 1597, but still tied to praise: "celebrate with due honour." The first citation of a verbal use that is closer to the relevant sense is Barrow, 1660: "As it is commonly cited and celebrated by all men."

20. Garth was not alone in disapproving of what happened at the Old Bailey: "The Sessions House... was gaining a national and sinister renown under the familiar name of 'the Old Bailey'" (Babington, 1971, 59).

21. In the first two editions, IV.1 read "that most famous Theatre." Garth changed "most famous" to "frequented" in the first revision of 1700, and left it so in all subsequent editions. One also notes several correlations between the "angry Justice" of I.8 and the "wand'ring Punks" of IV.2. For the Old Bailey–theater connection, see Rogers (1972, 248–49).

22. In discussions of heroic art, *awful* was a technical term for the emotional response to representations of heroes and their deeds, a response that was thought to explain the didactic efficacy and thus the social and moral value of heroic art. Readers would be filled with awe (wonder) at the godlike deeds of the epic hero and, awestruck, would be moved to emulate the qualities of such awful figures.

the inappropriateness of an angry Justice cannot be suppressed. The sense of the whole underscores the dissonance of the parts and undoes any expectation of a positive, valorizing reading. *Awful* comes to mean something much closer to its present sense (first *OED* citation from 1834), a sense that is closer to the original ("causing dread") than to the dominant seventeenth-century meaning ("worthy of, or commanding, profound respect or reverential fear"). The unrealized potential of the words stands as an indictment of so two-faced a justice that cannot uphold its celebrated standards.

The second couplet ("Where little Villains must submit to Fate, / That great Ones may enjoy the World in State") is more explicit, but it also harbors a hitch for the reader in the apparent over-specificity of "little." Why *little* villains? Little villains as opposed to what? Big villains, it would seem; but in the verse the little villains are answered by the "great Ones" of the second line, and it is not obvious that they should be villains. With the strongly paired noun phrases, the perspective on the Old Bailey's awful Justice is doubled again, but this time by a doubled reference.

On the one hand, "great Ones" is synonymous with "the great," a transparent reference to the aristocracy who, in fact, live "in State" and will never appear at the Bar in the Old Bailey. In this case, the couplet presents an urban version of a universal, if dismaying truth: it is the fate of the low-born, villains (from the Latin *villanus*, a farm laborer or servant), to labor, to want, and, if they steal, to die so that their betters can live well—a truth allied to one of the poem's more explicit themes, the exploitation of the poor and ignorant by those who are, or should be, their betters.[23] To readers who know the habits of the Old Bailey, this reference has a sharper edge. For the Lord Mayor and Sheriffs daily put on notoriously sumptuous feasts (at three and five o'clock) for the judges, their guests, selected counsel, and any person of quality enjoying a visit to the court. Oft-confirmed Old Bailey lore held that the course of many a trial was shaped by a judge's longing for the awaiting feast.[24] From this angle, the Old Bailey stands as both the ultimate defense and the ultimate display of the rights of property and privilege.

---

23. E. P. Thompson (1975) demonstrates how widespread was the manipulation of the legal system by the government and others who live "in State." Although Rogers (1985) corrects Thompson on details, the general point still stands.

24. Hooper (1935, 130–37). This is how these lines were later used by Pope, "The hungry Judges soon the Sentence sign, / and Wretches hang that Jury-Men may Dine" (*The Rape of the Lock*, III.21–22), and Gay, "For petty rogues submit to fate / That great ones may enjoy their state" (*Fables*, 36.39–40). Thornbury (1897), who does know the ways of the Old Bailey, sees

On the other hand, the strong parallel structure and the otherwise unnecessary specificity of "little Villains" attract the pronoun "Ones" to "Villains"—little villains, big villains. In that case, the couplet depicts in its reduplicated design the hierarchy among thieves in which lesser, laboring thieves stole and died for their thief-taker masters. In this angle, the Old Bailey represents the world of the criminal underground, as Newgate would in *The Beggar's Opera*. This underground was more closely associated with Newgate, but Newgate and the Old Bailey were in more than one way joined, and the drama of the Sessions House was essential to maintaining the criminals' code. Thus an angry Justice is a justice of informers and scapegoats, and the Old Bailey's drama shows the inevitability of subordination among men.

For readers who can maintain the double perspective, the result is a species of referential pun. Held in suspension, the two references generate something like an epitome of the thematic structure that Gay would later exploit in *The Beggar's Opera*. The villains, moved to emulate their betters, reproduce in their microcosm a model of social relations that helps us to see more clearly how the great, in exploiting the little villains, emulate them. Eventually Garth will develop in the poem a two-layered instance of such vicious emulation both up and down the social scale. That pattern of emulation involves three parties—mountebanks, apothecaries, and Apothecaries Physicians—arrayed in the concentric circles typical of mock-epic, a configuration that expands metonymically to indict all reaches of English society. The result in Garth is the same as in Gay: readers are left to wonder just where distinction lies.

The act of judgment that these couplets demand is first and foremost an act of suspicion. To resolve the sense of the whole is to adjust the sense of its parts, all the while correlating the depiction in the lines with the facts of their reference. Doing so, the reader constantly revises and revalues—*great* declining to the coarse interestedness Walpole would later give it, and *villain* gaining from our pathos. Most complexly revised is *enjoy the World in State*: like their buskined counterparts of the "frequented Theater" who "rule imaginary Worlds for Bread" (IV.4), the actors in Old Bailey's drama of judgment also rule for bread, as *enjoy* shifts toward *ravish*. Through these revisions, we learn to suspend judgment, distrust expectation, withhold resolution, and generally refuse to

---

both the connection between Pope and Garth and the importance of the feasts to Garth's point: in his survey of London, Thornbury introduces his account of the feasts by quoting Pope's line and ends it with Garth's Old Bailey couplets (II.468–69).

take partial views at face value. Everything about these lines leaves us suspiciously looking forward in hopes of some *future* source of linguistic stability.[25] In order to settle the referent of this locative prepositional phrase, the reader is cast forward to the main clause and its "Dome," itself unnamed. And in struggling to identify the Dome, we are cast forward to its "Pious Patron" (I.15), whose identity is itself a puzzle, though also a key to the poem's moral and social diagnosis.

Although any satirist would be wary of naming the persons he attacks, Garth would need a special reason to occlude names of places so elaborately. In each of the settings in *The Dispensary*, Garth withholds names, substituting instead some selective set of specifying properties.[26] Drury Lane is "that frequented Theatre / Where wand'ring Punks each Night at Five repair" (IV.1–2); Covent Garden is "this darling Quarter of the Town" which "Long has . . . For Lewdness, Wit, and Gallantry been known" (IV.17–18); Apothecaries Hall is "a Structure on a rising Hill, / Where *Tyro's* take their Freedom out to kill" (III.128–29); and Horoscope's shop in Little Britain is "the Mansion where the Vulgar run, / For ruin throng, and pay to be undone" (II.102–3). Clearly in none of these cases is the point to obscure or otherwise hinder the reader's efforts at identification. Garth may make the reader work through a few lines to identify these places, but his purpose is not to leave the reader in doubt. Quite the contrary: these sometimes extensive periphrastic settings are designed to remove doubt, to settle the matter at hand, which is not mere location.

The pattern Garth sets is followed by Pope in the major settings in the *Dunciad*s. After the dedication to Swift, with its plays on names and identities, the three-book *Dunciad* also opens by setting place:

> Where wave the tatter'd ensigns of Rag-Fair,
> A yawning ruin hangs and nods in air;
> Keen, hollow winds howl thro' the bleak recess,

---

25. The syntactic structure of these couplets is thoroughly forward looking. These couplets constitute a long locative prepositional phrase whose cohesive ties with the rest of the text are exclusively cataphoric (i.e., the syntactic and semantic features refer forward to features of the text that will be encountered in subsequent lines). The prepositional phrase's internal structure is equally suspensive. The syntax of the noun phrase appended to the preposition (demonstrative determiner + noun + restrictive clause + restrictive clause) is itself highly cataphoric, each item looking forward to the next to settle its referent.

26. The one exception is the introduction of the Elysian Fields in Canto VI, since none of Garth's readers would have the kind of knowledge of that location that Garth typically draws upon in his periphrastic settings.

> Emblem of Music caus'd by Emptiness:
> Here in one bed two shiv'ring sisters lye,
> The cave of Poverty and Poetry.
>
> (A I.27–32)

This opening setting, which continues another ten lines, works precisely as Garth's had. As in Dryden and Garth, there are two locations. The preliminary location, Rag-Fair (structural counterpart to the Old Bailey), is named outright, although *Rag-Fair* is already a descriptive name that designates the objects and activities associated with the place. The main location, the "cave of Poverty and Poetry" (counterpart to Barbican and the College of Physicians), remains unnamed[27] and is placed by those particulars associated with it.

In the final *Dunciad*, the preliminary location (counterpart to the Old Bailey and Rag-Fair) is handled just as in Garth's poem, even down to the surprising and disconcerting detail about a statue:

> Close to those walls where Folly holds her throne,
> And laughs to think Monroe would take her down,
> Where o'er the gates, by his fam'd father's hand
> Great Cibber's brazen, brainless brothers stand.
>
> (B I.29–32)

Now the cave is a cell in Bedlam (Bethlehem Hospital), and the details are richer in associations than those in the *Variorum*.[28] The surprising detail is in the epithet "brazen": the statues were in fact stone, and Pope knew as much. Most critics have thought this simply an error that Pope was too careless or too taken with to change, but it was not. This setting requires the same kind of retrospective, wholistic understanding that Garth's Old Bailey demands. There will be a delay before the reader can know why Cibber's brothers must be brazen (see Chapter 9). And there will be a rather longer delay before we can know what it means in this final *Dunciad* that "Folly holds her throne" or what it means "to think

---

27. This place may be only a fiction, but, given Pope's characteristic practices, it is perfectly possible that the "yawning ruin" is a particular place. Rogers has plausibly suggested that the cave is Grub Street itself (37–70).

28. I think we must ignore Warburton's attempt in his note (B I.33n) to associate this cell with nearby Sion College. It is beside, even contrary to, the point. See Rogers's evidence against Warburton's identification (57–63).

Monroe would take her down."[29] In the course of that delay, the reader must master a strikingly complex network of relations and is likely to value Bedlam wrongly, to take it too lightly. This Garthean procedure continues in the time setting, which in both versions follows soon after the place setting. It too employs the kind of value-setting periphrasis Garth had established in his poem:

> 'Twas on the day, when Thorold, rich and grave,
> Like Cimon triumph'd, both on land and wave:
> (A I.84–85 [B I.85–86])

The pattern of deferral and substitution that characterizes Garth's and, later, Pope's settings reveals their deep distrust of the power of names. That distrust is the doubt to be removed, the matter to be settled. It does not doubt the power of names to name or refer, but their power to convey values and say the truth: the power of predication and its accompanying judgment. Indeed, *The Dispensary* is largely animated by the gnawing contradictions between the physician's fear of the power of the mountebank's art, where words like nostrums can cozen and kill, and the poet's confidence in the power of his art, where words can be made to speak themselves and proclaim their truth. And the bite of those contradictory feelings is only sharpened by the propagandist's recognition that there is not such a great difference between the two arts.

The reader has been warned. Garth's first, almost unspeakable line informs us that the drama of the mock-epic is the drama of being able to tell, of seeing and saying the truth: "Speak, Goddess! since 'tis Thou that best can'st tell" (I.1).[30] It will take the inspiration of a muse and the discernment of a goddess to tell what's what and who's who in this drama of a corrupted discourse in which all terms of value have been so

---

29. For an account of what it means, see Morris's discussion of madness in *The Dunciad* (279–85). For an earlier account of this madness, see Spacks (210–53). For madness in Augustan literature generally, see DePorte (1974) and Byrd (1974). For eighteenth-century views of madness, see Foucault (1961).

30. After much puzzling, I cannot say with certainty whether Garth means this line to be as funny and as harsh in the mouth as it is—as though we begin not only mystified but tongue-tied. Since the formula was common enough, I like to think that Garth knew what he was doing. Garth could certainly do better (and seldom does as bad), and he never changed this line—even after he had the example (and presumably the advice) of a young Pope to guide his later revisions. Defoe paid Garth the compliment of imitating this line in "The True-Born Englishman" (1700; *POAS*): "Speak, Satire, for there's none can tell like thee" (1).

abused that they have lost the power to speak the truth. And since value, identity in the fullest sense, is the matter at hand, Garth ostentatiously avoids names, toying with the matter of identification, which is never really in doubt, in order to settle the matter of identity, which is.

"*Dullness* by Its Proper Name"

3

A strange thing this! that a Man must be an Atheist, only for calling Dullness *by its proper Name.*
—Tom Brown, "To Sir W. S——," *January 8 [1700]*

Again I insist, you must have your Asterisks fill'd up with some real names of real Dunces.
—Swift to Pope, *16 July 1728*

The Censure they pass [on The New Dunciad*] is, that the Satire is too allegorical, and the Characters he has drawn are too conceal'd: that real Names should have been inserted instead of fictitious ones.*
—The Universal Spectator, *3 April 1742*

Mock-epic emerges at a point when satire's ancient ties to magic and ritual punishment were most in disrepute.[1] The reasons were many: political preferences for moderation and accommodation over factional confrontation; social preferences for refinement, delicacy, and "good manners"; literary and philosophical preferences for a general, preceptual didacticism. Yet to survey the great satires of the eighteenth century is to find satire after satire that is immoderate, unrefined, ill-mannered, particular, and personal. For immoderation, who can match Pope's supremely elegant and supremely distasteful image of a daisy chain of courtiers: "From tail to mouth, they feed, and they carouse" (*Epilogue to the Satires,* II.179). The muse of late Augustan satire

---

1. For satire's primitive origins, see Elliott (1960). For early satire, see Knoche (1949); Renaissance satire, Kernan (1959) and Korshin (1973); Augustan views of satire, Elkin (1973). For modern approaches to satire, see Feinberg (1968) and Paulson (1971).

prefers particular victims and is, as Erskine-Hill, Morris, and others have argued, a "Muse of Pain."[2]

The shift to particular, punitive satire is, however, a larger cultural phenomenon. It was no accident or quirk of personality that led Pope to name names in his satire. Nor was it an accident that Pope broke the taboo on names in a mock-epic, since in large measure Pope's move was required by the poetic momentum of the genre. Elements of particular satire are already evident in Dryden's later work; Oldham offers a wealth of immoderation;[3] and other influential models are found in popular political satire, including works by the likes of Waller and Marvell. More important, Pope's kind of particular satire is fully present in Garth's mock-epic. What from the perspective of Pope's career looks to be a major turning point—the first *Dunciad*—only completes the generic pattern established by Garth in the last year of the previous century. More than any other work of the turn of the century, *The Dispensary* marks the transition from the satiric poetry of Dryden to that of Pope.

In both literary and legal circles, the preferences for moderate and refined satire found expression chiefly in bans against satire that was "particular" and named names. Though the second *Dunciad* would break through to a relatively unrestrained use of proper names, Garth's poem is already fully particularized. Like *MacFlecknoe*, *The Dispensary* avoids the actual names of its victims to keep within the laws of the kingdom and of decorum, but Garth's techniques for naming his persons are specifically designed to ensure correct identification, and Garth helped his friends make keys.[4] His coy disclaimer in the "Preface" only affirms that the poem is "directed at ... particular Person[s]"—and dares the reader to find them.

---

2. Morris (214). Erskine-Hill (1975) showed in great detail how Pope relies on the particulars of his victims' lives, an argument further developed by Morris. Also see Carretta (1983) and Guilhamet (1987).

3. For Oldham's satiric poetics, which Pope called "indelicate" and "too much like Billingsgate" (Spence, 43), see Korshin (1973, 145–74).

4. One MS key to *The Dispensary* is found in a letter from Garth to Arthur Charlett (Sena, 1974a, 93–94). Other MS keys were circulated very early on, and surviving copies are filled with readers' attempts (largely successful) to identify the figures. Interestingly, the one identification Garth does try to obscure is that of his major villain, Horoscope, whom he identifies in his letter as James Houghton but who is certainly (as most key makers saw) Francis Bernard. Ellis rightly notes that Bernard's recent death made Garth reluctant to name him (1699, II.69n). In *A Satire Against Wit*, Blackmore complains, "They dig up learned *Bernard's* peaceful Grave" (109).

There is more to the mock-epic effort to particularize its victims than proper names. When Pope added names to the *Dunciad*, he also added the *Variorum* notes with their wealth of particulars, another case in which Pope refined and developed a structure already present in *The Dispensary*. As is the case with the mock-epic's place names, the poets are unwilling to trust to the efficacy of a simple, direct identification. They fill the poems with particulars that supplement the proper name they do not trust, exposing the interests that make the name empty. Here too is the Augustan distrust of language as an instrument of truth-telling, and the poets' attempt to engage the knowledge and experience of their readers as instruments of the poets' moralizing. Here is also the special problem that faces the particular satirist who relies so heavily on readers' knowledge and experience as his instruments, the problem always awaiting those who would make instruments of persons.

Name and Reputation

"Poets," said Shelley in *Defense of Poetry*, "are the unacknowledged legislators of the world." Dr. Johnson thought much the same: "The poet must write as the interpreter of nature, and the legislator of mankind" (*Rasselas*, X). The youthful Pope saw himself as a legislator who "*restor'd* Wit's *Fundamental Laws*" (*Essay on Criticism*, 722),[5] adding that the poet-legislator interpreted Nature: "*Nature* and *Homer* [are] the same" (135). Even the laws of the critics replicated nature: Aristotle was so influential a lawmaker that even "*Nature* did his Laws obey."[6]

As Augustans saw it, the natural genre for the poet-legislator was the epic. They saw epic chiefly in terms of matters of state: "*Theologians, Philosophers,* and great *Law-givers* every where fell into this way of instructing and cultivating the People."[7] The epic's subject was leaders of men; its moral, the proper conduct of civil affairs; its originals, full of lessons of statecraft. Dryden saw in the design of the *Iliad* a lesson in

---

5. For other mentions of law in the *Essay on Criticism*, see lines 91, 132, 162, 168, 270B, 651, 679, 715.

6. This line was inserted into an early edition of the *Essay on Criticism*; the final version has the more modest claim that poets "[r]eceiv'd his Laws, and stood convinc'd 'twas fit / Who conquer'd *Nature*, shou'd preside o'er *Wit*" (651–52).

7. Blackmore, Preface to *Prince Arthur* (1695, A2v).

"the necessity of Union, and of a good understanding betwixt Confederate States and Princes engag'd in a War with a Mighty Monarch: as also of Discipline in an Army, and obedience in the several Chiefs, to the Supream commander of the joynt Forces" (Ker, II.167). Although Dryden here makes it all sound rather more like a training manual than do most critics, this reading was endlessly repeated and seldom challenged.[8] Later, Pope would choose for his first published translation from Homer Sarpedon's "admirable Speech" on the heroic's lessons of state—the speech to which he returned when he felt compelled "to open more clearly the Moral" of *The Rape of the Lock* (V.7n). Even the ballad of Chevy Chase becomes, in Addison's ingenious reading, a poem to instruct princes (*Spectator* 70). Thus the aim of the epic was to inculcate by attractive representations the "Theology [or 'Publick Faith'] of the Country" (Blackmore, 1716, 74)—what Addison calls "the Constitution of the Country," but what we would call ideology. In its turn, the mock-epic naturally looked to matters of law as a source of authority to enforce its judgments.

Note, however, that the mock-epic does not settle for mere law*giving*. While it retains from the epic and the panegyric an interest in statecraft, a claim to legislative power, and a desire to instruct, the mock-epic also embraces satire's power to punish. Legislation is finally not enough. The institution of law to which Garth immediately turns in *The Dispensary* is the seat of an angry, enforcing justice.

> Where angry Justice shews her awful Face;
> Where little Villains must submit to Fate,
> That great Ones may enjoy the World in State;
> (I.8–10)

If judges who cannot judge must be judged because their interests blind them, so too healers who cannot heal. Garth will put his readers in a position to judge and himself in a position to heal the healers, both in the pacific political counsel of his surrogate, Harvey, and in the corrective, penal force of his satire.

In order to have its force, punitive satire must be particular. For a judge to pronounce sentence, he must first name names. But few were

---

8. For a convenient review of many positions on this matter, see Swedenberg, "Fable and Action" (166–92) and "Moral" (193–215), especially Dryden (nos. 4, 12, 13), *Athenian Mercury* (no. 5), Pope (nos. 18, 19), Dennis (no. 25), Gildon (no. 27), Trapp (no. 28), *Gentleman's Magazine* (no. 33), Goldsmith-Newbury (nos. 39, 40), Kames (no. 41), Wood (no. 43).

willing to give poets a judge's right to use names. Bolstered by strong preferences for moderation and refinement in civil affairs, these sentiments ran deep, both in criticism and in the law. The laws against satire and libel were severe and vigorously enforced right through the seventeenth century.[9] The law, however, was characteristically literal minded, and the satirists characteristically resourceful. The law protected only names, and satirists found other ways to identify victims and particularize an attack. As Swift explained, the wealth of writing in political and other controversies generated a ready body of well-established conventions for circumventing the law "so that although everybody alive knows who I mean, the plaintiff can have no redress to any court of justice."[10]

Critical censures against particular satire were broader, though the penalties rather less severe. Dryden held that "[w]e have no moral right on the reputation of other men," although he exempted criticism of his work: "I speak not of my poetry, which I have wholly given up to the critics: let them use it as they please" (Ker, II.80; also see II.22). Addison's gentle Spectator was also "very scrupulous in this particular of not hurting any man's reputation," though with a similar qualification: "[N]or shall I look upon it as a breach of charity to criticise the author, so long as I keep clear of the person" (*Spectator* 262). This distinction continues to appear as late as Pope's second *Epilogue to the Satires,* in the voice of Pope's concerned, conservative friend:

> *F.* Yet none but you by Name the Guilty lash;
> Ev'n *Guthry* saves half *Newgate* by a Dash.
> Spare then the Person, and expose the Vice.
> (II.10–12)[11]

---

9. As late as 1599 the archbishop of Canterbury and the bishop of London issued orders to burn books and prohibited all future satires (*A Transcript of the Registers of the Company of Stationers of London,* 1876, III.316). For a brief account of the history of satire and law, see Elliott (260–62).

10. Swift, *Political Tracts, 1713–1719* (14–15).

11. Pope's "Bill of Complaint" prefaced to *Arbuthnot* announced his new commitment to naming names: *"I had no thoughts of publishing it, till it pleas'd some Persons of Rank and Fortune to attack in a very extraordinary manner, not only my Writings (of which being publick the Publick judge) but my Person, Morals, and Family."* Compare the language of Thomas Cooke after his appearance in the *Dunciad:* admitting that he did "converse with many who have wrote against you," he adds that his associates were not "such as take those methods of writing slander in the dark. Your moral character I never heard attacked by any with whom I converse" (*Corr.,* II.509, 520). Soon after, Cooke wrote that Theobald "attacked

As the critics complained, the poets named names. In 1693, Dryden already thought that modern satire was overrun with libels and lampoons.[12] In 1720, John Dennis attacked Steele's good name by bemoaning the increase in personal satires.[13] But where the standard complaints blamed the liberty of the press and the hacks it encouraged, Dennis blamed the "violence and virulence of the contending Parties in *England*" and pointed to Dryden: "We have since had Libels which have pass'd for Satires, as *Absalom* and *Achitophel*, the *Medal*, *Mac Fleckno*, and the *Dispensary.*" Not since *Hudibras* could Dennis find a "just Satire" that only "exposed the Vice" (II.201). Dennis's horizon may be too long, but the fact remains that in the last quarter of the seventeenth century more and better poets turned more and more to particular satire.[14]

Although Garth could count on "the Pleasure which we find that the Generality of Mankind takes in particular Satire" (Dennis, II.396), using actual names would nevertheless expose him to significant risks. Since the laws against libel stated a cause of action in terms of the name itself and were, in 1699, still strictly construed,[15] Garth dared not name his persons outright. Pope had the advantage of nearly three decades of increasingly particular satire, and the greater advantage of the standing as a poet and social critic that he so carefully cultivated. Still, it took courage for Pope to use names in the *Variorum*, even with no legally traceable paper trail from the publisher to himself. Friend Swift, experienced propagandist that he was, knew full well the import of his insistence that Pope use "real names of real Dunces" (*Corr.*, II.504–5), although he also knew that there were few dangers to purse or person in a purely literary quarrel. What Swift could not know was how thoroughly the

---

Mr. Pope, regarding him only as the Editor of that Author [Shakespeare], without any Reflections on either his Person, his Morals, or Family" (*The Letters of Atticus*, 1731, 34; quoted in Weinbrot, 1982, 241n).

12. Ker, II. Dryden's complaint very closely follows that of Robert Wolseley's 1685 "Preface" to *Valentinian* (Spingarn, III.13–14).

13. See, for example, William Ayloffe's "Preface" to Sedley's *Works* (1707).

14. For a study of Dryden's "typological" solution to the ban against particular satire, see Zwicker (1972). Korshin (1973) offers a useful history of seventeenth-century satire.

15. The rule of law was to construe allegedly libelous texts *in mitiore sensu*, in the least harmful sense. Not until 1711, in the case of *Queen u Hurt*, was libel successfully prosecuted for anything less explicit than full mention of the victim's name—and the Queen was the plaintiff (Kropf, 1974, 164). By 1724, courts had held that "[w]ords are now to be taken by the Court as they import and mean in the Sense of the Bystanders, and in common Parlance, and understanding of Words" (*Aston u Blagrave*; see Reynolds, 1975, 475–77). For other accounts of the legal history, see Downie (1979) and Davis (85–101).

Variorum would mark a new phase in his friend's career, a phase in which Pope would pride himself most of all on naming names even when his victims did have stings. By the final *Dunciad* (as in the Horatian satires), few names were safe from Pope's sentence; and for those few whose names he never dared utter, Pope's indirections became perilously explicit.[16]

Pope's turn to proper names comes rather late in the game. In many ways that turn marks the end of the game of Augustan particular satire, the last and most explicit step across the bounds of good manners. The game began early in the popular "sub-literary" press and in such marginal genres as the advice-to-a-painter poem. It continued through Dryden, although Dryden never quite gave his satire over to particulars. It was Garth who first fully particularized his satire, as Dennis's genealogy recognizes: "*Absalom* and *Achitophel,* the *Medal, MacFleckno,* and the *Dispensary.*"[17] It was also Garth who first formulated the complex relation between names and particulars characteristic of the mock-epic.

Names and Particulars, Identification and Identity

Garth had to rely on the standard techniques for creating surrogate proper names because his poem was already more than daring enough for a respected physician without a poetic track record. But the need for those surrogate names does not explain the elaborate relation Garth develops between proper names and identifying particulars. Eventually Pope would use full proper names with none of the standard shifts to surrogates, but he matched those names with notes full of particulars. Those notes complete the logic of the mock-epic's union of names and

---

16. See Weinbrot (1982, 270–75) for an excellent discussion of Pope's daring play on names in the Midas episode in *Arbuthnot* (69–82), whose unspoken conclusion would soon be spoken in *Epistles* i.1: "a Minister's an *Ass*" (96). For the danger of such boldness, see Mack (1969, 130ff) and Morris (236–40). Also see Pope's well-known reply to one of Arbuthnot's several admonitions against using names (*Corr.,* III.419–20).

17. Even in *MacFlecknoe,* Dryden did not name living persons, although both the Oldham and the Yale manuscripts have all names fully spelled out. But like Garth, Dryden called attention to those names—in the *Mac,* which so confused Shadwell (Oden, xv), and in such games as the scatological joke on Shadwell's name: "But loads of *Sh*——almost choakt the way (101–4; see Wilding, 1969).

particulars, already fully realized in Garth's poem. That union follows from two strands of the mock-epic's poetics. One is the distrust of language, especially its power of predication. The second is the special role of identification in particular satire, a role largely ignored by critics and poets alike as they focused their commentary exclusively on the problems of general satire.

These problems concerned Garth and Pope very little in their mock-epics. The task of a general satire focuses chiefly on the question of the identification of appropriate targets. A general satire reserves for itself sole authority over its represented persons, a power akin to the magical utterance of primitive satire. Since Aristotle, that power had been understood as the poet's special advantage over those, chiefly historians, who were tied to particulars. Fool, madman, jealous incompetent, cunning charlatan, satanic rebel—the general satire expects to have the last say about its represented persons. Thus the general satire sets its reader an interpretive task at whose center stands the word the poet will not use, the proper name. The poet has to rely on the reader's powers of identification and on his poem's ability to engage the reader's moral judgment and social scorn. For the poet to succeed, the reader must apply the satire correctly—to himself and to the world.

For the particular satire of the mock-epic, the roles of identity and identification are reversed. Now the work of identification—application—is the province of the poet, and the work of identity—judgment—must be shared with the reader. A text truly functions as a particular satire to the degree that the reader has, whether by report or by experience, some idea of its persons that is independent of, and so different from, that offered by the poem. In that difference are the seeds of a struggle rooted in satire's primitive, magical past. Although the particular satirist cannot as a matter of course claim power over his persons, he will have designs on them, designs on that authority. He will, as Pope said, want what he cannot easily have: persons made for the poem (TE, V.205). He will want to have over his actual persons the power that the general satirist claims over his.

The particular satirist risks chiefly disbelief, that his readers will fail or refuse to see how his representations are true of his persons. Without the kind of social, institutional standing that gives juries the right to find facts and judges the right to pronounce sentence, the poet will be hard pressed to find in himself, as the history of *Dunciad* criticism shows, the fund of authority to make his readers surrender their own judgments and become instruments of his moralizing social stigmata. Only perfect virtue will do, and that no reader of judgment will grant—despite any show of poetic genius, of the mantle of tradition, of well-crafted life and house and gardens. Pope and his friends, grumped Dr. Johnson, expected one to think that they "had engrossed all the understanding and virtue of mankind, that their merits filled the world" (*Life of Swift,* VIII.225). Indeed, the very attempt to assume such virtue has for many readers been proof against it: "Pope finds himself unable to resettle the equilibrium in his nervous system," complained de Quincey of Pope's acts of judgment and execution, "until he has taken out his revenge by an extra kicking administered to some old mendicant or vagrant lying in a ditch" (XI.126–27). Just such resistance lies at the root of much of the effort to see Pope's persons in *The Dunciad* as fictions or metaphors or ciphers: we rightly resist the surrender Pope seeks from us.

If, then, the power to make readers cede their right to judge cannot be found in the genre, or in the poet's role, or in the poet's person, it must be found in the design, the power of the poetry itself. Poetry has access to truths beyond "bare representation" (Ker, I.153), and it needs them. In traditional terms, that power is the power of affect, of the special vitality of poetic representations. Readers can indeed be dazzled, cajoled, frightened, persuaded, or otherwise moved to surrender to the poet the authority of their independent knowledge of the person in question. If Belinda's beauty can benumb our rational powers to judge her faults of character—"you'll forget 'em all" (*Rape,* II.18)—so can the incantatory beauty of a verse compel us to accept its characters at face value. In the mock-epic, however, with its particularly demanding claim on the readers' judgment, the poet does more: he also engages the specifically cognitive powers of poetry.

Garth and Pope both understood how a particular satire that rises above simple invective demands a stable language of judgment, just as they understood how unstable their language really was. Such stability now seems to us a pipe dream, the product of a necessary, though futile longing for simple truths and pure, unmediated communication. But it was then widely taken as an ideal, lost yet still a viable goal even in a fallen world. In the court of law, a relative stability for the language of judgment was and is achieved by an elaborate institutional system that gives special power to words precedent, a system best captured in the concept of *stare decisis.* In the mock-epic, where it is institutions that seem most unstable and most at risk, the language of judgment was given the best protection that poetry affords, the power to engage the knowledge and experience of its readers. The cognitive dimension of the poet's craft helped to stabilize its judgments, by fixing the judged, not only in amber or even in words, but also in thought.

Gilded Pills

Although every major mock-epic was popular on its first publication and for decades thereafter, over the years only *The Rape of the Lock* continued to please with its exquisite and delicate detailing, its apparently trivializing machinery, and its domestic subject. Largely because the mock-epic demands so much of the knowledge and experience of its readers, the gilding of the *Rape* came to define the genre, making the other poems all the less palatable. This gilding is one of the livelier pleasures of the mock-epic, as are the pleasure of knowingly engaging in the mock-epic's pretenses and the pleasure of watching a public, ritual punishment. But what the mock-epic offers its readers most aggressively is the bitter truth and a larger and more reliable understanding: larger, because the poem embeds the particulars of its interest in a larger network, not of "abiding ideals and values to which lesser realities might be referred with ease,"[18] but of other particulars, other realities; more reliable, because that network of particulars enables poet and reader to fix those ideals and values whose abiding is so much in doubt. Such benefits, however valuable, are hard on readers—hard because the bitter truth is seldom welcome and hard because the path to that truth ranges them through a world of particulars few are prepared to negotiate. The mock-epic's offering has been especially hard on readers who have shied away from the claims to truth, been put off by the bitterness and the name-calling, and preferred not to care about the particulars.

While the densest collection of particulars correlated to names can be found in the notes to *The Dunciad,* those notes have proved too radical an innovation for most critics to accept. We have proved unable to accept their weighty presence on the page and equally unable to ignore the weight of the signs that mark them as marginal, ancillary, beside the point. With so much baggage, the relation between names and particulars in *The Dunciad* is especially hard to sort out. Fortunately, however, the relation that Pope makes a key to his masterpiece replicates a structure that was fully formed in Garth's less troublesome poem. In *The Dispensary* we see both the role of particulars in identifying persons already named and the point of giving particulars a role as a de-

---

18. Earl Miner, closely following Aubrey Williams's lead, says this of *MacFlecknoe* (84). Rothstein says much the same about *The Dispensary:* "The traditional heroic represents an ideal that can be consistently applied" (21). This assurance may be true of some of Dryden's work. I do not see it in *MacFlecknoe,* and it is no part of *The Dispensary.*

fense against the malleability of language and those who self-interestedly manipulate it.

There is a truth and a roundabout of particulars in Garth's opening Old Bailey couplets, a bitter truth that concerns both the Old Bailey and the College of Physicians. From their poetic and topographical contiguity grows an identity of dishonor between them. This first hint at their connection grows out of Garth's extended analysis of the College's own failings in the battle of the Dispensary. Readers from Dr. Johnson to Frank Ellis have accepted Garth's extensive propagandizing for the College as the main—and effectively the only—business of the poem.[19] But Garth's concerns are more general, focused on his exploration of the nature of civic responsibility and on the personal, political, and economic interests that cause its failures. In this larger compass, he finds the College moved by the same failings that motivate its enemies. Although it will take an understanding of the whole to know the full significance of Garth's analysis, that analysis begins forcefully—though with decorous indirection—in the first setting.

As we have seen, Garth locates his first action—the construction of the Dispensary, which rouses Sloth, who had taken possession of the College's library—by fixing first on the Old Bailey. He then moves on to the College's most prominent physical feature, the dome of the Cutlerian Theatre:

> Not far from that most celebrated Place,
> Where angry Justice shews her awful Face;
> Where little Villains must submit to Fate,
> That great Ones may enjoy the World in State;
> There stands a Dome, Majestick to the Sight,
> And sumptuous Arches bear its oval Height;
> A golden Globe plac'd high with artful Skill,
> Seems, to the distant Sight, a gilded Pill:
> This Pile was, by the Pious Patron's Aim,
> Rais'd for a Use as Noble as its Frame:
> Nor did the Learn'd Society decline
> The Propagation of that great Design;
> In all her Mazes, Nature's Face they view'd,
> And as she disappear'd, their Search pursu'd.

---

19. Johnson swallowed the propaganda wholesale: both project and poem are the work of "great liberality, and dignity of sentiment, very prompt effusion of beneficence, and willingness to exert a lucrative art, where there is no hope of lucre" (*Life of Garth*, II.384).

> Wrapt in the shades of Night the Goddess lies,
> Yet to the learn'd unveils her dark Disguise,
> But shuns the gross Access of vulgar Eyes.
>
> (1.7–23)

As in the case of the Old Bailey couplets, this description raises more questions than it answers: which Dome? which Patron? what Use? what Design?

The questions begin with the dome. The representation helps us feel the epic grandeur of the dome's physical and poetical prominence. With its "sumptuous Arches," "oval Height," and "golden Globe plac'd high with artful skill," the dome is truly "Majestick to the Sight." But readers prepared for mock-heroics know such elevation must be headed for a fall. Fall it does when we learn that the topmost ornament, the golden globe, "Seems, to the distant Sight, a gilded Pill"—a characteristically Garthean deflation that introduces a dissonance resolved only in succeeding lines. Since pills were generally spherical and, in the better circles, gilded, the "gilded Pill" can be taken as an elegant detail specifying this as a place of medicines. But nothing in mock-epic is so simple. Pills fell in the apothecary's proper sphere, not the physician's, and gilding pills had the same bad name it has now. Pills were gilded, powders dispensed in gilded paper or even gold foil, and liquids dispensed in gilded bottles—none of which affected the usually noxious quality of the nostrums. The chief effect of the purely cosmetic practice of gilding was to increase prices. For a seventeenth-century physician committed to the new science and flushed with its successes, this hocus-pocus and the ignorance it fed was the first enemy. To those who see aright, the "gilded Pill" is a sign of disease.

Here the mock-epic pattern of assertion, uncertainty, and reversal is more complex than in the Old Bailey couplets. Garth has enfolded the epic description ("And sumptuous Arches bear its oval Height; / A golden Globe plac'd high with artful Skill,") within lines that speak less of what we see than of how we react ("There stands a Dome, Majestick to the Sight... Seems, to the distant Sight, a gilded Pill"). As in the Old Bailey couplets, the lines enact the characteristic paradigm of mock-epic delay: the sense of the two central, descriptive lines is left suspended between the sense of the introducing and concluding lines. The first and last lines themselves form an extended chiasmus composed of two sets of carefully paired phrases:

> There stands a Dome, Majestick to the Sight,
> . . . .
> Seems, to the distant Sight a gilded Pill:

The outer paired phrases—"There stands a Dome" and "a gilded Pill"—generate the mock-epic conflict of values by offering readers a conflict of reference and focus. Which is to be decisive, Dome or Pill? The inner paired phrases—"Majestick to the Sight" and "Seems, to the distant Sight"—represent the same conflict, now in terms of perspective. Is it to be the magisterial, assertive, majestic sight or the mere seeming of the distant sight? As always, caution is in order, and we must not judge too quickly or on appearances. Many have shared the wariness of one of Garth's best modern readers, Frank Ellis, who cannot bring himself to accept the idea that so loyal a member of the College can mean this to be the serious attack it might seem (1699, I.15n). Yet an attack is precisely what these lines, and the poem as a whole, become.

One factor in deciding the matter is the key allusion to Denham's *Cooper's Hill*, an important model for the extensive georgic strain in *The Dispensary*. Denham also sets the first scene with a dome, "that sacred pile," St. Paul's.[20] That dome, too, sparks only uncertainty: "whether 'tis a part of Earth, or sky, / Uncertain seems" (B 15–18). Of course, the cathedral is both, and the seeming is the proper sight. Turning to the city and its preoccupation with "luxury, and wealth" (B 33), the poet continues:

> Under his proud survey the City lies,
> And like a mist beneath a hill doth rise;
> Whose state and wealth the business and the crowd,
> Seems at this distance but a darker cloud:
> And is to him who rightly things esteems,
> No other in effect than what it seems.
>   (B 25–30)[21]

From the distant sight, Denham's poet can see truly those who

---

20. Many contemporary visual representations of the Old Bailey contrive to have St. Paul's prominent in the background, presumably because it was the dominant topographical feature of the neighborhood.

21. The emphasis on seeming and poetic sight is first present in the revisions for the *B* text in 1655.

> Toyle to prevent imaginarie wants;
> Yet all in vaine, increasing with their store,
> Their vast desires, but make their wants the more.
> As food to unsound bodies, though it please
> The Appetite, feeds only the disease;
>
> (A 30–34)

Garth echoes Denham's conservative critique of the early modern tendency to accept as natural the appetites that fuel self-interest.[22]

Garth's reader also gains from the distant sight, truly valuing the appetites and interests reflected in the golden globe. Gold is a sign of no good throughout *The Dispensary.* Here a conventional token of greed, gold will eventually become the center of a sustained exploration of the socially disruptive power of money and the moneyed interest—a theme that will later inform the political and social analysis in the final *Dunciad.* Thus Garth's chief villain and undoer of the vulgar, Horoscope, knows both "the sacred Charms, that in true Sterling dwell" (II.107) and the magic of gilding: "How Gold makes a *Patrician* of a Slave, / A Dwarf an *Atlas,* a *Thersites* brave" (II.108–9).

From the distant sight, we can easily see how gold's corruptions can become general. We are invited to make a number of metonymic scale expansions, globe-Dome-College-Realm-World, that make this gilded pill even harder to take with equanimity. Moreover, the golden globe comes to the poem with a prepackaged association. It was the trademark of the infamous Dr. Case, mountebank *par excellence* and a master of advertising. By another easy metonymy, the golden globe becomes both a stigma for a whole range of mountebanks who had joined the apothecaries' party and a diagnostic sign of their infiltration of the College.

The other decisive factor also centers on the golden globe but is, characteristically, developed only in the subsequent lines:

> This Pile was, by the Pious Patron's Aim,
> Rais'd for a Use as Noble as its Frame:
> Nor did the Learn'd Society decline
> The Propagation of that great Design.
>
> (I.15–18)

The test in these lines lies in the ambiguous references to "This Pile" and its "Pious Patron." Garth's editors commonly assume that the "Pile"

---

22. See McKeon (200–205).

refers to the entire College complex and so to the College as an institution. Accordingly, they take the "Pious Patron" to be the College's founder, Linacre, whose house had been the College's first meeting place. This reading carries the cataphoric ties of "Pious Patron's Aim," "Noble Use," and "great Design" forward to equate the aim and design with the *ars medendi* (I.24–67) that follows. There Garth instructs the reader in the proper, scientific practice of medicine and presents a history of the College (albeit a slightly distorted one) as a center of the growth of scientific knowledge. This is the role Garth wants to cast for the College, both in response to its critics and in exhortation to its members. In this respect at least, he portrays the College as above reproach: this "ancient League" is represented as originating as a home of scientific innovation from which had come most of the new science on which medical progress was based. This is an aim and design that does justice to a Linacre.

But, as always, there is just enough dissonance. The pile Garth has actually described is the dome of the Cutlerian Theatre, a relatively new building in the new complex erected on a new site after the great fire. Linacre had nothing to do with raising this particular structure. Nor is Linacre suited for the role, since he was an active member of the College—its first president, not its patron. Moreover, the Cutlerian Theatre had its own patron, Sir John Cutler. His statue dominated the rotunda, its inscription—"Omnis CUTLERI cedat Labor Amphitheatro"—clearly laying claim to the title of patron.[23] Thus, if we take Cutler as the "Pious Patron," we make sense of the anaphoric ties back to the pile and the dome—but we do so only at the expense of the strong cataphoric ties to the "great Design" celebrated in the paean to scientific progress that dominates the first Canto.

To resolve this dissonance is to come to see it as Garth's mock-epic point. Here is another instance of a double reference, another of Garth's referential puns. In his presentation copy of the 1706 edition of the poem, now located at the Huntington Library, Pope identified the pious patron as Cutler.[24] Ellis tries to correct Pope's identification because "the irony of this attribution is apparent" (1699, I.15n). Even if Pope did not have special knowledge of his friend Garth's intentions (though it seems likely that he would), Pope could see that "the irony of the attribution" is precisely the point, since Garth's mock-epic scorn depends

---

23. Strype's 1720 *Survey* records two architectural features of the College of Physicians: a statue of Charles II and the statue of Cutler, complete with inscription (III.193).

24. Pope would give Cutler his due in the *Epistle to Bathurst*, both as old Cotta (179–98) and by name (314–34). See Erskine-Hill (1975, 250, 262–63).

on the correlative praise of Linacre. For Sir John Cutler had his own designs. He had funded the theater and had been celebrated for his pious generosity; he had lent his name to his gift and his likeness to adorn its rotunda; and he had secretly, artfully entered his gift to the College in his private account books as a loan. His heirs sued, and in October 1695, obtained a writ of error ordering the College to repay the entire amount.[25] From the distant sight of 1699, Cutler's theater must have seemed a gilded and a particularly galling pill.

Cutler was known to pride himself on his piety, and he alone of Garth's great villains earns the right to demean that most honored Virgilian epithet. Just to make sure we know what company Cutler keeps, Garth uses *pious* twice more. In the tableau of social evils added in 1703, we find "sly Hypocrisie with Pious Leer" (II.34). To drive home the tie between hypocrisy and piety, Garth adds a note to Dryden's *Palamon and Arcite:* "Next stood Hypocrisy with holy leer" (II.564). The second use of *Pious* participates in the same network of associations. In the consult of the Apothecaries Physicians, the first to agree to violence (later, the first in battle) is Querpo (George Howe).[26] In 1699 Querpo's hypocrisy and his association with social upheaval is explicit:

> Drain'd from an *Elder's* Loins with awkward gust,
> In Lees of Stale Hypocrisie and Lust.
> His Sire's pretended pious Steps he treads,
> And where the Doctor fails, the Saint succeeds.
> (1699, IV.96–101)

From the distant sight of the whole poem and of the company Cutler keeps, we know what to make of his pious patronage.

So must the character of this patron have seemed clear from the perspective of 1697, when Garth delivered the Harveian Oration in Cut-

---

25. Royal College of Physicians MS. 274, 18 October 1695; cited by Ellis (1699, I.11n). Thornbury (1897) indignantly tells the story of Cutler's loan, mentioning Pope's attack on Cutler in *Bathurst.*

26. Pope identified Querpo's salient characteristic: "Dr. How Son of a Non Con Preacher" (1706, Huntington Library Copy). Howe was satirized as Querpo in *The Second Tunbridge Lampoon* (1699; BM MS, Sloane 1731A, f113; Ellis, 1699, IV.96n). *Querpo* is formed from *in cuerpo* (*OED:* without the cloak or upper garment). Garth's satiric use is almost certainly derived from that in another satire on hypocrisy, *Hudibras,* IV.iii.201. There may also be echoes of Cleveland's Royalist satire, "Character of a London Diurnal" (1644).

ler's auditorium. On this occasion, Garth felt compelled by the presence of Cutler's newly repaid heirs to mention him among his list of royal patrons, "Ornaments of our Societie," and other "Benefactors." Garth speaks of Cutler with praise that is not self-evidently ironic. But I think it easy to see in Garth's mention of Cutler a subdued, but bitter inside joke, carefully designed not to offend the friends and family of this "Pious patron" of the College at a time when the College needed all the friends it could get, but just as carefully designed to damn him in the eyes of those in the know.

In the oration, which rehearses the key themes of the poem, Garth turns to Cutler after praising Hamney, who "preserved this Building from the rage of the Civil Warr" (*HO*, 119) and before mentioning "some Benefactors yet living" (140). These benefactors Garth praises as "noble," "no lesse courteous than bountifull," and "being of approved integritie and prudence" (140–45). In praising Hamney, Garth compares his "Bounty" to that of Garth's idol, William Harvey, who "[l]ike to the heavenly Inhabitants [,] stood need to few, but was beneficial to very many, even to posterity" (113–14). Garth emphasizes that Hamney's bounty was equal but less known: "Some {desire} covet Offices, some Estates, some honour, some other things," but "It was his desire rather to be than to seem bountifull" (120–24). After such praise of this man of "plain integritie," Garth immediately turns to Cutler: "Neither may I here omit Baron Cutler. If I should pass him over in Silence, these Walls, these Benches would reprove me"—not to mention Cutler's likeness in the rotunda (126–27). Then follows praise that is in this context carefully measured. That praise includes none of the key words that Garth repeats so often in praising others, words notably associated with an older code of virtue. Instead, Garth presents only a picture of a man careful about money, with all the merchant virtues of the frugal and precise: "A man neither covetous of what belong'd to others, nor prodigal of his own ... he took care of the publick good, and in the interim neglected not his own private {concerns} Interest" (127–34).[27] Surrounded by so much bounty, this praise is faint at best. Those of Garth's auditors in the know about the Baron's sharp practices could not help but notice that Garth's description of Cutler mentions not generosity but "private Interest," the key to mock-epic scorn. They would

---

27. As a wealthy merchant and a "city" man, Cutler would have been closely associated with Garth's chief villains—Bernard, Gibbons, and Blackmore. The City is an important source of allegiance for the Apothecaries Physicians.

understand why "[i]ts not meet for me to say more {of} and I cannot justly speak lesse of him"(134–35).[28]

This gilded pill will be seen aright only by those who can attain the proper, distant sight *and* who are in the know. With the gilded pill, the first signpost to the poem's evaluative stance, Garth bifurcates his readership. Because it relies on particulars, the indirection—"allegory"—of the mock-epic was often an insiders' game. But unlike traditional allegory, which self-consciously veiled its truths so that only the fit few could know them, the mock-epic is also very much a public genre. This contradiction has effects everywhere in the mock-epic line. The most notable instance is the bifurcated form of *The Dunciad Variorum*, whose apparatus incorporates, among other things, some of the obscurer particulars that only insiders would know. In *The Dispensary* Garth uses this contradiction to keep his criticism of the College itself a College affair: his intention is not, he says, "to persuade Mankind to enter into our Quarrels" ([A5v]).[29] For those who lack the requisite insider's knowledge, the golden globe stands as a token of his dissatisfaction with the venality that threatens the College (as it always threatens mankind), and it stands so in virtue of its role as a conventional sign of greed, of its likeness to a gilded pill, and of its general, public association with the signpost of an infamous quack. The golden globe and its gilded attractions are just vulgar enough for a self-aggrandizing city merchant and for those outsiders whose "vulgar Eyes" Nature "shuns" (I.23). For those who know the particulars because they can see past the "dark Disguise" (I.22), the golden globe betokens a highly specific dissatisfaction with the College itself, one that rests not only on a detailed knowledge of the College's internal, "state" affairs, but also on a public-minded, civic understanding of the College's role and duties, its stewardship of the public health. With this first distinction between readers in the know and readers not, Garth begins what will develop into an extensive, though largely covert, diagnosis of the ills of the College itself, a diag-

---

28. For a very similar discrepancy between measured praise in the oration and blame in the poem, compare the two mentions of Lady Grace Pierrepoint. This is the oration: "There remains also some Benefactors yet living, as Madame Grace Pierrepoint [,] a most noble heiresse of a noble paternal dowry" (*HO*, 15). This the poem: "How Gold makes a *Patrician* of a Slave ... Finds Sense in *Br*[ownlow], Charms in Lady *G*[rac]*e*" (II.108–11).

29. Garth also uses such veiled truths to protect readers from matters they are unlikely to care about and are unprepared to understand. *The Dispensary* includes a running commentary on the nature and purpose of medical practice. Grounded in allusions to the controversial literature associated with the dispute, that commentary almost certainly went unnoticed by many of Garth's readers, as it has gone unnoticed by all of his critics before Frank Ellis.

nosis that can remain largely covert (and therefore seemly) precisely because in this poem, as in all mock-epics, evaluation will be intimately tied to local, detailed knowledge of the particulars of the case.

In the setting that Garth here imitates, Dryden tells us that Barbican was

> A Watchtower once; but now, so Fates Ordain,
> Of all the Pile an empty name remains.
> (*MacFlecknoe*, 68–69)

So too with "This Pile," the Cutlerian Theatre. The name remains, as does the likeness with its aggrandizing inscription. As Garth had said, "If I should pass him over in Silence, these Walls, these Benches would reprove me." But the name, like the inscription, is now empty. It stands, not as a monument to Cutler's bounty, but as a monument to one who looked to his private interest and desired rather to seem than to be bountiful. Like the "golden Globe plac'd high with artful Skill," this "Ornament of our Societie" also stands as a token of the many private interests that threaten to overrun the College. The College was itself a watchtower once, a guardian that protected the public against those who would practice a mere seeming medicine for personal gain. And like Barbican, the College is an "antient fabric rais'd t'inform the Sight"—both the sight of those threats from without and science's penetrating sight into Nature's "dark Disguise." But now the College too is in danger of becoming a ruin. Not the buildings—those monuments will stand—but the "great Design" that was the original patron's aim is threatened by the "great Design" of its new patrons. Garth saw that the College's stewardship was being undermined by those members whose allegiance was divided—divided by gold and commerce, Garth says in his poem. And he saw that its "searches into Nature," which for Garth were its glory, had been all but lost. Thus do "ancient Leagues" to modern greatness fall—to a greatness not of bounty but of consumption, a greatness that does not serve but "enjoys the World in State."

Urban Gravitation

4

> Natural Philosophy, *in the large Sense I now use it, does not only comprehend all those* Appearances of Natural Bodies, *which we know from Experiment, but also inquires into the Nature of our Souls.*
>
> —*Cumberland,* De Legibus Naturae

The *Dunciad*s are full of circles, circles that point the way to the poems' common conceptual center. As was usual for Pope, the significance of these circles became more evident with each new incarnation of the poem. It was not until the 1742 appearance of *The New Dunciad* that the relationship between those circles and duncehood was made explicit in the almost cinematic image of Dulness with her "conglob'd" disciples spread across the land—an image echoed by the equally cinematic close, transported from the *Variorum,* in which our perspective slowly widens to encompass the spread of "Universal Darkness." By then, Pope wanted to make sure his readers understood that the mechanism of the expanding (and contracting) circles of dullness was the "One instinct" that transports all dunces and fuels social and cultural decay: "None need a guide, by sure Attraction led, / And strong impulsive gravity of Head" (B IV.75–76). Of course this "gravity of Head" is part of the extended play on the dunces' sometimes weighty, sometimes weightless profound. But it is much more. This "gravity of Head" defines the class dunce and carries the largest measure of Pope's diagnosis of the aesthetic, social, and moral work of Dulness. It is "moral gravitation."

The phrase "moral gravity" does not appear in Pope's poetry, nor, so far as I can determine, in his correspondence, but Pope would have encountered the concept and the phrase regularly in the writings and versation of his friends and admirers. The phrase itself is associated with Thomson. In *Liberty* it describes the relation between self- and public interest:

> Without this
> This awful Pant, shook from sublimer Powers
> Than those of *Self,* this Heaven-infus'd Delight,
> This *moral Gravitation,* rushing prone
> To press the *public Good,* my System soon,
> Traverse, to several *selfish* Centers drawn
> Will reel to Ruin.
> (*Liberty,* V.254)[1]

Underlying the phrase is an analogy between the design of the cosmos and the design of society that is endemic in moral philosophy, the typically Augustan cross between traditional ethics and a faintly dawning social science. "Moral gravitation" lent a suitably philosophical—which is to say, scientific—cast to accounts of social and moral order, phenomena that were poorly understood and more poorly explained. It also lent a suitably modern cast to conservative arguments marshaled to oppose the growing influence of early modern capitalist social theories. With the extraordinary success of Newton's cosmology, the analogy of moral gravitation gained both intellectual power and popular appeal—at least until Hume recast for moral philosophy a "scientific" language not so notably grounded in analogies with purely physical phenomena.

As early as 1703 Peter Paxton found moral gravitation essential to civil polity: "the pursuit of happiness is as inseparable from the Nature of Man, as the Tendency towards its own Center is to unthinking Matter."[2] Hutcheson uses the analogy often, comparing gravity both to benevolence,

> This universal Benevolence toward all Men, we may compare to that Principle of Gravitation, [which] like the Love of Benevolence, increases as the distance is diminish'd, and is strongest when Bodys come to touch each other.

---

1. Herbert Drennon (1938) argues that Thomson found the phrase in John Norris's *The Theory and Regulation of Love* (1688), but Thomson's use is pure Newton. It builds on one of Newton's more important though not popularly recognized innovations: his recognition that *all* matter exhibits gravitational attraction, not just especially massive bodies such as stars and planets.

2. *Civil Polity, A Treatise Concerning the Nature of Government* (1703).

and to self-interest,

> Self-love is really as necessary to the Good of the Whole ... as that Attraction which causes the Cohesion of the Parts, is necessary to the regular State of the Whole, as Gravitation.[3]

Addison went so far as to explain instinct in animals in terms of gravitation (*Spectator* 120), and Bolingbroke stopped just short of assigning instinct to matter:

> Nay, there is a further analogy between animated and inanimated bodies. The former have, by instinct, a sort of moral gravitation to one another, by which they adhere together in society. I will not apply instinct to the latter; but this I may say, that a force as unknown as instinct, produces a gravitation of the several parts of matter to each other, and keeps them together in a kind of physical society.[4]

In *Guardian* 126, Pope's friend George Berkeley offered the general reader painstaking instruction in using and understanding the analogy.

For almost half a century, the analogy of moral gravitation showed remarkable life and versatility. It appeared in serious philosophical works, which testifies to the intellectual power of the Newtonian example. It also had relatively widespread popular currency, appearing not only in Berkeley's didactic popularization in the *Guardian* but also more casually in the *Spectator.* But not too casually. That the terms of the analogy were so consistently spelled out, point for point, is a sign that it had not been fully assimilated as a habit of thinking, a sign of its vitality as a metaphor.[5]

---

3. *An Inquiry into the Original of our Ideas of Beauty and Virtue* (1726, I.74, 164).

4. "Fragments or Minutes of Essays," *Works,* 4.363. These essays, from which I shall draw several examples, were written to guide Pope in composing *An Essay on Man.* Also see *A Dissertation upon Parties,* Letter IX, *Works,* 2.83ff. Another of Pope's friends who was taken by the analogy was George Cheyne, whose *Philosophical Principles of Religion, Natural and Revealed* (1734) includes many examples.

5. Although Newton has been much studied, this particular use of cosmology has been little noticed. McKillop briefly discusses Thomson's analogy, and Kinsley (1975) traces its relation to physico-theology in *The Dunciad.* Kramnick mentions two examples from Bolingbroke to show "the imprint of Newton's ideas on political thought in this period" and "the mechanistic phraseology of Augustan Commonwealthman thought" (139, 255). Although he quotes the relevant passages, White mentions the analogy hardly at all.

In his study of Thomson, Alan Dougal McKillop stresses the role of the analogy in physico-theology, where it serves as an authoritative and convenient illustration of the argument from design: "The Newtonian principle of gravitation was from this point of view simply the most cogent form of unity in variety" (31). In fact, though, the analogy had a wider currency and a more specific use: it was most often brought to bear on the tangled question of the role of self-interest in social organization (Meyers, 1983). This use was particularly apropos for the mock-epic, which rested its social diagnosis on the operations of self-interest in its subjects/victims. For the mock-epic poet, for Thomson, or for that matter anyone concerned to explain the design of social organization, the analogy offered more than unity in variety, although it offered that too. The special value of Newtonian cosmology was that it seemed to solve in the physical world the kind of problem that self-interest posed in the study of the social world: how to explain action at a distance.

One defining question of Augustan moral philosophy was, What is the nature of social obligation? But that question was complicated because early modern economic thought had carried the day in making self-interest the central indisputable fact of human interrelations and a primitive of social analysis (Appleby, 1978). The problem was to connect personal relations with wider social relations by bridging the gap between self-interest and social obligation. Moving beyond self-interest created conceptual difficulties closely analogous to the puzzle that had plagued all theories of gravitation: how, without resorting to "occult qualities," can one explain the action of interest at a distance from the self? How can the motive forces behind self-interest and familial obligations be extended to those with whom one has only the most distant, most impersonal relations?

One response of conservative thinkers (such as Dryden, Garth, and Pope) was to model wider social relations on familial relations. But so serious was the problem of self-interest that it eventually became hard to explain even the "natural" affections within the family. Consider, for example, the plight of Richardson's Clarissa, who cannot reconcile self-interest and filial duty—notably in situations in which she is denied personal encounter with her parents. There is no better emblem of the rift between personal and social obligation than the image of Clarissa vainly striving, through letters and other intermediaries, to reconcile her personal and her familial obligations by presenting her parents with "pictures" of her distress, hoping that affect will overcome the distance between them.[6] With such wedges dividing self- and familial interest, social theories could rely less and less on personal and familial models of social obligation.

Most Augustan philosophers and moralists understood these questions of social relations and social obligation as a challenge posed by Hobbes and made urgent by continued political strife. But the hold of this question ran deeper, fueled as it was by new economic realities and increasingly powerful political interests. To the question of social obligation were offered many different kinds of answers. Philosophers, including Hobbes and Locke, offered contract theories of social obligations. "Moralists" such as Shaftesbury preferred to identify social obligation as a species of instinct, calling it natural affection or sympathy. The most enduring solution was provided by Mandeville and others who looked to economic relations as socially definitive. Mandeville's *Fable of the Bees* (1714)—with its most un-mock-epic fable—gave memorable expression to a key tenet of early modern economic thought: it equated self-interest and the public good, defining the market as a mechanism for mediating from one to the other. Such solutions were anathema to conservative thinkers for whom markets were too egalitarian and too free-form—they would say, too vulgar—to serve as a foundation for social order. In the case of the conservative thinkers who wrote mock-epic, the challenge was both to explain corruption at a distance and somehow to enforce the distant obligations that maintain the relations that comprise the good order of society. Although the problem of action at a distance had not in fact been solved by Newton, his countrymen thought it had.[7] Thus British social theorists and poets found in the Newtonian cosmology a wealth of analogies that, if they did not reason away the mystery of social obligation, at least confronted it with the authority of nature.

As important as the Newtonian model was, moral gravitation was only the dominant one of several analogies drawn between cosmology and social organization. As early as 1672 Richard Cumberland offered a

---

6. Fielding also gravitated to stories of personal and social obligation told against a backdrop of familial disorder. In *Tom Jones* affection and obligation grow for Tom and fail to grow for Blifil until Fielding ultimately restores the blood tie so that affection and obligation remain strongest within the family. By the time of *Amelia*, there is little left but the affection of one's family.

7. Acceptance of Newton's theory came more slowly on the continent. The French scientist Saurin wrote in 1709 that Newton "likes to think of weight as a quality inherent in bodies, and to revive the discredited ideas of occult quality and of attraction" (quoted in Hesse, 157n).

mechanical analogy without the nice unity of the Newtonian model.[8] More than half a century after Cumberland (and nearly as long after the *Principia*), Bolingbroke could still mix Cartesian and Newtonian elements.[9] What we see in this wider compass is a *range* of explanations of social order that rest on, are illustrated by, or are merely decorated by analogies between social structures and mechanical explanations of the cosmos. Newtonian mechanics held pride of place: it was English and less suspected of the atheistical tendencies attributed to the new sciences.[10] But all of these analogies offered a causal, non-market mechanism for social phenomena. From the earliest glimmering of the new science, the first duty of a modern was to seek out the causes of things; pseudo-causes such as Aristotle's "occult qualities" became the emblem of the old science and the favorite whipping boy of the new.[11] For serious scientists, the stress on causes was in fact a stress on mathematics. Galileo had said so in *The Assayer* (1623), and every major physical scientist followed suit. For the popular understanding, however, the crucial fact of science's search for causes was that it offered readily intelligible models that equated cause with mechanics. Mechanical models continued to have an important, though secondary, role in the primary sciences (Hesse, 1961, 156), and in the popular mind models, cause, and science were the same.

Although mechanism still carried the threat of atheism (and in that respect is a target of the final *Dunciad*), for the most part these mechanical explanations did not presuppose a mechanistic social order

---

8. Cumberland's cosmology mixes Cartesian and Epicurean notions, and his social analogy centers on the Cartesian vortex (*De Legibus Naturae,* 1672). Magnetism had served as well as gravity in Norris's early use of the phrase "Moral Gravity" (*Theory and Regulation of Love,* 1688). For magnetism as a motive force, see Korshin (1971).

9. "We love ourselves, we love our families, we love the particular societies, to which we belong, and our benevolence extends at last to the whole race of mankind. Like so many different vorticies, the centre of them all is self-love, and that which is the most distant from it is the weakest" (4.165). Bolingbroke's mixture is scientifically uninformed: Newton's inverse square law disproved the Cartesian hypothesis of the vortex. Nicolson and Rousseau show that Pope, too, favored the figure of the vortex (200ff).

10. J. T. Desaguliers's political poem, *The Newtonian System of the World, the Best Model of Government* (1728), strives to prove that just as the English Newtonian cosmology is superior to that of Ptolemy and Descartes, so the English Hanoverian government was the best form of civil polity (see Kinsley, 1975, 25). For an account of how Garth's atomistic science was suspected of atheism, see Ackerman (1979).

11. In one early, apposite example, Marchamont Nedham launched the attack on the hegemony of the "Gownmen" of the College with the rallying cry to search for "the Causes of things." Nedham's program is an amalgam of Bacon and Boyle: "[A] strict and constant observing of [Nature's] Motions and manner of Operations, is that which gives a man light how to trace her in the darkness of obscure Causes" (1665, 227–28).

any more than Newtonian mechanics was thought to presuppose a mechanistic cosmos:

> Eventually gravitation came to be regarded as a purely mechanistic principle, and the world view developed from Newtonian physics excluded human values. But for much popular thought of the eighteenth century, even when the deterministic or mechanistic aspects of the system are noted or stressed, they do not terrify, for they point to an active and omnipresent intelligence. There had been a campaign against Cartesian mechanism and of course against the Epicurean teaching of a "fortuitous concourse of atoms," but Thomson is not interested in fighting these battles over again. (McKillop, 34)

Neither was Addison much interested in fighting the battle over mechanism. He takes as evident that gravitation is like instinct and that both manifest the direct hand of God: "For my own part, I look upon it [instinct] as upon the principle of gravitation in bodies, which is not to be explained by any known qualities inherent in the bodies themselves, nor from the laws of mechanism, but, according to the best notions of the greatest philosophers, is an immediate impression from the first mover, and the divine energy acting on the creatures" (*Spectator* 120). While McKillop is right to call his modern reader's attention to the role of theism in these mechanical explanations, in the original context the theism was expected and the mechanical explanation stood out as distinctive. Addison may deny that either gravitation or instinct can be explained by "the laws of mechanism" (by which he means *mere* mechanism), but he holds to a standard of explanation that gives pride of place to the mechanics of things.

So did just about everyone else. In philosophy—already becoming "the science of MAN"[12]—mechanical models were essential. Hobbes, Locke, and Hume, each in his own way, assumed that to explain the mind was to explain the mechanism by which it operated. That Hobbes and Hume came to conclusions widely considered dangerous is here less relevant than that all three—and most others in between—assumed a standard of explanation that made the mechanics of things the ground of knowledge. To be able to say what a thing is, one must be able to say how that thing works—and so Addison offers us a mechanism, a divine mechanism, for instinct and gravitation just as Thomson

---

12. Hume, *A Treatise of Human Nature* ("Introduction"). Hume was also influenced by the analogy with Newtonian cosmology; see *Treatise*, I.i.iv.

offers a divine mechanism for benevolence, Bolingbroke offers a divine mechanism for the balanced state, and all these moralists offer one or another mechanism of social order.

So too did the mock-epic poet concentrate on the cause or mechanism of the relations that generate social disorder. There were several good reasons. For one, the traditional poetic account drew social obligation as an outgrowth of interpersonal, familial relations. Dryden, for example, consistently drew on Senecan "benefit theory" to explain social relations in terms of the exchange of personal favors or gifts, that is to say, benefits, which create for the recipient a corresponding obligation. Thus the social order is constructed and stabilized through this network of personal relations—generosity and gratitude—especially through the network of obligations owed to rulers for the benefits they provided all (Wallace, 1980). Such conceptions had been central in Garth's *Harveian Oration,* which describes the College's "Benefactors" as "noble," "courteous," "bountifull," "beneficial," and "Like to the heavenly Inhabitants." But that occasion was a family affair, and Garth's understanding of the appropriate genre for the occasion was particularly tradition-bound. The mock-epic poet, on the other hand, addressed a *national* culture with national (even international) means of distribution and control—of goods, of ideas, of literature, of medical knowledge and practice, *and* of social obligations. The language of personal relations just could not account for the facts of life in a national culture as physically, economically, and socially mobile as that of late Augustan England.

Also, the mock-epic is urban poetry. When life is predominantly urban, most human relations never rise to the level of personal encounters—think of Swift's *City Shower* or Gay's *Trivia,* or think of the adventures of Moll Flanders in London. The city dweller is an adventurer, an idler, and above all a spectator. When that urban life is shaped by the centralized institutions of a commercial society, the few personal encounters that remain are for the most part commercial transactions in which personal obligations play a lesser part. The great institutions of commercial life were, Bolingbroke's *Craftsman* warned, "monstrous members and societies in the Body Politic," which "have bodies, but no souls, nor consequently consciences" (Kramnick, 288, 426). Even the small tradesmen for whom *The Craftsman* spoke experienced most of their personal relations as commerce. For them to think otherwise was to court disaster, as shown by exemplars as different as Moll Flanders and the Heartfrees in *Jonathan Wild.* In such a modern social organization, it is impossible to found social obligations on purely personal relations.

Other reasons for the mock-epic's reliance on mechanism rest in the nature of the genre's mix of satire and natural philosophy. A satiric form given initial shape by a scientific physician, the mock-epic strives for more than the pseudo-diagnosis that merely labels the disease and displays its symptoms. A scientific physician knew that the diagnosis that cures reaches beyond symptoms to causes, and that such a diagnosis rests on a theory of the disease—what we now call its etiology. Of course this was also thought to be the greatest power of the traditional epic—to display the "Causes creative" (TE, V.50) of its subject.

When it came to representing the causes of social corruption, the mock-epic poet relied partly on the depiction of character, but the chief work of diagnosis was less direct, was reserved for the "furniture" of his story, in the locations of the action, in the settings, in the disposition of the scenes. In these diagnoses, the poems use spatial relations to model social and moral relations just as moral gravitation does. By representing the scene and the action in terms of the relations that generate social disorder, the mock-epic poet defines for us a Newtonian space in which the contrary forces of attraction and repulsion can figure the mechanism of that disorder so that, understanding its motive forces, we know not only its agents but its causes as well. And best of all for the poets' agenda, those causes remain personal, in keeping with the traditional account of social obligation. In the mock-epic, social disorder does not arise from the failure of institutions, the failure of a culture, the failure of an economic system or a system of social controls. Instead, social disorder is very much a matter of personal failures—in the extreme case, personal failure on a massive scale, but personal failure nonetheless. Moral gravitation allows the poet to represent such mass personal failure in a way that is modern, mechanical, and poetically powerful.

Although there are fewer explicit cosmological analogies in *The Dispensary*, Garth had there laid the ground of the mock-epic's explanation for social disorder using the language of mechanics. Because *The Dispensary* predates most uses of a specifically Newtonian analogy, Garth nowhere explicitly directs the reader's attention to a Newtonian precedent for the configuration of his space. The specifically Newtonian ground of mock-epic's "point-field" representations is most evident in *The Dunciad*. After all, Pope would give moral gravitation its most memorable expression. In *An Essay on Man* the great chain of being has a point-field structure: "Drawn to one point, and to one centre bring / Beast, Man, or Angel, Servant, Lord, or King" (III.301–2). And, "Self-love and Social" form a planetary system:

> On their own Axis as the Planets run,
> Yet make at once their circle round the Sun:
> So two consistent motions act the Soul;
> And one regards Itself, and one the Whole.
> (III.313–16)

For Pope, the mechanism of social relations is a human analogue to Newtonian mechanics, the social order an image of the order of the heavens:

> God loves from Whole to Parts: but human soul
> Must rise from Individual to the Whole.
> Self-love but serves the virtuous mind to wake,
> As the small pebble stirs the peaceful lake;
> The centre mov'd, a circle strait succeeds,
> Another still, and still another spreads,
> Friend, parent, neighbor, first it will embrace,
> His country next, and next all human race,
> Wide and more wide, th'o'erflowings of the mind
> Take ev'ry creature in, of ev'ry kind;
> Earth smiles around, with boundless bounty blest,
> And Heav'n beholds its image in his breast.
> (IV.361–72)

This image had first, however, explained in the original *Dunciad* the mechanism not of social order but of social disorder:

> As what a Dutchman plumps into the lakes,
> Once circle first, and then a second makes,
> What Dulness dropt among her sons imprest
> Like motion, from one circle to the rest;
> So from the mid-most the nutation spreads
> Round, and more round, o'er all the seas of heads.
> (II.373–78)[13]

---

13. Brown suggests that this obscene version imitates a parody of Pope's *Temple, Aesop at the Bear Garden* (1715). "Why," she asks, "does this ambivalent image of energy and stasis seem to convey so much significance in Pope's corpus?" While her focus on this as an image of imperialism is surely relevant, moral gravitation is the answer to her question.

Earlier still, in *The Temple of Fame* Pope had found that the same mechanism explained the ways of rumor. This time, however, using a procedure more like that of Garth or Thomson, Pope takes care to make sure that his analogy is also a scientifically correct description of how rumors, or any other sounds, spread:

> As Flames by Nature to the Skies ascend,
> As weighty Bodies to the Center tend,
> As to the Sea returning Rivers roll,
> And the touch'd Needle trembles to the Pole:
> Hither, as to their proper Place, arise
> All various Sounds from Earth, and Seas, and Skies,
> Or spoke aloud, or whisper'd in the Ear;
> Nor ever Silence, Rest or Peace in here.
> As on the smooth Expanse of Chrystal Lakes,
> The sinking Stone at first a Circle makes;
> The trembling Surface, by the Motion stir'd,
> Spreads in a second Circle, then a third;
> Wide, and more wide, the floating Rings advance,
> Fill all the wat'ry Plain, and to the Margin dance.
> Thus ev'ry Voice and Sound, when first they break,
> On neighb'ring Air a soft Impression make;
> Another ambient Circle then they move,
> That, in its turn, impels the next above;
> Thro undulating Air the Sounds are sent,
> And spread o'er all the fluid Element.
> (428–47)[14]

It should not surprise that Pope reused this image in such different contexts. Repeating a small set of key images in widely varying contexts and to widely varying ends was among Pope's favorite procedures, just as the attendant questions about continuity in change and especially about continuity of identity in changing circumstances were among Pope's most common concerns (R. Cohen, 1974, 1977). Nor should we find it surprising or contradictory that Pope would rely on mechanical

---

14. Pope's preference for the example of expanding waves in a fluid raises questions about his understanding of the science. What was most distinctive about Newton's cosmology was not motion-as-collision but motion *without* collision, i.e. action at a distance. Pope thought of his example of waves in a fluid as connected to Newtonian astronomy. Whether he also recognized its relation to Aristotle and pre-Newtonian mechanics, using it to unite ancient and modern science, I do not know.

explanations in a work that takes mechanism as a major enemy.[15] *Mere* mechanism, the mechanism of a purely mechanistic cosmos of material first causes, is the nightmare vision of *The Dunciad*. But what damns the dunces is not the fact of their mechanism but its emptiness. Pope found himself again and again attacking those whose unwelcome likeness to himself was perhaps their chief fault. He attacks mechanism that leads to atheism and free-thinking. He bothers to attack it because the kind of mechanical explanations that led freethinkers to atheism are not distinguishable in kind from those that the whole culture, Pope included, took as natural. Thus the attacks on mechanism—like all the attacks in mock-epic—are a way to establish difference, always a difference of source and of ends, never of means. The mechanism by which Dulness spreads her nutation is the very same mechanism in which "Heav'n beholds its image": it lacks only God, "the all-extending all preserving Soul" (*Essay on Man*, IV.372, III.22).

The circle spreading round a fixed point of corruption is the dominant image, the dominant structure of representation, and the dominant social mechanism of the *Dunciad*s. There Pope exploits, refines, and makes more explicit the pattern of contracting and expanding circles that Garth had established in *The Dispensary*. The opening setting of *The Dispensary* depicts a series of expanding circles of attention, starting with the golden globe atop the dome of the College's Cutlerian Theatre, and expanding metonymically (globe-dome-College-realm-world). These expanding circles give a Newtonian order to the poem's spaces as they expand the scope of its social diagnosis.

Even more significant are the cycles of attraction and repulsion by which Garth represents the spread of the apothecaries' disease. Note the progress of the representation of Horoscope-Bernard—he of the "Planetary Schemes" (II.133). First we locate his home/shop (in Little Britain, near Smithfield) as a center of attention and attraction for all around.

> Onward she [Envy] hastens to the fam'd Abodes,
> Where *Horoscope* invokes th' infernal Gods;
> And reach'd the Mansion where the Vulgar run,
> For Ruin throng, and pay to be undone.
> (II.100–3)

Then after a description of the shop and its value-fixing particulars, we and Envy move into the "inner Room" which "receives the num'rous

---

15. Battestin gives the definitive case for Pope's attack on mechanistic cosmologies (113–18).

Shoals, / Of such as pay to be reputed Fools" (II.130–31)—a social grouping defined by their relationship to Horoscope. A short description of the room and an extended description of the various fools follows, and the first movement of the picture is complete: pleased Envy hovers over "*Horoscope* environ'd by the Crowd" (II.163). When Envy's speech terrifies Horoscope with the prospect of a lawful, if not virtuous life, the crowd he had attracted is now repulsed, and disperses over the surrounding territory:

> At this fam'd *Horoscope* turn'd pale, and straight
> In Silence tumbl'd from his Chair of State.
> The Crowd in great Confusion sought the Door;
> And left the *Magus* fainting on the Floor.
> (II.204–7)

The pattern of Horoscope's levee is specifically recapitulated in the action of *The New Dunciad,* which has proved so puzzling.[16] First Dulness gathers her subjects, whose connection to each other is their relationship to her:

> Now crowds on crowds around the Goddess press,
> Each eager to present the first Address.
> (IV.135–36)

Then she sends them back into the world with confusion renewed:

> Then blessing all, "Go Children of my care!
> To Practice now from Theory repair."
> (IV.579–80)

More than this, all the *Dunciad*s are overcome by spreading circles of nutation.[17] These circles are the end—both goal and final resting place—of Dulness: the spreading darkness at the close of the *Variorum* (A III.335–56), which is all the more frightening in *The Dunciad in Four Books* because it is preceded first by the spreading dunces and

---

16. For a very different explanation of the action, or lack of it, in Book IV, see Sitter (87–97).

17. *Nutation* had just acquired a new meaning most apposite to Pope's case. The *OED* records a 1715 usage in which *nutation* refers to a disturbance in the earth's regular rotation: "Another Nutation arising from another Cause may produce all this diversity in the distance of the Pole-star from the Pole" (*Gregory's Astronomy* [1726, I.302]).

then by the spreading yawn (B IV.579–626). Once we understand the motive forces behind this cycle of attraction and repulsion (the personal motives that center the portraits), then we know the cause and the cure of the social disorder it displays. But since disorder and order share the same mechanism, and since evil is counterfeit good, both cause and cure are ultimately personal, resting wholly in the elusive qualities of individual motive. What is easy to see on the cosmological scale, the difference between God and Dulness, is obscure in the smaller compass of the personal scale, demanding the poet's greatest skills.

The poem's other representations are also dominated by Newtonian circles. In Book I, Tibbald/Cibber sits "Studious... with all his books around" (A I.111), his altar a point source from which Dulness will "spread a healing mist before the mind" (A I.152). Such circles are especially prominent in Book II, which is centered on the May-Pole/Church of the Strand, the point around which the Dunces' progress ranges. Book II begins with Tibbald/Cibber enthroned:

> All eyes direct their rays
> On him, and crowds grow foolish as they gaze.
> Not with more glee, by hands Pontific crown'd,
> With scarlet hats, wide waving, circled round,
> Rome in her Capitol saw Querno sit,
> Thron'd on sev'n hills, the Antichrist of Wit.
> (A II.7–12 [B II.7–16])

Then the dunces gather at the May-Pole for the first round of games—circled, Pope twice reminds us (A II.49, 149; B II.53, 157), round their Queen. This round of games ends with the noise-making contest, in which Blackmore's strains circle round the western reach of Dulness's influence. After the turn at Bridewell, the diving contest produces with each new dive an instance of expanding circles, and from Smedley we learn how the Fleet, "tinctur'd" by a "branch of Styx," supplies Dulness's eastern influence: "Each city-bowl is full / Of the mixt wave, and all who drink grow dull" (A II.313–20). The book ends with the expanding circles of sleep quoted above. This book of circles itself centers the *Variorum*. In *The Dunciad in Four Books*, the circles of Book II are answered by the encircling levee of Book IV:

> And now had Fame's posterior Trumpet blown,
> And all the Nations summon'd to the Throne.
> The young, the old, who feel her inward sway,

> One instinct seizes, and transports away.
> None need a guide, by sure Attraction led,
> And strong impulsive gravity of Head:
> None want a place, for all their Centre found,
> Hung to the Goddess, and coher'd around.
> Not closer, orb in orb, conglob'd are seen
> The buzzing Bees about their dusky Queen.
>   The gath'ring number, as it moves along,
> Involves a vast involuntary throng,
> Who gently drawn, and struggling less and less,
> Roll in her Vortex, and her pow'r confess.
>   (B IV.71–84)

This "gravity of Head" represents more than Pope's long-running joke on the profundity of bad writers and the massive solidity of the dunce. This attraction distinguishes a dunce because, like gravitation, duncehood is a relational concept.[18] Duncehood is not defined by any specific family of features, though looking to features is a necessary first step in comprehending it (as, for example, in Rogers, 1972). A dunce is one—any one—who shares in the relation to Dulness. Their "gravity of Head" simply names their dullness, the universal attraction among dunces. Queen Dulness is no more than the massed forces of her collected sons and daughters, and King Tibbald/Cibber, the earthly center of her system:

> As man's maeanders to the vital spring
> Roll all their tydes, then back their circles bring;
> Or whirligigs, twirl'd round by skilful swain,
> Suck the thread in, then yield it out again:
> All nonsense thus, of old or modern date,
> Shall in thee centre, from thee circulate.
>   (A III.47–52)

---

18. In a 1743 addition to the P. W. note to these lines, the relational character of Newtonian connection is made explicit. Isolating "three classes in this assembly," the note adds, "The *first* drawn only by the strong and simple impulse of Attraction, are represented as falling directly down into her ... and resting in her centre.... The *second*, 'tho within the sphere of her attraction, yet having at the same time a different motion, they are carried, by the composition of these two, in planetary revolutions round her centre.... The *third* are properly *excentrical,* and no constant members of her state or system: sometimes at an immense distance from her influence, and sometimes again almost on the surface of her *broad effulgence.*"

In this image Pope achieves the fullest, most perfect representation of Dulness and her powers of negation—"Music caus'd by Emptiness" (A I.30; B I.36). Born of privation, both mythic ("Daughter of Chaos and eternal Night" [A I.10; B I.12]) and personal ("Who hunger, and who thirst, for scribling sake" [A I.48; B I.50]), Dulness "marks her image" (A I.105; B I.107) in a spiritual privation that opens the way for material causes such as an empty gut or ale. Dulness is also just emptiness. Queen Dulness has no existence apart from dunces, no existence apart from particulars. Dulness does not inform *The Dunciad* in the way that God informs the *Pastorals* or would inform what we can imagine as the epic counterpart to *The Dunciad.* It's not so much that Dulness stands in stead of God, as that she gives name to the void of the Godless. When she spreads her "broad Effulgence" (B IV.18) she covers the land, but only with her minions. Her mists are only so many duncical papers; her influence only so much flowing ale or resounding air or waters of the Fleet. Her generality is the generality of her mass—her mass of Nonsense, her massed dunces, her mass culture, the crowds at her empty parody of the Mass. Dulness "conglob'd" is a picture of a Newtonian universe, overflowing with particulars but emptied of God.

Ranging Afield

5

God loves from Whole to Parts: but human soul
Must rise from Individual to the Whole.
—*Pope*, Essay on Man

Moral gravitation brings the social diagnosis of the mock-epic into the mainstream of Augustan moral and social philosophy. The figures of moral gravitation also enable the mock-epic to indulge, to a degree unprecedented in high Augustan poetry, the modern's fascination with all the particulars of urban life, which it depicts with a level of observational detail reminiscent of the new science. In this respect, the figures of moral gravitation answered to the chief technical challenge of the genre. In traditional terms, that challenge was to generalize its significance without generalizing its materials. Moral gravitation gives the poem something like the didactic power of moral philosophy, while it preserves the ties between the poem's satire and the particulars of history. Through the particulars, the poet achieves the general instructive force of the precepts of philosophy by a surer route than the traditional preceptual fable that must be applied, a route that uses poetry's sensuous, affective powers not only to reinforce but also to stabilize its judgments.

The matter can, however, be put a little differently. Moral gravitation also gives ready ideological significance to a more general representational pattern found throughout the poems. This pervasive representational pattern is metonymic in that single points—places or persons—center fields of attention that range across a variety of details brought into relation to those centers. In the prototypical scene of moral gravitation, persons are collected to be brought to the door, or even to the feet of the poems' central figures, there to add to or draw from their stores of corruption. This is, of course, a reenactment in small of the prototypical scene of mercantile imperialism, in which Father Thames collects and disperses the goods that bring Britain its wealth and global preeminence—with the difference that the mock-epic transactions are characteristically empty, circulating only gilded pills or nonsense. The mock-epic's point-field ranging thus depicts the social and moral identity shared by the arrayed particulars, using their equivalence to mark them and to mark off their difference from its virtuous and knowing readers. Doing so, it confirms the essential assumption of conservative political theory, that social and economic structures are neutral instruments of interaction, and differences in value arise from the quality of the persons and the inherent value of the goods arrayed in them. As the poem ranges, it exposes the varieties of interest, presumed to be self-interest, that are the motive forces of the field and that threaten the interests of a wide range of readers—threaten, in short, the public interest. In this way, the poem reaches toward a kind of generality, both the generality of its social and moral taxonomies and the generality of the public interest. Thus the seemingly narrow interests that motivate the poem and give it such particular subjects are differentiated from those of the self-centered victims because they are a species of public interest—particular in matter and in focus, but general in truth and appeal.

Multiplying Reference

The traditional preference for generality in poetry could not be ignored by a fledgling poet such as Garth. Serious public poetry was general, and the eminent doctor certainly intended his to be a serious poem. That need to appeal to a general audience explains the germ of truth in Garth's protest that he does not intend "to persuade Mankind to enter into our Quarrels" ([A5v]). That protest is clearly disingenuous: by the time Garth wrote the preface, he knew full well that the poem had already interested "Mankind" in the College's troubles. Blackmore had already responded with *A Satire Against Wit* (23 November 1699), which prompted Tom Brown and his coffee-house companions to produce *Commendatory Verses on the Author of the Two Arthurs and the Satyr against Wit* (1700; see Boys, 1949), which in turn prompted other rounds of response and counterresponse. On the Wits' side, these responses adopted language, images, themes, and arguments from *The Dispensary*. These responses drew the poem into the center of the ongoing skirmishes between the Cits and the Wits and thus into the continuing cultural struggle that occupied Augustan England at least until the final *Dunciad*. This literary and political axis is only one of several fields of interests that Garth traces out in *The Dispensary*, interests meant to move Mankind, not to enter the College's internecine quarrels, but to see—judge—them rightly.

Garth's solution for achieving a measure of epic generality without compromising the mock-epic's particularity is born of his disadvantages. Garth lacked, for example, the kind of relatively automatic public investment that *The Dunciad's* subject brought with it. Literature already held a prominent position in the cultural repertoire for describing the health of society, and Pope's literary villains were seen by both poet and readers as major sources of culture: the dunces were persons native to the public arena and of wide influence. Literature also offered the institution of the laureate. The succession plot gives *The Dunciad*, as it gave *MacFlecknoe*, both temporal and spatial extension in the "kingly" rule of the hero.[1] Finally, literature had already incorporated a rich language of political and social controversy, with ready political implications that carried "long trains" of generalizing associations already correlated to Pope's literary subject.[2] Even Swift and Boileau had the advantage on Garth. *The Battle of the Books* found in Parnassus / St. James's Library an institutional, public property that was at once historical origin and "cause creative" of culture, and Boileau's clergy offered a story centered on the church lectern—the site of their public, institutional, educational, and ceremonial role.

The Dispensary project offered no such public, institutional scope. Garth might look to the wide-ranging influence of the two official bodies charged with the health of the nation, but that is only so much legalism. The practice of medicine was an activity of the closet, a private transaction between doctor and patient, or at most the patient's family. Because Garth's resources for finding an easy general significance were comparatively meager, he had to rely on purely poetic resources far

---

1. Seidel analyses *The Rape* and *The Dunciad* as succession poems (226–49).
2. See Mack (1969, 128–29). Systematic political use of the press had begun with the Harley administration (see Downie), and the kind of paper warfare that develops such linguistic resources was by Pope's time nearly a century old.

more than any other mock-epic poet. And so he turned more determinedly to particulars, and found that through the figures of moral gravitation even the smallest particular could be made to engage the attention and interest of a wide range of readers.

For example, standing at the center of the opening setting is the golden globe atop the dome of the Cutlerian Theatre. The setting's smallest particular, the globe gains an elaborate network of relations as the poem progresses and the reader's understanding grows. This crowning point of the physical College locates it for the widest range of viewers and viewing points. It stands as the fixed point around which readers range through the field, along two axes: one spatial, in which time is held fixed as the poem ranges through a map of simultaneous corruptions; the other temporal, in which place is fixed as the poem ranges through a line of inheritances either preserved or perverted. The field of particulars thus becomes an *ordered* collection of objects and events that are seen in relation to the globe.

In presenting his poem's field of battle, Garth gives us a focal point (the globe) which centers a field of other points, each of which addresses other interests and so other readers. However, as the relations among those points of interest become more prominent, the field reconfigures itself as something more like a field of social forces. In the now-familiar process by which topographical and poetic contiguity is projected into a moral equivalence, what is true of the globe comes to be true of its dome and theater, but also of the Old Bailey and its villains little and great, and of the College's designs and patrons, past and present. All these are drawn by a kind of poetic gravitation to the golden globe, arrayed in a field of forces whose chief vectors are corruption (private interest), civic duty (public interest), and the progress of knowledge (both scientific and civil).

Because it centers the field of forces, the golden globe thematizes the setting, unifying the particulars whose *range* widens the appeal. Since this is the *opening* setting and so thematizes the whole poem, the golden globe draws all the poem's major concerns into its orbit, marking the spot where in Garth's diagnosis the College's problems begin and end—in the College itself. The breadth of concerns in its orbit is considerable. The most important aspects are announced as dominant themes: the danger to traditional institutions from the chaos of individual interests; the responsibility that should but does not follow privilege; and the corruption that ensues when economic interests become sources of social and political actions. Other aspects depend on an insider's knowledge of the particulars, including Garth's attacks on the self-interested benevolence of the College's "pious patron" and on the apothecaries' infiltration of and corrupting influence in the College (see Chapter 7). Three others are developed only later in the poem: as a pill (bullet), the globe betokens the violence that the apothecaries bring to the College and that the College, to its shame, embraces; as a globe, it betokens the abuses of science and learning in the "Planetary Schemes" of Horoscope (II.132–33); and in its golden glow, it betokens Apollo's domination of the poem's machinery and the poem's concern with the power of science and poetry to penetrate the "dark Disguises" of Nature and of men. That is a lot of significance for so small a thing to carry, and it takes the whole of the poem to endow it so.

The technique of using topographical particulars to enforce values has been discussed from Courthope to Rogers, and these discussions have yielded reliable, though partial accounts of its poetics. The first to recognize Garth's key role in developing the technique was Geoffrey Tillotson, who notes that Garth's "descriptions ... enforc[e] his scale of values by pretending not to have one" (TE, II.113). Quoting one of Garth's temporal settings ("With that, a Glance from mild *Aurora's* Eyes ... " [III.53–60]), Tillotson admires the valuative "method of laying down parallel stripes of the beautiful and the sordid," though he fails to see that the ranging particulars are the point of the exercise and so thinks them out of place in the poem. Tillotson was also early to recognize that Garth's practice is a key to mock-epic poetics, not only to its "descriptive-satiric methods" but also

> to more concentrated effects:
> To stain her Honour, or her new Brocade ...
> or to that line which has troubled so many inattentive readers and for the offending word of which one editor ventured to suggest the emendation "baubles":
> Puffs, Powders, Patches, Bibles, Billet-doux.
>
> (TE, II.113)

The lines Tillotson selects for our attention seem specially designed to illustrate the general principle of poetics, that in poetry contiguity projects equivalence (Jakobson, 1960). Since then, these lines have been much discussed, becoming not only the critics' examples, but also their theme. The result has been a body of standardized interpretive procedures for finding moral equivalence. The interest in Popean zeugma is never in the figure itself—that is, in the verb whose sense is wrenched by the contrary objects—but in the projected equivalence of those objects. Similarly, the surprise, at once delighted and disapproving, that we find in Pope's piebald lists comes from the moral equivalence that contiguity leads us to expect.

These witty representations of a contiguity that marks equivalence rely on a highly refined, elaborately configured conceptual schema that defines the Augustan concept of place.[3] Normally expressed in spatial language, this schema articulates a network of social relations by which all things human—persons, their language, their products, their possessions—are correlated to a hierarchy of value. One group of ideas configured by this schema has been investigated in a substantial body of work, beginning with Arthur Lovejoy's *The Great Chain of Being* (1936) and including a substantial line of literary studies.[4] Most of the literary studies have bypassed the social uses of the great chain, emphasizing instead its relation to the body of religious/philosophical beliefs known as "physico-theology." But that focus only reflects the sometimes narrow limits of literary scholarship. The great chain is one of a number of hierarchies of value, whose variety and depth show that they are a feature of the general cultural semiotic, including basic conceptual structures more entrenched and so more powerful than any explicitly avowable beliefs. In that sense, the poet can justifiably claim that these equivalences are found—albeit found in an ideological projection—not made by the poem.

The point of the schema of place, however, is not to discover equivalences. In the poems, as in the culture, its ideological function in the social-semiotic repertoire is first and foremost the sanction of difference. It is deployed in all the discourses of social, economic, or political life, both to justify and to enforce distinction, *in*equality. In mock-epic, the poet polices the good order of the social world, and so uncovers the dark underside of place. What he finds— equivalence, lack of distinction—are marks of social violation and disgrace. Worst of all, he finds that those who fail to observe distinctions think and act as through they were of a kind with those who do. Uncovering these failures to observe difference, the mock-epic poet displays the essential equivalence of all corruption.

---

3. Like the "implicit or incompletely explicit *assumptions*, or more or less *unconscious mental habits*" that an earlier history of ideas called "unit ideas" (Lovejoy, 7, 15), this schema offered a ready-to-hand way of configuring explanations for natural and human phenomena. See Lakoff and Turner.

4. Another important early work was Spitzer (1944–45). Later these studies included work in social and political theory (Viner, 1972). The line of literary historical studies begins with McKillop. Particularly relevant here are Williams and Battestin.

It is a disgrace that the Apothecaries Physicians are no more than apothecaries, and the apothecaries no more than quacks. It is a greater disgrace that the quacks, apothecaries, and Apothecaries Physicians all think themselves on a par with the gentlemen of the College. Garth explores their shared identity only in order to stigmatize them with the mark of their kind and to preserve their social inequality. So too is Belinda-Arabella stigmatized by the equivalence in her mind of her honor and her new brocade. By failing to observe the difference between them, she measures her difference from those readers who do. Even more pointed, because less pure, is the example of Belinda-Arabella's Bible. Not only is her Bible in the place where baubles should be, but she has inverted the "natural" relation, putting religion in the service of beauty, reducing the Bible to an instrument of her charms.[5] In each case, whether the poet sees simple equivalence or the more complex inversion, the schema of place gives us equivalence in order to make us enforce difference.

The Designs of the City, I: The Dispensary

Though written by an amateur author, *The Dispensary* is a poem about professionals and is steeped in the ideology of the professional. For all its traditional features and mythic machinery, *The Dispensary* is the first insider's look at the modern, secular profession and its establishment as an economic and political institution. In this context, the question of place or identity is a particularly anxious one, beset by the contradictions in the establishment of any profession. A profession demands from its members a nearly tribal allegiance, but is in principle open to all with the requisite knowledge and know-how. A profession needs for its establishment to have the force of law, but wants to reserve to itself the power to police its members and borders. A profession must have the most obvious, publicly ratified marks of membership, but rests finally on a badge no more durable than a license. That anxiety is why the scene of *The Dispensary* is configured by law and its villains are all

---

5. The nasty truth of these schemas of place is that those who occupy lower stations are in service to, at the pleasure of those above (who, to be sure, owe some duty in return): in addition to her Bible, the furniture of Belinda's dressing table includes her Betty, who in Pope's elegant way is denied both her name and the credit of her ministrations ("And *Betty's* prais'd for Labours not her own" [I.148]). These consequences were endorsed by Soame Jenyns, *A Free Inquiry into the Nature and Origin of Evil* (1957); only the upstart Sam Johnson was wise enough to see the truth about Pope in Jenyns ("Review of *A Free Inquiry*," 1757).

counterfeit professionals, Apothecaries Physicians whose license is genuine but whose allegiance is misplaced.

As Garth elaborates the poem's hierarchy of counterfeit practitioners, he finds two kinds of identities. The first is the "vertical" identity that grows out of the relationship among all those who have joined the army of unlicensed practitioners. Holding the uppermost place are the Apothecaries Physicians, those "amphibious Fry" (II.118) who might have stood among the first of their kind, but elected to align themselves otherwise. Though they include both physicians turned apothecaries (Mirmillo-Gibbons) and apothecaries turned physicians (Horoscope-Bernard), both prove no more than apothecaries at the last. Next are the apothecaries themselves, who might have found an honorable and secure place in an established hierarchy, but who together with their physicians have made themselves the great ones, the "Chiefs" in the army of mountebanks, empirics, and other quacks. All these, from the degraded physician to the lowest quack, share the identity of their mutual interest and corruption.

There are also identities across the scales. The Apothecaries Physicians share a relation and an identity with others of the great who stand in corresponding positions on other scales in the poem's field of corruption. Thus the ill-gotten luxury of Mirmillo and Horoscope is identical to that of the "great Ones" of the Old Bailey, who "enjoy the World in State." "Fam'd" Horoscope is the "great *Alcides* of our *Company*" (II.169) who dispenses his medicines and advice from a Satanic "chair of State" (II.205). Like both the jurymen and the thief-takers general of the Old Bailey, these Apothecaries Physicians reap all the benefits while the "little Villains must submit to Fate."[6] The fate of these little villains is to submit to these counterfeit practitioners: deprived of the good offices of the Dispensary, they "[F]or ruin throng, and pay to be undone" (II.102–3). Other little villains include the unlicensed practitioners who do the dirty work of openly disrupting the social fabric while the apothecaries and their physicians work safely behind the scenes.[7] In these identities we find the germ of a summary of the argument or diagnosis that motivates the poem.

---

6. Oldham told a similar story in *A Satyr... Dissuading the Author from the Study of POETRY*: "Here a vile Empirick, who by Licence kills, / Who every week helps to increase the Bills, / Wears Velvet, keeps his Coach, and Whore beside, / For what less Villains must to *Tyburn* ride" (*Works*, III.176).

7. The apothecaries know that "War's rough Trade shou'd be by Fools profest, / The truest Rubbish fills the Trench the best" (V.163–64), and they trust that "Tho' such vile Rubbish sink, yet we shall rise; / Directors still secure the greatest Prize" (III.245–46).

The identities along and across the poem's hierarchies provoke a more global set of metonymic expansions. Guided in the first instance by Garth's three names for the College—globe, dome, pile—these expansions grow by sheer momentum to an ever-wider compass: globe-dome-theater-College-City-realm-world.[8] This movement expands the poem's range of reference in two ways: first in these figural expansions and, more directly, in the ranging tour through the particulars of London's field of corruption. By so expanding its range of reference, the poem also expands its claim to relevance. As the particulars multiply and their shared identities emerge, the representation of the battle of the Dispensary speaks to the interests of larger and larger communities of readers.

This analysis is supported by the evidence of reception, which though scant is clear. The poem did appeal for many years to the interests of a large community of readers, and contemporary commentary on the poem was focused less on medicine than on Garth's larger concerns— on the ranging particulars. Modern commentary, however, has been largely ignorant of the particulars, medical and otherwise, and so perpetuates the charge that the poem is unreadably topical.[9] But even as they blame it, the poem's few careful critics clearly register the effects of the poem's expanding range of reference. They are evident, for example, when Tillotson both identifies *The Dispensary*'s point-field episodes as the poem's best strokes, and simultaneously complains that they "lose their value in the general chaos of the poem," calling them "litter" that "in a medical satire in mock-heroics should not be there at all" (TE, II.114–15).

Were *The Dispensary* in fact only "a medical satire in mock-heroics," its wider field of corruptions would be extraneous. Because it is a mock-epic, the wider field is essential. Tillotson is certainly right to sense a disjunction between the poem's narrow focus and its expansive interests. For instance, the golden globe that dominates the observer's view of the College (within and without the poem) is a focal point that must—from the proper, "distant Sight"—come to seem absurdly small and all too trivial. Indeed, from a sufficiently distant sight, the globe would have shrunk to a vanishingly small point, so small that an observer might wonder (productively for the poem's purposes) whether

8. One of the knottier issues for Garth is how far this blame reaches. Garth consistently praises William and, later, Anne—often in contexts that directly contrast his blame of others (see Sena, 1986, 37–68). If the kingdom as a whole escapes the corruption, however, it is clearly in peril.
9. Ellis's edition (*POAS*, vol. 7) and Sena (1986) are notable exceptions.

it was the globe or the dome that seemed "a gilded Pill" (I.14). Even as the globe serves to shape the poem's emerging *ordonnance* and the reader's growing understanding, it invites, even demands resistance. In the distant sight, the *ordonnance* asserts itself, so that each point of focus becomes comprehensible chiefly in terms of its relation to other points in the field, in terms of the lines of force that define the field. The poem is no longer a medical satire in mock-heroics, and Garth has ensured that his attempts to generalize the relevance of his poem do not force him to generalize its materials.

The fullest examples of how Garth generalizes by building relationships and identities are the passages Tillotson praises for setting values and blames for being irrelevant. These are the passages locating the homes/shops of the chief villains, Horoscope-Bernard and Mirmillo-Gibbons. Although intelligible as they stand, these settings ask a detailed knowledge of topography and its social and economic significance. Bernard's house is located in Little Britain, near Smithfield and his practice at St. Bartholomew's Hospital. Gibbons lived and practiced in King Street, Covent Garden. Both physicians are marked by their patients, who are marked by the locales. Mirmillo-Gibbons's house, where the Apothecaries Physicians gather to plot their strategy, is

> Not far from that frequented Theatre,
> Where wand'ring Punks each Night at Five repair;
> Where Purple Emperors in Buskins tread,
> And rule imaginary Worlds for Bread;
> Where *Bently* by old Writers, wealthy grew;
> And *Briscoe* lately was undone by New,
> There triumphs a *Physician* of Renown,
> To none but such as rust in Health unknown.
> None e'er was plac'd more fitly to impart
> His known Experience, and his healing Art.
> When *Bur*——*ss* deafens all the list'ning Press,
> With Peals of most Seraphick Emptiness;
> Or when Mysterious *F*——*n* mounts on high,
> To Preach his Parish to a Lethargy:
> This *Aesculapis* waits hard by, to ease
> The *Martyrs* of such Christian Cruelties.
>   (IV.1–16)[10]

10. Excluding the first and last framing cantos, the first half is given over to apothecaries (presided over by Bernard, apothecary turned physician), the second half to physicians (pre-

Thus opens the longest and most elaborate setting in the poem, again centered on unnamed places: Covent Garden, that grocers' home[11] with its vulgar, energetic, commercial, and most attractive bustle, its mountebanks and charlatans, its coffee-houses and bagnios; Drury Lane Theatre; Russell Street, home of the booksellers Bently and Briscoe; Russell Court and Burgess's popular, strikingly theatrical nonconformist sermons, late of Bridges Street; St. Paul's, site of Freeman's inept performances. All these present a wealth of debased and debasing activity that provides Gibbons with patients and Garth with the field through which we are to see Gibbon's place in the poem's structure of values: "None e'er was plac'd more fitly."[12]

The attention to detail here is exquisite. If we locate each of the places and actions, we find Covent Garden something like a funnel, gathering patients from the eastern and southern edge as far as Bow Street and Drury Lane, and channeling them through the open square, past St. Paul's to the northwestern corner and down King Street to the well-placed Gibbons. And just to reinforce the point that more is at stake here than the corruption of the College, Garth extends the setting with the longest and best of his world-upside-down *topoi:*

> Long has this darling Quarter of the Town,
> For Lewdness, Wit, and Gallantry been known.
> All sorts meet here, of whatsoe'er Degree,
> To blend and justle into Harmony.
> The Criticks each advent'rous Author scan,
> And praise or censure as They like the Man.
> The Weeds of Writings for the Flowers they cull;
> So nicely Tasteless, so correctly Dull!
> The Politicians of *Parnassus* prate,
> And Poets canvass the Affairs of State;
> The Cits ne'er talk of Trade and Stock, but tell
> How *Virgil* writ, how bravely *Turnus* fell.
> The Country-Dames drive to *Hippolito's,*

---

sided over by Gibbons, physician turned Apothecaries Physician). This setting marks that transition, representing the apothecaries' temptation and corruption of the College's weaker, more vulnerable members.

11. Apothecaries were originally part of the grocers' company; and until the chemical revolution that precipitated the controversy, an apothecary's wares would be little different from a grocer's.

12. Tom Brown reports that Gibbons "got all his Patients by taking Dr. *Lower's* House" in King Street, Covent Garden (quoted by Ellis, IV.7n).

> First find a Spark, and after lose a Nose.
> The Lawyer for Lac'd Coat the Robe does quit,
> He grows a Madman, and then turns a Wit.
> And in the Cloister pensive *Strephon* waits,
> 'Till *Chloe's* Hackney comes, and then retreats;
> And if th'ungenerous Nymph a Shaft lets fly
> More fatally than from a sparkling Eye,
> *Mirmillo,* that fam'd *Opifer,* is nigh.
>
> (IV.17–37)

As the poem ranges through the field of particulars, centering on the point that the setting is meant to locate, an identity begins to develop among those particulars. As the politicians and poets perversely exchange roles, the former prating of Parnassus, the latter writing on Affairs of State, we begin to see that they are both "Politicians of Parnassus." In this sense Covent Garden is the poem's carnival, with all the anarchic carnival reversals born of the mountebank's natural setting, the trading fair and market square, now naturalized as the home of the professions.[13] By these reversals, all come to share an identity: "All sorts meet here, of whatsoe'er Degree, / To blend and justle into Harmony," the harmony not of a well-disposed design but of simple equivalence. It hardly matters whether it is a Cit or Politician or Lawyer who tells "How *Virgil* writ," they are all beyond their professional ken and so are sure to be equally unenlightening. All the denizens of Covent Garden—including especially Mirmillo-Gibbons—have, by abandoning their talent and their place, lost all distinction and degree. They are all the same, all Politicians of Parnassus.

This uniformity of professionals who forget their proper sphere extends the relationship established at the beginning of the poem between politicians and physicians. That shared identity and its carnival implications had been suggested twelve years before in Lord Rochester's contribution to the large literature of quacks and mountebanks, *The Famous Pathologist or the Noble Mountebank* (1677). Living in the

---

13. Bernard's shop is also near a carnival setting, Smithfield. In Covent Garden, the carnival has both come out into the open and moved significantly up the social scale. Covent Garden had already become identified with carnival reversals in popular verse. One example is purportedly by Dennis ("A Day's Ramble in Covent-Garden" [20 March 1691], in *Poems in Burlesque*, 1692): "But which were Wits, and which were Beaus, / The Devil sure's in him who Knows, / For... These look'd like those, who talk'd like these." In "The Swan Triple Club in Dublin" (1705), attributed to Swift, the reversals are described in a passage that imitates *The Dispensary* extensively, even to locating one coffee-house in terms of another.

mountebank's underworld in order to escape the entanglements of justice, Rochester delighted in its uncertain, free-form identities, its theatricality, costuming, and elaborate props, its general habit of thumbing the nose at social convention and decorum, and most of all the opportunity it afforded for a double dose of the kind of aggressive deceit that put the libertine above all social convention and sanction. By deceiving the gullible populace, Rochester also deceived his aristocratic and powerful enemies, who if they saw through Bendo, never saw through him to Rochester. By accepting at face value (and so tolerating) the mountebank's deceit, they made themselves fools to their supposedly superior understanding.[14]

Meditating on how nice is the distinction between the "Counterfeit" and "his Original"—and in the process destroying the distinction in a cascade of self-reflection—Bendo-Rochester writes,

> Reflect a little what kind of Creature [the Mountebank] 'tis: he is one then, who is faine to supply some higher ability, he pretends to, w[i]th Craft, he draws great companies to him, by undertaking strange things w[hi]ch can never be Effected.
>
> The Politician (by his example no doubt) finding how the People are taken w[i]th Specious Miraculous Impossibilities, Plays the same Game. . . . thus are [the people] kept & established in Subjection, Peace & Obedience, He in Greatness, wealth, and Power: so you see the Politician is, & must be a Mountebank in State Affairs, and the Mountebank no doubt, (if he thrives) is an errant Politician in Physick. (34)

But where the libertine finds in such collapse of distinctions only a cruel delight in the charlatan bond between men of state and those who play the fool for the mob, the professional gentleman Samuel Garth—even though allied with the wits against sober men of the city—finds only ruin. Garth would have it that Rochester's "Mountebank in State Affairs" and his "Politician in Physick" share an identity with the "Politicians of Parnassus" and all others whose professions are false, including those other Politicians in Physick, Apothecaries Physicians such as

---

14. The "Epistle Dedicatory" by Thomas Alcock is quite explicit on this matter. He offers an epigraph from Rabelais, "Si populus vult decipi decipiantur," gloats over Rochester's "Laughing at, & deluding his Ignorant and Malicious Enimies," and describes their "perpetual Jangling . . . in a Jargon of damn'd unintelligible Gybberish all the while, & indeed we judged it not convenient, in our Circumstances, to do anything in plain English but Laugh" (29).

Mirmillo-Gibbons. By so relating themselves, the Mountebank in State Affairs, the Politician in Physick, the Politician of Parnassus, the Apothecaries Physician and the others lose all distinction except the shared distinction of their corruption.

The Designs of the City, II: The Dunciad

Schemas of place lend themselves, as McKillop pointed out, to enumeration. Although the Augustan habit of multiplying particulars need not employ schemas of place, the schemas invite expansion up, down, and across their "scales" or "chains."[15] Their work of extending relevance is crucial to both the polemical and the punitive aims of the mock-epic. Until "Mankind" is engaged on the side of virtue, neither the poem's teaching nor its chastising can succeed. And yet, to rest the work of extending relevance on these procedures for extending reference is to hazard the poem's appeal and so its life, chancing success on the knowledge—and the memory—of readers. Garth did rely on the attempt to extend relevance by extending reference, believing that "Such poor Supports" serve as a "Stay." "The Tree once fix'd," he hoped, would stand when its "*Rest* is torn away" (III.245–46). The hazard in that belief is evident when we remember that the best mock-epic, *The Dunciad,* comes to us with its "Rest" so intricately intertwined in the main body of the poem that to tear it away is to uproot the tree. The hazard is also evident in the subsequent fate of Garth's mock-epic, which faded with the fading memory of its readers. Now that the science and medicine of the past have begun to be a viable part of our cultural memory, there may be life in *The Dispensary* yet.

Garth had little choice but to hazard his poem in this way. He had few other resources since his subject did not offer the kind of "institutional" bases for extending relevance that Pope found in the dunces. And yet, even though Pope did have greater latitude, he elected to particularize his mock-epics, and especially the *Dunciad*s, in just the way Garth had shown him, extending the relevance of the poems without generalizing their materials. Of course in using Garth's techniques Pope refined them as only he could.

---

15. Ehrenpreis (1970) argues that *The Dunciad* is composed chiefly of such lists and blames them for disrupting the poem's narrative and arguments (235–36). Brown argues that in *The Dunciad*'s lists all are reduced to objects (132–39).

The most innovative, most Popean of those refinements is the apparatus of *The Dunciad*. With his unerring technical insight, Pope recognized that the only solution for a poem that must depend on its readers' knowledge and memory was to memorialize that knowledge *in the poem itself,* not merely as a key in the manner of *The Dispensary* or as a witty appendage in the manner of, say, *A Tale of a Tub,* but as an essential feature of the poem. As memorials of what the reader is presumed to know, Pope's notes are perhaps his most important tool in the struggle to control his readers' judgments. Unfortunately Pope's recent editors have thought the notes something of a nuisance (Sutherland's distaste is palpable; other editors have decided, and to this day continue, to abridge or eliminate the notes altogether). Pope's best critics, persons notable for the depth of their knowledge and the reach of their memory, have thought the notes only "an implicit admission of a kind of failure."[16] Of course, the failure they have in mind is, on the one hand, Pope's failure to confine himself to the limits of their knowledge and memory and, on the other, their own culture's failure to know and remember what the critics have taken the trouble to learn.

Pope's notes are most important in relation to his portraits, where he uses them to let the dunces speak for themselves. In this chapter's examination of how Pope refined Garth's point-field settings, we will see how even there Pope conjoins notes and verse, making the two together into a poem.

Pope's uses of settings and topography in *The Dunciad* have received so much attention that there is little to add to establish the fact that topography and value correlate in *The Dunciad*. We know, however, rather little of how they do so, and what has been said on the subject of poetics has been wrong. From the most distant view, the scenes of *The Dunciad* are mapped onto two kinds of locations identified clearly enough in Pope's *exordium:*

> Books and the Man I sing, the first who brings
> The Smithfield Muses to the Ear of Kings.
>   (A I.1–2)

---

16. "Pope refused to attempt the kind of integrative process he undertook when he incorporated the epic machinery into *The Rape of the Lock*; he attempts instead merely to shore up the earlier structure of his poem" (A. Williams, 77). Griffin defends the notes (221–27), but he sees them almost solely as opportunities for Pope's aggrandizing self-display; this is Sutherland's position (TE, V.xl) and offers little basis for integrating the notes and verse.

Courthope recharacterizes this action as "the removal of Dulness from the City to the polite world" (E-C, IV.24) of the West End. Courthope is good, though brief, on the significance of this distinction, even mapping out the area between the City and the Court in which most of the events occur: "Just beyond the western and northern sides of the wall lay a district in which most of the Dunces themselves found their homes and amusements" (E-C, IV.25). Aubrey Williams adopts Courthope's characterization of the relevant topography more or less wholesale, adding such impor tant details as Blackmore's role as the spokesman for the City's westward influence. Since Blackmore's reechoing strains define the boundaries of the polite world (A II.251–53), Blackmore is the fixed point in that field of corruption. Rogers offers an important reevaluation of the evidence of the poem's details, arguing that in the opening setting "Pope explicitly states that the City connections of which Aubrey Williams makes so much ('her own Guildhall') are secondary" (1972, 39).[17] Dulness, Rogers convincingly argues, is not a City but a "Suburban Muse."

These conflicting readings of the significance of this topography are nicely sorted once we recognize that this map is designed around points and fields. The simple distinction between City and Court or Whig and Tory is too crude as history and as interpretive scheme to explain the complexities of Pope's poem. The Smithfield muses are, indeed, suburban creatures who are all the more dangerous for it. That the dunces are intermediate, liminal beings makes them at once more grotesque— more place-less—and more able to circulate and spread their corruption. Their ability to circulate and spread generates, as Williams shows, the essential movement of the poem.[18] At the same time, the theme of the City and the "moneyed interest" *is* an essential feature of the poem's value structure. While the dunces "cannot be *simply* equated with the brokers and stockjobbers, the merchants and importers, the shopkeepers and moneylenders" (Rogers, 1972, 76; emphasis added), they are in fact equated in the poem. They have the equivalence of their contiguity,

---

17. Carefully charting the poem's locations, Rogers finds them concentrated in four general areas (Rosemary Lane, St. Giles' Cripplegate, Fleet and Farringdon, and St. Giles' and Covent Garden) which "ring the ancient walled City": "[T]he Dunces, for the most part, did not invade the City, narrowly defined ... [and] they themselves had no real stake in the life of the City" (1972, 75–76).

18. Doody suggests the "charivari" is the dominant topos of the dunces' progress (and of the mock-epic in general). The charivari does involve important carnival elements of mock-epic, but Williams's emphasis on the progress is more to the point of Pope's interests and of other mock-epics.

of their shared identity in a field of forces that preserves their particular distinctiveness and displays their general interrelation.

The Dunciad is a poem first and foremost about literature; the suburban sites of the literary trade are its central locations. The City and its corrupting money are brought into the poem as elements of the poem's field of corruptions. The City is *never* the central point in that field; it only adds importantly to the particulars through which the poem ranges. Even the Lord Mayor's procession on which Williams rests so much of his reading is introduced only as one of the many contiguous particulars by which Pope sets the time of his first episode:

> 'Twas on the day, when Thorold, rich and grave,
> Like Cimon triumph'd, both on land and wave.
> (A I.83–84)

So too is the rest of Courthope's and Williams's evidence for the importance of the City (and for that matter, the Court) grounded not in the poem's central, focal points but in the field through which the poem ranges. Pope engages our concern for the City in the same way that he engages our concern for the breakdown of the law, which is to say, in the way Garth had shown in *The Dispensary*. In *The Dispensary* Garth leads the reader to construct a valuative map through which a minor scuffle in the basement of the College of Physicians addresses the interests of the nation. In the *Dunciad*s Pope progresses through such a map, addressing *seriatim* the varied interests of the nation and making that progress the central fact of his poem.[19] The City and its corrupting moneyed interest are key to Pope's diagnosis, but the City is only *one* element in the poem's expanding range of reference and relevance. Much of our best criticism of *The Dunciad* finds its evidence in the ranging particulars. There is perhaps no better evidence of how well Pope succeeded in extending relevance by extending reference.

---

19. Even without any very exact correspondence between the dunces' procession and that of the Lord Mayor, Williams's emphasis on the progress of the dunces is an essential insight. An important feature of that progress is its predictive force. Both *The Dunciad Variorum* and *The Dispensary* end, like *Paradise Lost*, in imitation of *Aeneid* VI. But where the *Aeneid*'s predictions are in something of a future perfect (predicting what is in the poem's future but the reader's past), the mock-epic predicts a less certain future. *The Dunciad in Four Books* adds another layer of prediction, since Book IV represents a fulfillment of the predictions of the *Variorum* but is itself yet another predictive, future-directed moment. In terms of epic precedent, *The New Dunciad* is to the *Variorum* as *Paradise Regained* is to *Paradise Lost* (and it includes several key imitations of *Paradise Regained*).

How deeply that effort to extend relevance penetrates *The Dunciad* can be seen in what at first looks to be a minor incident, the shift of scene from the Strand to the Fleet as a noise-making contest ends with "sonorous Blackmore's strain."

> This labour past, by Bridewell all descend,
> (As morning pray'r and flagellation end.)
> To where Fleet-ditch with disemboguing streams
> Rolls the large tribute of dead dogs to Thames,
> The King of Dykes! than whom, no sluice of mud
> With deeper sable blots the silver flood.
> (A II.257–62)

This passage is discussed by both Aubrey Williams and Rogers. Williams cites it because its note on Bridewell advances his claim that the action of the poem follows the progress of the Lord Mayor's procession; Rogers is more interested in the representation of Fleet Ditch, whose "ecology" he explains in useful detail (1972, 145–66). Here I want to examine Bridewell as the point on which Pope turns between the two centers of duncical games, the church/May Pole on the Strand and Fleet Bridge.

The detail on which Pope turns this setting is noise. As Blackmore's reverberations die down, we hear and turn our attention to the morning sounds of Bridewell—prayer and flagellation. The note singling out these sounds ends with a description of the dunces' progress, but it begins by explicating one significance of these particular sounds:

> 258. [*As morning pray'r and flagellation end*] It is between eleven and twelve in the morning, after church service, that the criminals are whipp'd in *Bridewell.*—This is to mark punctually the Time of the day: *Homer* does it by the circumstance of the Judges rising from court, or of the Labourer's dinner; our author by one very proper both to the *Persons* and the *Scene* of his poem. (A II.258n)

Pope could not come closer to explicating for us how he uses setting to extend reference and so relevance. Why, we are told to ponder, is this circumstance so "very proper both to the *Persons* and the *Scene*" of this poem? Rogers presents a general topographical warrant: the region of the Fleet was a natural and especially dangerous home of the dunces. Williams gives us a temporal warrant: " 'between eleven and twelve' was apparently the time at which the Lord Mayor customarily journeyed to the Thames" (39). Pope suggests two warrants, both of which draw us back into the particulars of this point in the dunce's playing field.

First, Pope tells us, "between eleven and twelve" was the time when criminals were whipped in Bridewell. This first warrant is simple fact. The second lies in previous poetic practice. Homer is Pope's authority for the general practice of locating time by another "circumstance" ("What-time the Judge forsakes the noisy bar / To take repast" [*Odyssey*, 12.519–20]; "what time in some sequester'd Vale / The weary Woodman spreads his sparing Meal" [*Iliad*, 11.119–20]). But here Pope indulges his habit of alluding to a classical source by way of intermediate English sources. Nearer to hand is Pope's own practice of setting time by the contemporaneous activity of judges and laborers:

> Mean while declining from the Noon of Day,
> The Sun obliquely shoots his burning Ray;
> The hungry Judges soon the sentence sign,
> And Wretches hang that Jury-Men may Dine;
> The Merchant from th' *Exchange* returns in Peace,
> And the long Labours of the *Toilette* cease.
> (*Rape*, III.19–24)

And, if we are paying attention, we cannot fail to recognize that both the allusion and its significance find their roots in Garth's opening setting and its point-field configuration of judges and laborers.

If we follow the note's instruction to consider how these circumstances are "very proper" and take its suggestion to focus on technique, then the reference to Bridewell opens up in several directions. First, it participates in *The Dunciad*'s general attention to the failures of the law by recalling the similar theme in *The Dispensary*. In that respect, *bridewell* functions in both its senses. *Bridewell* was the proper name of one particular prison, Bridewell Palace (presented to the City by Edward VI in 1552); but it was also a generic name for all prisons. Thus the Garthean connection reminds us that when the dunces turn toward the Thames they are entering a district of bridewells—the Fleet, Newgate, Ludgate, and the Old Bailey are all hard by. The Garthean connection also reminds us how to read such particulars: the dunces are not unique in their corruptive powers, as the story of Bridewell shows. Bridewell Palace (rebuilt since the fire) was originally named for St. Bride's Well, a holy place near which Henry VII had built a palace. When Edward VI gave this structure to the city, it was first intended as a hospital. Later it became a House of Corrections, still called a hospital, a place to cure the spirit of vagabonds and beggars, especially women.[20] By 1728 it had become only another prison, where the lesser offenders for whom it was intended were intermixed with hardened criminals, with the inevitable corruption and hardening of the (relatively) innocent (Webb and Webb, 1922). This is the classic mock-epic story of decline and of the spread of corruption through the indiscriminate mixing of the worst with the rest. Now, all that remains of correction in this house is the empty music of an empty ritual of enforced prayer and enforced contrition.

This story and these sounds aptly value the persons and scene that follow (the diving dunces) and those that have come before (Blackmore and all who heed his voice). The connection between the divers of the Fleet and the inhabitants of Bridewell is chiefly their shared vagabondage.[21] But with the persons and scene that precede Bridewell, the connections are rich and specific. Empty noises are the stuff of duncery, and Blackmore's braying victory is heroic example. Both the prayer and flagellation of Bridewell and Blackmore's noise replace, so displace and degrade, the genuine items—prayer and poetry. (Pope's long, lashing note on Blackmore highlights his religious poems in addition to his epics.) Moreover, Blackmore had already been branded by Garth as a dunce known by his sound. As one of the great ones in physic, notable among them for "the Dissonance of [his] untuneful Verse" (IV.202), Blackmore was already identified with the great ones of the Old Bailey. Now, some thirty years later, that identity is updated. The bounds of Blackmore's "strain" include two more legal institutions:

> Long Chanc'ry-lane retentive rolls the sound,
> And courts to courts return it round and round:
> Thames wafts it thence to Rufus' roaring hall.
> (A II.251–53)

In a nice example of the vagaries of cultural memory, Pope feels he needs a note on the delays of Chancery (which Dickens and others later

---

20. The pretense that Bridewell was a hospital was bolstered by its extensive ties to another house of confinement important to the poem, Bedlam, whose officers also administered Bridewell's care. See the "Gazetteer" in Gordon (1976).

21. There is also the connection between the submerged, rather prurient image of whip on bare flesh in a woman's prison and the rather more openly prurient images of the mud-diving (A II.301–28).

made legendary), but he expects his reader to know that "Rufus' roaring hall" refers to the din of Westminster Hall.

In this way, the great ones in physic and of the Old Bailey share their identity first with the great ones among the dunces—Blackmore was long since known for a dunce who made it big[22]—and second with the great ones of Bridewell, who, as they notoriously enrich themselves on the suffering of those who fall into their House of Correction, force their victims into a show of prayer and contrition.[23] Thus Bridewell becomes one of the prominent points in Pope's field of corruption, one that further extends the poem's range of reference. How like Pope to make his notes the source of so complex an allusion, and how like the mock-epic to use allusion to multiply its particulars.

Mapping Mock-Epic Gravitation

Early in our century Ezra Pound saw "Pope and the eighteenth-century writers" as exemplars of the power of poetry to engage the play of abstraction, *logopoeia*, the "dance of the intelligence among words and ideas" (1918, 394). In *The Dunciad*, Dulness is the center of that dance, mazy though it be. Mock-epics center again and again on abstractions—on civic virtue, on civil polity, on the personal integrity of true virginity, on the obligations imposed by a cultural estate, on the influence of literature on civil order. But Dulness's abstraction is of a different sort. Hers is the abstraction of classification, of any Lockean general name, the abstraction that comes from knowing many particulars and knowing what is common to them all. In Garth's point-field gravitational model Pope found a form of representation—an image, if you will—that on a grand scale collects particulars in order to display their common features. We see the shared identity of the dunces in their ale, their dirty haunts, their affinity for prisons, their cells in Bedlam and Grub Street,

---

22. The emblem of Blackmore's material success was his coach, memorialized in Dryden's joke, which Pope in turn cites: "Sir *Richard Blackmore*, Kt. who (as Mr. *Dryden* express'd it) *Writ to the rumbling of his Coach's wheels*" (A II.256n). The idea of dunces making good on the labor and corruption of others is prominent in Book II. The noise contest immediately follows the contest of the booksellers, those dunces who above all enrich themselves on others.

23. The corrupt practices of the jailhouse bureaucracy were a long-standing scandal (Babington, 47–58; Rogers, 1972, 154).

in all the particulars of the poem's settings and its portraits. This abstraction must, however, rest its claims to truth on what are now called "natural kinds." According to Augustan philosophers, my idea of dog can be well founded—can rise to knowledge—only if there is such a thing in nature as the kind dog and only if I have ideas of enough particular dogs to know the distinctive features of the kind. So, too, my idea of a dunce. What such abstraction produces is the taxonomies of natural history. And in the poem's many changes of scale more than one dunce is presented to us enormous, parts clearly labeled, like the fleas that illustrate the natural histories of the time. Dulness names the natural kind *dunce,* and *The Dunciad* is its class portrait.

Dulness's two kings hold a special place in that class. They are centers, collection points, point sources that in the ebb and flow of attraction and repulsion spread the very forces they collect: "Shall in thee centre, *from thee circulate.*" Thus Dulness at the end of Book IV sends her children back into the world to spread her dark nutation. Thus the dunces range round their May Pole, spreading their influence east (via the waters of the Fleet) and west (via the less dense fluid of the air). Thus Horoscope's collected patients are dispersed out his door to spread their uncured diseases. And thus Horoscope collects in himself the corruption of the apothecaries only to spread it, first among the Apothecaries Physicians gathered at Mirmillo's, and then among the physicians of the College.

To be able to say what a thing is, one must be able to say how—and why—it works. In the mock-epic judgment is all, and judgment is a matter of identity. Identity, in turn, is a matter of place, of mechanism, and of motive. The motive forces of corruption—the gravity of the mock-epic vision—sustain these circles, keeping physicians in the orbit of apothecaries and keeping the dunces in the orbit of their Queen. The mock-epic leads its reader to a vision of such a corrupt cosmos by the arrangement—and the particularity—of its parts. Though it teaches us to know wholes, the mock-epic understands that, to rephrase the *Essay on Man,* "God [knows] from Whole to Parts: but human soul / Must rise from Individual to the Whole." The mock-epic also knows that its proper study is man, and so it diagnoses those motive forces of corruption in yet another of its point-field designs, that found in its portraits.

Part Two

The Figure in the Portrait

Prologue

[T]is only by hunting One or two from the Herd that any Examples can be made.
—Pope to Arbuthnot, 2 August [1734]

The mock-epic disrupts the steady, hierarchical progression from the Moral, through Fable, Allegory, Action, Episodes, and Persons, down to Descriptions. The mock-epic builds upward from Descriptions and Persons, overturning the neoclassic story of epic ontogeny by finding episodes, actions, allegories, and morals to suit its prime matter, persons and places. The Morals underlying the Actions (those metaphoric statements literalized into actions) are already sentences about the Persons: "Theobald/Cibber brings the Smithfield Muses to the ear of kings"; "The dunces deal in dirt"; "Horoscope is mercenary"; "The apothecaries indulge in rebellious violence"; etc. So in the mock-epic the Action is divided, grounded in what still seems to many a contradictory logic. Looking downward from the Moral, the poem evaluates its Persons by characterizing their acts. Looking upward from the Persons, the poem generates its actions by characterizing—portraying—those who act. Part I focused on the kinds of description that are characteristic of the genre, showing how those descriptions both ground and extend the relevance of the poets' judgments. In this part, I shift from description to depiction, focusing on the contribution of the Persons to the Action, which is to say, on their portraits.

I begin, in prologue, with a portrait. Though not from a mock-epic, this is a portrait of a dunce. Found in *The Egotist: Or, Colley upon Cibber* (1743), which purports to be the second Cibberian response to *The New Dunciad*, this is explicitly a revised counter-portrait: *His Own Picture retouch'd to so plain a Likeness, that no One, now, would have the*

Face to own it, But Himself.[1] With brassy, good-humored self-deprecation—Cibber's most engaging trait—our Author discusses with one Mr. Frankley the abuses of Cibber's character perpetrated by an unnamed Satyrist. In an extended dialogue, the Author gives what is "intended as the last Sitting to my Picture" (A2v), a stance reinforced in the epigraph from Dryden: "But one Stroke more, and that shall be my last." There is a certain rhetorical complexity in a self-portrait that aims to have the last word, especially a counter-portrait whose superiority is meant to rest on simple likeness.

Throughout the dialogue, the Author recapitulates the stand Cibber had taken in his first response to *The New Dunciad*, the pose of one genuinely saddened to see so great a talent succumb to an excess of Spleen, but who is unaffected by a satire that cannot bite because it is not like. Urged by the acrimonious and vengeful Mr. Frankley to assent to an abusive characterization of the Satyrist and his motives, this Author shows only an equanimous restraint.

> I hope a satirical Picture, whether like or unlike, is not an equal Disgrace? And when the Features are not yours, will not the Name be a Misnomer? As for the Satyrist, let him be as able an artist as you please, if he is reduced to those low Shifts, and dares not trust to the Truth of his Colours, he debases himself to a dirty Dawber of Sign-Posts. (18)[2]

Though mild by Cibber's standards, the epithet Author allows himself is insulting enough. Its pedigree, which Pope surely knew, would also add to the insult. The first *OED* citation is from Dryden's "To Mr. Lee, on his Alexander." There, Dryden ends his praise of Lee by defending him against his critics:

> Your beautious Images must be allow'd
> By all, but some vile Poets of the Crowd;

---

1. Cibber's first response was *A Letter from Mr. Cibber, To Mr. Pope* (1742). His first public self-portrait was *An Apology for the Life of Colley Cibber* (1740), in which he glanced briefly at Pope and his satiric treatment of Cibber.

2. Cibber's conceit spread quickly. A month later, Lord Hervey's *Difference Between Verbal and Practical Virtue* (1742), in which Cibber had a hand, says that Pope "Dawb'd minor Courtiers, of a minor Court" (5) and calls Pope's body "A Symbol and a Warning to Mankind: / As at some Door we find hung out a Sign, / Type of the Monster to be found within" (6). In the same month *Sawney and Colley* (1742) calls both Cibber and Pope daubers.

But how shou'd any Sign-post-dauber know
The worth of *Titian,* or of *Angelo?*
(49–52)

Between Dryden and Cibber, satirists used the figure steadily, though not extensively. The figure was drawn into the discourse of the sister arts, and the poor skills of the signpost painter were used to demean the skills of the poet, as in Dryden's original use. The figure was brought into the mock-heroic strain by Marvell. Taking a hint from the anonymous "Answer of Mr. Waller's Painter to His Many New Advisers" (1667),[3] Marvell opens his *Last Instructions to a Painter* by turning in despair to a signpost painter, who better "suit[s] our great debauch and little skill" (7–8). By 1730, the signpost painter had, through the example of *The Dunciad,* been naturalized into the republic of Grub Street:

No *Venus* shou'd in Sign-Post Painter shine;
No *Roman* Hero in a Scribbler's Line:
The Monst'rous Dragon to the Sign belongs,
And *Grub-Street's* Heroes best adorn her Songs.[4]

A second, less pronounced strain in the use of the figure emphasizes the semiotics of signpost painting. In the Augustan account, the signpost is an indexical sign whose chief source of meaning is simple contiguity. Signpost painting seems more ostensive, more referential—and so in some ways less representational—than true portraiture. In the "Epistle to the Whigs" prefaced to Dryden's blistering counter-portrait of Shaftesbury in *The Medal,* Dryden characterizes signpost painting as chiefly mnemonic: "I must confess I am no great Artist; but Sign-post painting will serve the turn to remember a Friend by; especially when better is not to be had" (38). Unlike *The Medal* but like the medallion ("so counterfeit and light" [9]), the signpost is a mere pointer, a sign whose meaning is purely ostensive and lacks the accessory ideas that are the poet's stock-in-trade. Dryden sees the signpost as a memorial, mere testament to an absent object. By some of our standards, such is the paradigmatic instance of the sign, but it is anathema to any eighteenth-century

---

3. In the "Answer," the painter complains that his "advisers" would be better served by a "dauber": "Look out some canvas-stainer, whose cheap skill / With myths and stories alehouse-walls doth fill" (95–96).
4. Henry Fielding, "Prologue" to *The Tragedy of Tragedies* (18–27).

semantics. It makes the signpost painting a travesty of the sign, its dauber a travesty of the artist, and its subject the travesty of a person—Oldham calls one signpost subject *"Man anagrammatized."*[5]

Cibber rests his case for the justness of his epithet and the unjustness of Pope's signpost portraiture on a simple question that Cibber thinks has a simple answer: "And pray, Sir, why my Name, under this scurvy Picture?" Cibber first asked this question in the first *Letter... to Mr. Pope,* adding, "I flatter myself, that if you had not put [my name] there, nobody else would have thought it like me, nor can I easily believe that you yourself do." And so, he puts forward his chin: "Now let me hold up my Head a little, and then we shall see how far the Features hit me!" (31–32).

Though only a blockhead can afford to offer his jaw to a counterpuncher as talented as Pope, Cibber does have an argument that he is especially well situated to make. Cibber's *Apology* was already an important document in the growing debate over the nature of the written character, and would soon be drawn into Fielding's extended exchange with Richardson.[6] The central issue in that debate was how characters were to be drawn. Where the Theophrastan character was grounded in well-defined character traits, perceived in largely external views that make character a product of judgment,[7] Cibber's brand of self-defining character forged a ground of interiority on which to write a "life." Just as early modern social theory had increasingly explained social action in terms of appetites, desires, interests, and other "internal" motive forces, so literary theory emphasized the interior dimension of character. The shift posed a problem for the satirist: since no person could speak authoritatively of the interior life of another, the self-defined character was reserved for the autobiographer, the diarist, and the writer of fictions and was denied to the satirist or any other outside observer. We see in Pope's letters his own attraction to the mode of self-defining characterization, and some critics have found traces of it in his verse.[8] But for a satirist to move into the ground of interiority and write the life of his victims is the nicest of tasks.

---

5. "Character of a Certain Ugly Old P――." For another version of the signpost as empty sign, see Wycherley's joke about Horner as "a sign of a man" (*Country Wife,* I.1).

6. The title of Fielding's first entry is *An Apology for the Life of Mrs. Shamela Andrews... by Conny Keyber.* Cibber would continue to represent for Fielding one extreme of the new mode of characterization.

7. The standard Augustan guide to the Theophrastan character is Gally (1725). Also see Boyce (1947).

8. See, for example, Griffin and also Russo (1972).

Cibber's question, "Why my name," seeks to limit Pope to the stable, trait-bound Theophrastan character of general satire. The question draws its force in the first instance from a correspondence theory of resemblance: a picture, verbal or visual, resembles what it depicts to the degree that it has "the same" features. As Cibber says, when "the Features are not yours," neither is the picture. There are difficulties in treating resemblance as a matter of toting up common features, even more in the idea that a representation and its object can have common features. But the process of understanding objects and representations in terms of features comes so easily and "naturally" that it (and Cibber's question) feels unavoidable—certainly most critics have thought so. Insofar as Cibber's question taps our tendency to think in terms of correspondences between features, it succeeds in undermining the mock-epic's complex, relational representations with their emphasis on wholes. But in order to have the full force Cibber wants for it, the question must also be tied to a theory of reference: a picture depicts when it resembles *and* refers to an object. To equate reference and resemblance is yet more difficult,[9] but again there is great appeal in Cibber's negative formulation. When there is no resemblance,"will not the name be a Misnomer?"

By his own lights, which are far less dim than Pope's depiction has made history believe, Cibber has a case. If we accept anything like Cibber's correspondence theories, Pope must indeed seem to have fallen to "low Shifts." In the grip of such theories, we find ourselves scouring Pope's portraits, comparing them feature by feature to the original, and sorrowfully (or angrily) tut-tutting any departures from our norm—a practice common enough, even among Pope's admirers. Cibber thinks that his portrait in *The Dunciad* is so unlike him that his less-than-generous inquiry into Pope's motives is enough. Critics who have largely accepted Cibber's correspondence test have thought the portraits in *The Dunciad* so unlike that they are not portraits at all, only embodiments of abstractions or notes toward a supreme fiction.

Although we must reject Cibber's correspondence theory, we can agree with him in this: Pope and Garth are signpost daubers. In the figure of the signpost dauber Cibber has hit on the aptest image for the kind of portraiture these poems pursue: the popular, commercial art of the streets in which the sign marks the spot. Cibber's simple correspondence test cannot settle the matter, since the portraits, as all the representations in *The Dispensary* and the *Dunciad*s, pose an important

---

9. For an account of resemblance and depiction, see Goodman (3–43); for an account of resemblance and reference, see Putnam (22–48).

alternative to correspondence theories of truth. Of course Cibber is shrewd enough to see something of this. He insists on simple resemblance precisely because he rejects Pope's right to any other form of representation, especially Cibber's own kind of interior representation. Cibber's test would license only the general satirist, who must rely on the compelling resemblance of his portrait to lead the reader to make correct identifications. Cibber wants to deny Pope the right to make Cibber's name the center of Pope's portraiture, reducing it to a supplemental label that adds insult to injury.

Naturally enough, Cibber's argument addresses only part of the issue. It fails to notice that signposts are not grounded solely in resemblance. A signpost might be, as we now say, representational, but as an "utterance" it is only incidentally descriptive. Cibber's test ignores those indexical elements of the signpost that Dryden had noted. Signposts fall into the same category as those utterances known as *performatives*, utterances whose truth lies in the utterance itself. Take, for example, warning, promising, and blaming. If I utter the appropriate words in the appropriate circumstances, I will merely by my utterance have warned or promised or blamed. I can warn unnecessarily, break my promise, blame unfairly—but I have nevertheless truly warned, promised, or blamed. Similarly, if under the appropriate circumstances I place a signpost before my dwelling or business, the very act makes that signpost my true sign. Performatives are that class of utterances for which, if the circumstances are right, saying makes it so.

Cibber wants to take his portrait as purely descriptive, but Pope wants to have it both ways. He wants his portraits accepted as true descriptions at the same time that he wants them to have performative force. In this Pope returns to the central role of the law. Most performatives are either declarations about ourselves ("I warn you," "I promise you") or declarations of our social standing ("By the powers vested in me ... "). One of the few instances in which we give performative standing to statements that also stand as descriptions is in the court of law, where judges or juries are charged to "find facts." When a judge, in the appropriate circumstances, finds facts, his descriptions become social truth and no one—normally not even a higher court—has the right to say otherwise. This is, of course, just the power to which Pope aspired. The mock-epic poet stands before his public as legislator, judge, jury, and executioner—a stance that is complex and contradictory. It leaves him to shift between the calm purveyor of truth ("Be it as to the judicious reader shall seem good" [TE, V.39]) and the wrathful, god-like judge ("*Out of thine own Mouth will I judge thee, wicked Scribler!*"

[TE, V.21]). It also leaves readers to shift between two forms of judgment: the judgment that grounds the knowledge in every true sentence and the judgment that is a sentence to death or worse. This is the stance perfectly captured by the figure of an angry justice.

In part, this is the stance of the counter-laureate, the pose Pope had assumed by the time his translating was over and *The Dunciad* begun. Pope would in his poems—and in the public mind—displace the king's laureates, who had divorced themselves from the ancient line of authority and so disestablished themselves. In this, Pope departs from Garth's example. After administering his public punishment, Garth explicitly relinquished his authority back to those duly appointed (VI.334–51). Pope, however, had come to see himself as the only possible enforcer of his laws: "Law can pronounce judgment only on open Facts, Morality alone can pass censure on Intentions of mischief: so that for secret calumny or the arrow flying in the dark, there is no public punishment left, but what a good writer inflicts" (TE, V.14). The dominant figure for the rogue's gallery of *The Dunciad* would come to be the pillory, that signpost of public shame, and *The Dunciad*'s pillory would thereafter be the model for Pope's sense of his role as a poet.[10]

> I must be proud to see
> Men not afraid of God, afraid of me:
> Safe from the Bar, the Pulpit, and the Throne,
> Yet touch'd and sham'd by *Ridicule* alone.
>   (*Epilogue to the Satires,* II.208–11)

"The Bar, the Pulpit, and the Throne": these stands are indeed authoritative. The dunces were not wholly wrong when they so often called Pope a tyrant and a usurper. Some of the same bravado can be found in Dryden, who fell easily into the comparison of his surgical satire to the good offices of Jack Ketch, whose "fineness of a stroke" gives him the power—and the right—"to make a malefactor die sweetly" (Ker, II.93). These poets, and especially Pope, made for themselves an Augustan version of the myth of an outpost civilization, now best known in the American myth of the Old West, whose lone Sheriff is the only law in the territory and the only bulwark between the helpless and hapless citizenry and the outlaw bands. We can, of course, trace direct lines of descent for both myths to Odysseus and others of Greek origin and to

---

10. See *Corr.,* II.341, III.316, 423. For a general discussion of Pope's practice, see Morris (214–40).

Aeneas and his outpost civilization. Among Pope's poses are more than one anticipation of Gary Cooper, alone at high noon.

It is one thing to assume the mantle of law. It is another to have the right to that mantle, and still another to have the power to exercise that right. Nothing can prevent the questions about the poets' right to take their stands and post their signs. Whence comes their power of office? Who was it that gave them the Mace? They will be asked, as the dunces did ask in their plays on Pope's name, Who died and made you God? And face it, the dunces have a case. We, too, wonder about the poets' right. To wrap oneself in the mantle of the law and to plant signposts at others' doors is a gesture worthy of a Virgil—but also of a son of Flecknoe. Who indeed *"would have the Face to own it"?*

Resistance to Pope's presumption was always at the heart of his troubles after *The Dunciad*, and it has shaped critical opinion from the time of Johnson to the present.[11] Pope may have been willing to bear the likes of Addison as "brother near the throne" (*Arbuthnot*, 198), but from the first he beat back every Phillips, Dennis, Tickell, Theobald, or Cibber who challenged his preeminence and his right to give laws. Pope's first entanglements with the dunces began when the young poet's older friends, seeing his genius, talked him up to another Virgil, and he first gave laws in *An Essay on Criticism*. It was his presumption—"this Youngster is pretending to give Laws"—more even than the portrait of Appius that so set Dennis against the *Essay* and began their lifelong quarrel.[12] Youngsters who give laws, geniuses or not, and counter-laureates of any age or station must inevitably face questions about their right to speak for us all.

Garth had a ready answer. He speaks for his College because it has charged him to do so; he speaks for the spirit of Harvey and a line of physician-scientists stretching back to Democritus; he speaks for Somers, who does "ha[ve] the Mace." Pope too had a ready answer, one he gave again and again—a long line of poet-legislators, beginning with Homer and Virgil and ending with Milton and Dryden, died and left

---

11. Johnson presents a telling case in the *Lives of the Poets*. In responding to *The Dispensary*, he reacted chiefly to its claims to truth, fully accepting Garth's propaganda. But in the case of *The Dunciad*, about whose subjects he knew a little something, Johnson reacts most strongly to Pope's presumption.

12. Though excessively irascible, Dennis's criticisms of the *Essay* are not entirely unjust. Pope is, for one of his age and position, presumptuous (*Reflections*, I.397–98). He is manifestly wrong to claim that only poets can be good critics (I.398). He is self-serving in "the servile Deference which he pays to the Ancients" (I.399). He is often obscure in yoking ideas through a kind of word-play that we have since learned to value (and to explicate), but that then seemed difficult at best (I.397–400).

their mantle specifically to Pope. Of course that answer is itself presumptuous, though it is also meant to be humbling, as we see in the sense of mournful, but prideful limitation that suffuses the final *translatio studii* in the *Essay* (643–744)—in which Pope is "The last" but also "the meanest of [the Muse's] Sons" (196).

These answers have had and have now enormous appeal.[13] To have heard us tell it, only dunces would dispute Pope's claim. But the mock-epic poet is *not* the laureate. He is a signpost painter and a propagandist—and his discourse rests on a myth. That myth is what gives him the badge of office without which the sheriff is only another slinger of arrows in the dark. And as we learn from Virgil as from Gary Cooper, the one on whose shoulders civilization rests must be pious, humble, disinterested, and self-sacrificing.

So the mock-epic poet would have us believe in his piety and disinterest. He would also have us believe that his is a territory whose social institutions are too decayed and corrupt to support the rule of law without the violence of his satire. The satire grounds the high moral stance, even as that stance legitimates the satire. Supplanting the bar, the pulpit, and the throne, the mock-epic is a poem of signposts, of descriptions that are also sentences. It is a portrait gallery in which the pilloried victims stand with the poet's judgment *"pinn'd upon the breast"* (TE, V.9).

These portraits are the topic of Part II. As with the settings, Garth set the generic pattern. Looking back to Dryden's practice, but also to popular political satire, Garth produces the kind of single-feature portraiture, closely related to visual caricature, which would mark the satire of the early eighteenth century (Hagstrum, 1972). But he also gives these portraits the stamp of mock-epic. First, he makes those single features motive forces, building the portraits around the appetites and desires that early modern social theory had legitimated under the name of interests. Thus the portraits and the persons are walking, talking refutations of an ideology that fails to distinguish private and public interests.

---

13. We have learned to understand these answers with no little depth. Following the lead of Maynard Mack's early essays, Aubrey Williams has helped us to understand how Pope's claim to authority in his mock-epics rests on the authority of the ancients as transmitted and enriched by Christian humanism, how it rests on a native tradition that culminates in Milton, how it rests on the authority of the divine logos. This work, which has its roots in the effort to rehabilitate Pope at the beginning of this century, has since been supplemented by many critics, a line culminating in Martin Battestin's magisterial *Providence of Wit*. On the biographical front Mack (1969, 1986) has shown us how Pope tried to make his life itself a claim to the mantle that he assumes in his later poetry, attempting to ground his claim in his acts, his social position, and finally in so much stone, vegetation, and soil.

Second, he unfolds those portraits through a narrative line. He takes the liberty of speaking for them their words and ideas, thus giving the characters some of the vitality and the particularity of the written life, and claiming for himself an authority over his persons that is reserved for the writer of fiction or autobiography. Finally, Garth subordinates the portraits to the general point-field designs of the mock-epic's social diagnosis. In the Augustan language of the sister arts, he gives the portraits all the coloring that description and local particulars can provide while preserving for them the stability and longevity of a proper design. Garth aligns the portraits with the forces that configure the poem's fields of corruption, exposing these supposedly individual interests as part of a larger pattern of personal greed, social overreaching, and political factions: these are class portraits. As in the settings, this pattern of portraiture became a generic pattern when Pope adopted and refined it, eventually adding the essential technical refinement—the notes and apparatus of the later *Dunciad*s.

From Caricature to Portraiture

6

The Dispensary is full of portraits. In a little more than eighteen hundred lines, Garth names or otherwise refers to some ninety identifiable contemporary figures, thirty-six of which are listed (a few incorrectly) in the "Compleat Key" bound with the Dublin edition of 1725. These references are of three kinds, ranging from mere mentions, to brief (ten- to thirty-line) sketches, to full-scale characterizations of the major persons in the action. All bear the stamp of Garth's portraiture, which, though tied to traditional Theophrastan practice, makes full use of the mock-epic's characteristic play with frames and perspectives—frames of reference, points of view, frames of judgment, frame-tales. In so framing his persons, Garth brings into play both the stable, single-trait caricature of high Augustan satire and the free-form, interior portrait of the written life. Since the two forms of character are associated with competing theories of social action, one based in the external demands of place and one in the internal dynamic of interest, Garth's portraiture is itself an argument about the nature of the social good and so participates in the poem's largest thematic designs. But since that portraiture also gives the fullest possible play to the ways of interest, it fuels mock-epic's heady flirtation with the dangers it seeks to contain.

A Catalogue of Portraits

Garth's portraits are everywhere in *The Dispensary*. Even when the persons are only mentioned as illustrations, there is yet the pervading attempt at portrayal:

> All Ice why *Lucrece,* or *Sempronia,* Fire,
> Why S—— rages to survive Desire.
> Whence *Milo's* Vigour at *Olympick's* shown,
> Whence Tropes to *F*—— or Impudence to *S*——
> (I.46–53)

Minimal portraits such as these are common in *The Dispensary*. They lie just at the juncture between the local detail used to ground the social analysis and the more extended portraits of the chief characters. Like so many extras in a Hollywood costume drama, they constitute a human landscape that Garth uses in the same way and in similar circumstances as the topographical particulars. These mini-portraits are ready-made because their characterizing details already belong to the public image of the figures, and they succeed to the degree that they carry the force of public, socially ratified judgments.[1] The mini-portraits are also related to the references to historical figures such as Lucrecia and Sempronia, drawing on characterizing details represented in the cultural encyclopedia, however temporarily, in the same way as Lucrecia's coldness or Sempronia's warmth.

As the value-laden human landscape, the mini-portraits are part of what Garth takes as given, as the known ground for his argument of values. But as portraits, they are part of what Garth sets out to reveal, the unknown or unappreciated facts that he seeks to expose. This dialectic is shared by Garth's brief sketches, for the most part of relatively unknown physicians. All but two of these (Urim, I.143–62, and Colon II.83–97) are grouped in Canto IV, where come in succession sketches of Querpo, Carus, Umbra, and Vegellius (IV.100–168). Ostensibly these portraits are included because these persons have a role in the action. But except for Querpo and Carus, who later take on larger roles, these figures too tend to fade into the human landscape of the poem.

Like the mini-portraits, these sketches are built of a single characterizing detail; but the detail is developed rather than merely mentioned:

---

1. In this passage, two instances are clear: the troping "*F*——" is Heneage Finch, solicitor-general and Tory member of Parliament; he was satirized as "Polytropos" in *An Essay upon Satire* (1699; *POAS,* 1.408). The impudent "*S*——" is James Sloan, representative of the rotten borough of Thetford, Norfolk; he was known as "blustr'ing Sloan" (*POAS,* 6.21). The "*S*——" who "rages to survive Desire" was identified in the "Complete Key" as Robert Leke, third earl of Scarsdale, but readers found at least four other appropriate candidates (Ellis, I.48n): desire was a trait shared by too many others.

> Nor must we the obsequious *Umbra* spare,
> Who soft by Nature, yet declar'd for War.
> But when some Rival Pow'r invades a Right,
> Flies set on Flies, and Turtles Turtles fight.
> Else Courteous *Umbra* to the last had been
> Demurely meek, insipidly serene.
>   With him, the Present still some Virtues have,
> The vain are sprightly, and the stupid, grave;
> The Slothful, negligent; the Foppish, neat;
> The Lewd are airy; and the Sly, discreet.
> A Wren an Eagle, a Baboon a Beau;
> C—— a *Lycurgus,* and a *Phocion,* R——.
>
> (IV.140–51)

The chief difference between the form of the portrait of Umbra and the form of the two mini-portraits it contains is the difference between exposition and reference. It is akin to the difference between proper and periphrastic names and is a consequence of the obscurity of the original of Umbra, Dr. William Gold.[2] Not only must Gold's trait be more fully identified—he is "obsequious," "soft by Nature," "Courteous," "Demurely meek, insipidly serene"—but so must its consequences be briefly elaborated. Garth's sketches are, in a sense, mini-portraits elaborated for the unknowing.

What sharply differentiates the mini-portraits from the brief sketches is the role of their subjects in the overall thematic design. Unlike the subjects of the mini-portraits, the subjects of the sketches are medical persons with a place, however small, in the fable and its allegory. Their traits are part of the pattern of actions and motives portrayed and so exposed. For example, the ultimate consequence of the trait that distinguishes "obsequious *Umbra*" is his inability to make proper distinctions ("With him the Present still some Virtues have"). That inability is particularly appropriate to one so yielding, but it is also shared (for Garth, almost by definition) by all Apothecaries Physicians. So too does Umbra-Gold share with his fellows the affiliation with death suggested both by his name and by his trait.[3] By giving Umbra-Gold a role in the

---

2. Gold or Gould was a good Apothecaries Physician whose specialty (venereal disease) earned him a satire entitled *On Don Quicksilver* (Ellis, IV.138n).

3. *OED: Umbra,* 1. The shade of a deceased person; a phantom or ghost. *Obsequious,* 1.b. Through association with Obsequy: Dutiful in performing funeral obsequies or manifesting regard for the dead. Also see *Umbrage,* 6. A pretext or pretence; a colour or false show.

action ("Who ... declar'd for War"), Garth unifies and thematizes these aspects of his portrait, making it yet another facet of the poem's family album of rebellion: "Flies set on Flies, and Turtles Turtles fight" (IV.143).

For those persons with a larger role in the story, the epic emphasis on action opens important vistas on the portraits. When two of the subjects of Canto IV's sketches, Carus and Querpo, reappear in Canto V arrayed for battle, they take a hand in characterizing themselves as their actions speak louder than Garth's words. They also have a quick but important exchange (V.154–94) added in the major revision of 1703. One last chance for the Apothecaries Physicians to undo the dire resolution formed in the earlier debates,[4] the exchange takes the form of the familiar epic topos of the superior eloquence of actions:

> Vaunt now no more the Triumph of your Skill,
> But, tho' unfee'd, exert your Arm and kill.
> (V.191–92)

Throughout the poem the dialectic of word and action is thematized: the poem's most important action is speaking, chiefly debate and deliberation over the merits of taking action. In this way, the portraits are themselves drawn into the extended exploration of the role of talk and action in the proper conduct of civil affairs, not only the usual juxtaposition of word and deed or profession and belief, but more centrally the question of when to talk and when to act. In this way too, the portraits are transformed because they are freed from the kind of distanced and static portraiture that is pinioned by the narrator's commentary.

Especially as the Augustans understood and practiced it, epic narrative inevitably stands apart from its subject—one feature shared by narratives as disparate as *Paradise Lost* and *Tom Jones*.[5] Mock-epic narrative stands farther off than most, with its irony that plays on extremes of scale, rejoices in the grotesque, and petrifies its victims. It might seem that the mock-epic narrator's claim to capture his persons in a single, all-telling trait, puts him at the greatest possible remove from

---

4. The exchange recapitulates elements of the earlier debates: it mirrors the contentions of the forces of peace and the forces of war; both Carus's boast and his fears mirror those of Mirmillo; and Querpo's reply places him squarely in league with the "Infidels." The exchange also recalls the Miltonic connection: Querpo's reply recapitulates Satan to Michael: "Nor think thou with wind / Of airy threats to awe whom yet with deeds / Thous canst not" (*PL*, 6.282–84).

5. For the distance of epic, see Lukács (56–69).

the (interior) life of his victims. At the same time, however, the mock-epic accepts the prescription of Rapin's Aristotle to look first to "the *Cause* of the *Action*":

> And why Physicians were so cautious grown
> Of Others Lives, and lavish of their Own;
> (*Dispensary*, I.3–4)

> Say what strange Motive, Goddess! cou'd compel
> A well-bred Lord t'assault a gentle *Belle*?
> Oh say what stranger Cause, yet unexplor'd,
> Cou'd make a gentle *Belle* reject a *Lord*?
> (*The Rape of the Lock*, I.7–10)

> Say from what cause, in vain decry'd and curst,
> Still Dunce the second reigns like Dunce the first?
> (*Dunciad*, A I.5–6)

> Of darkness visible so much be lent,
> As half to shew, half veil the deep Intent.
> (*New Dunciad*, 3–4)

> Say how the Goddess bade Britannia sleep,
> And pour'd her Spirit o'er the land and deep.
> (*Dunciad*, B I.7–8)

Since "the Poet represents the *Minds* of Men by their *Manners*," and "The sovereign rule for treating of *Manners* is to... study well the *Heart of Man* to know how to distinguish all its *Motions*,"[6] the pose of narrative distance is a feint that shrouds, like Jack Ketch's hood, a powerful psychological dynamic. The moment of execution may require that the victim be perfectly objectified, but it is for the executioner and the victim a moment of perfect intimacy. It was not only as payment for services rendered that the victim offered gifts to the executioner

---

6. The study of the heart is no easy matter: "[T]he *Heart of Man* is an *Abyss*, where none can sound the bottom: it is a *Mystery*, which the most quick-sighted cannot pierce into, and in which the most cunning are mistaken" (*Reflections*, I.25). Similarly, Gally says of the Theophrastan character: "The deep and dark Recesses of the Heart must be penetrated, to discover how Nature is disguis'd into Art, and how Art puts on the Appearance of Nature" (1725, 29).

that he might do his business, in Dryden's word, "sweetly." The mock-epic's portraiture lodges a claim of extraordinary understanding—both rational, objectifying knowledge, and sympathetic, personalizing identification.

In order to represent the hearts and minds of the persons who figure prominently in the action, mock-epic makes its persons speak their minds. In the talking portraits, exposition is replaced with (self-) exposure. By giving voice to its persons and correspondingly diminishing the narrative voice, the mock-epic adds dimensions to its portraits. But these multidimensional portraits do not generate multidimensional characterizations. They still tend toward caricature, and center on a narrow range of well-defined traits. In this one respect, even the most complex portrait, that of Horoscope, is little different from the many mini-portraits. The talking portraits gain depth through the multiple perspectives on how these few traits are to be judged. In the sketches and the mini-portraits, our value for the person in question is dictated by the narrative voice, with its stable and fully articulated system of values. In the talking portraits the persons speak their minds and voice values presumed to be their own.[7] Although there is no room for real or lasting doubt, to whatever degree the narrative voice recedes, evaluation remains unspoken. Even for the most compliant readers, the values voiced in the portrait call forth rather than dictate the reader's judgment.

Fixing Values

Nowhere is the reader's responsibility for judging more evident than in the apothecaries' consult in Canto III. As the first wave in the spread of corruption that Envy plants in Horoscope's "sickly Brain," this consult

---

7. Garth's practice here is very consistent, even when the representational logic conflicts with the narrative logic. Garth relinquishes his evaluative authority only when his villains speak, a representational logic evident in the problems that occasionally arise when his "machines" speak, as in Disease's *ars poetica* in Canto III. In the "Preface" Garth acknowledged the objection "That the Fury *Disease* is an improper Machine to recite Characters, and recommend the Example of present Writers" ([A4r]); and he offered a baroque justification, that Disease doesn't really approve of the examples, but only uses them to mortify Blackmore. This explanation has been unpersuasive, as it should be. The same problem arises with the portrait of Urim (Francis Atterbury) added in 1703 to Sloth's opening speech, although there Garth more carefully juxtaposes Urim's fault and Sloth's values.

has a central role both in the analysis of the conflict and in the action that embodies it. This and the consult of the Apothecaries Physicians dominate the two middle cantos. They are the chief means of characterizing the two rebel parties as parties. Here, more than anywhere else in the poem, Garth gives voice to his villains and effaces his own. And so here, more than anywhere else in the poem, the interplay of conflicting values throws readers back on their own resources, evoking the judgments the poet demands.

These judgments need not be much of a challenge, and so of much interest. They often involve no more than the simple inversion of values paradigmatic of the mock-heroic—as, for example, when Diasenna bemoans the new age when "S——rs [Somers] has the Seal, and *Nassau* reigns" (III.180) and in turn celebrates "those golden Days of old" (III.164) when Charles I ruled and degeneracy was the rule in the professions. But once set loose, this kind of perspectival play will not always be reined in by the voice of authority. The "double-vision" that we take as paradigmatic of the mock-heroic is not immune to the diffracting effects of the multiple perspectives of the mock-epic. It can, and here does, double in on itself. And when it does, the perspectival play of competing and complementary values can flash, however temporarily, to threaten the narrative authority and to blind the reader's judgment.

Such is the case when, in the apothecaries' consult, Colocynthis repudiates Diasenna's argument. He begins with invective:

> Thus He—Thou Scandal of great *Paean's* Art.
> At thy Approach the Springs of Nature start,
> The Nerves unbrace: Nay at the Sight of thee,
> A Scratch turns Cancer, Itch a Leprosie.
> (II.204–7)

and then moves on to an extended account of the world-turned-upside-down (II.208–21). In using this topos against Diasenna, Colocynthis employs an oratorical and poetic cliché that is, in its Augustan uses, a tool of social and moral domination. It draws rhetorical power from those social forces that underlie the stable values of a fixed, hierarchical order. The one who speaks this topos (and means it) knows what is natural, inevitable, in the nature of things, and knows the dangers of things unnatural and how to enforce order on them. This, then, is a topos to be used—as it was used—by the high against the low, by the moral against the immoral, by the agents of hierarchy against those who would subvert it, by the physicians against the apothecaries. As an agent of disorder and rebellion, Colocynthis has no place using it. For Colocynthis to speak this way is itself a scandal.

Colocynthis does, however, have what he thinks is good reason to use the topos. Since his reasons are for us fully intelligible, they present a challenge, however small, to our good judgment. For Colocynthis, Diasenna is a scandal to the art of those superior beings who have the power and the inner strength to "dispose of lives." For him, the topos is grounded in the stable, fixed hierarchy of the courageous:

> we, the Friends o'Fates,
> Who fill *Church-yards,* and who unpeople States,
> Who baffle Nature, and dispose of Lives.
> (III.208–10)

This ethic is disarmingly close to the ethic of martial heroism that is the ultimate ground of the epic, which is in turn one ground of the mock-epic's system of values. For Colocynthis to excoriate Diasenna on the grounds of an ethic of courage must unsettle any reader who has felt the epic awe and admiration in Garth's extensive celebrations of William's (and later Anne's) martial, though peace-loving heroism, and who has felt the glory in Garth's celebrations of Britain's martial domination of the globe. Such appeals to the civic virtue of the patriot strike deep, to emotions that are beyond, or below, the claim of reason. Their power to spark us to action, the power of emulation, is the very heart of the epic's grandeur. Thus, for them to be so easily associated with Colocynthis's mean appeal is no small matter—especially since the courageous Colocynthis counsels rebellion and Diasenna, due submission.

There is no comfort in the power of courage and glory to spark the forces of disorder to action, no ease in the thought that emulation can bring persons down to violence as well as up to virtue. Such contradictions make value deeply, irretrievably circumstantial: they draw the reader who would judge correctly into "the nastiest of all Places, A bad Mind" (*Tom Jones,* IV.i). Since "the *Heart of Man* is an Abyss, where none can sound the bottom," to judge motives is to be deeply embroiled in the uncertain and treacherous world of circumstances. Though one *is* courageous and the other cowardly, Colocynthis and Diasenna are *both* impelled by bad motives, greed and lust for undue power. (William and Anne fight for peace, due power, and for English prosperity.) These motives may be clear as they are represented in the poem, but as Garth certainly knew from his own experiences of being embroiled in circumstances, these motives were not so clear in the world the poem asks us to judge, and were not the whole truth in either the villains' or the heroes' cases.

The contradictions, and the reader's task, only deepen as the poem progresses. This flash in Canto III is but the opening gambit in Garth's serious and sustained effort to undermine the ethic of martial heroism that grounds the epic, his praise of William, and ultimately the state itself. This effort is grounded in an alternative ethic—one that fears the ethic of heroism as too vulnerable to the workings of desire and self-interest. This alternative ethic is, in the Augustan view, itself indigenous to the epic. It is civil virtue, which expects due submission and looks first to the public interest. By questioning the need for and place of violence in a civil society, this ethic only more deeply embroils the poem in the contingent and circumstantial.

As these scandals begin to play one against another, a new view on the matter presents itself—if, that is, we know the particulars. From the right perspective (of the physicians, the narrator, presumably the reader) the topos is quite simply, precisely true. Colocynthis may use it wrongly, without the right to do so; but seen rightly, Diasenna is in fact one who has turned the world upside down. Colocynthis is Thomas Gardiner, an apothecary who serves as renter warden of the Company of Apothecaries. However misguided, he is right to give his allegiance to his fellows, and there is a certain sense to his attacks on the College. The same cannot be said for Diasenna, Peter Gelsthorp. Originally an apothecary, Gelsthorp was an Apothecaries Physician who *after* he was admitted to the College served the Company of Apothecaries as renter warden, upper warden, and Master (Ellis, III.124n). Thus, as a physician who serves the apothecaries, he is precisely a "Scandal of great *Paean's* Art" who has turned the world upside down. From this angle, the truth of the topos, which is the truth, permanence, and natural force of hierarchy, is more powerful than Colocynthis's rhetoric, more powerful than *any* misuse.

There are other contextual pressures. Colocynthis's use of this topos is not the only or even the most prominent use. He uses the topos near the end of Canto III. This is followed, at the opening of Canto IV, by the narrator's world-turned-upside-down setting which locates Covent Garden. There are key differences. Unlike Colocynthis, the narrator can use the topos naturally, in a simple, purely conventional way. As spokesman and defender of hierarchy who polices those who lose or leave their place, the narrator has the position to make his rhetoric conform to the truth and the nature of the topos. Moreover, the narrator's use is at the outermost level of the discourse, the level of the ultimate, enclosing frame in which he can have the final, stable word.

There are also disconcerting similarities. Colocynthis's art, with its power to "dispose of Lives," is strikingly parallel to the narrator's portrait art, which also claims the power to dispose of lives. This is one of the poem's many parallels between "great *Paean's*" arts, poetry and medicine. Colocynthis does in the realm of action what the narrator does in words, and his violence is unhappily akin to the narrator's efforts to "dispose of Lives." And, as so often seems the case, action dominates. The narrator's use of the topos to locate Mirmillo and his house is followed immediately by Mirmillo's speech, which proclaims Colocynthis's ethic ("By this Right Arm what mighty Numbers fell" [IV.57]) and announces Colocynthis's triumph—Mirmillo's own rebellious betrayal of the College. So much for the stability of the narrator's word; and so much more for the attraction of martial glory.

Garth is poet enough and enough absorbed with the mock-epic's play of values to put in question even his most central beliefs. But he is not one to leave such questions of value open to just any interpretation. It is characteristic of his practice in *The Dispensary* that the flash of conflicting values at the change of the central cantos, which also marks the change of subject from the apothecaries to the Apothecaries Physicians, is contained by what purport to be closed structures of values. Because it trusts to such containment devices, the mock-epic gives the local threats to the reader's good judgment the fullest possible play. Because the mock-epic is grounded in a radical play of perspectives, such local disruptions can and do come to threaten the stability of the whole. These middle cantos invoke two global determinants of value, both of which figure to fix the play of values and neither of which is fully sufficient to the task.

The first and most evident global determinant of value is the structure of the poem itself. *The Dispensary* is arrayed in three concentric circles whose authorial control over questions of value lessens as we move inward to the center. The first circle is Garth's: its cantos contain most of the scientific discourse (all of it in the earliest editions); they contain Garth's most explicit statements of values and of their application to the situation; and they contain Garth's most extensive praise of William. The middle circle includes the second and fifth cantos. Here we see Garth's anatomy of the corruption that invades the College, a textbook account of how social strife is born—in the dis-ease of anxiety and desire, stirrings of a "restless" and "sickly Brain"—and of how it is transmitted—by a language infested with "policy" that finds a willing host in greed and pride. The inner circle is, by and large, given over to the apothecaries and the Apothecaries Physicians to speak their minds. Whatever uncertainty these middle cantos might entertain is presumably contained in two ways: retrospectively, by the enclosure of these cantos within the other pairs; and prospectively, by the extensive portrait of Horoscope in Canto II, where the anatomy of his corruption constitutes a value-fixing prologue. In either view, we find an extensive authorial design to limit the play of values at the center of the poem. This design is, of course, always there, already infused into every word. The middle cantos' play of values is just play, a pretense. The pretense of letting the apothecaries speak their minds does not surrender the authorial voice, which speaks through and for them. And to speak *for* them is an act of domination far greater than to speak *of* them.[8]

Within the confines of the design, the reader willing to play the role of the naïf is offered vicarious moral danger and the self-justifying pleasure of the inevitable, predetermined return, from the Pious Patron's "great Design" to Harvey's vatic assurances as he reenacts the ceremony of Anchises, Aeneas, and Augustus. These structural determinants of value allow readers to enact and exhibit as objects of contemplation the values that ground the stability and justify the domination of the authorial voice—as, for example, Fielding's poetic justice gives us "Virtue" as "an Object of Sight" ("Dedication," *Tom Jones*). In the retrospective view, we see in the array of parts a token of the closed and enclosing order that is hierarchy. In the prospective view, we see an instance of the predetermining power of origins that is at once the measure and the guarantee of domination. The pleasure of the return is the pleasure of enacting the rewards and of feeling the security of so safe a test of those values, pleasures available only to the compliant and complicitous. Because this design merely assumes consent, it is helpless before the truly resisting reader—one who can see Colocynthis's rallying of the "legions of quacks" as valuable in itself, as (say) the work of social justice.

The second global determinant of value is, though less direct, more interesting because it works within rather than outside the pretense of letting the apothecaries speak their minds. Thus it furthers the chief rhetorical aim of these portraits—self-exposure. In their debate, the

8. Compare Fabricant (1979) on domination in portraiture and in depictions of landscape.

consulting apothecaries expose themselves by what they speak,[9] but they also brand themselves as they speak by arraying themselves in a configuration already charged as a sign of evil. In this, one of *The Dispensary*'s two careful, extended imitations of epic models (both originals located in hell), the apothecaries follow the example of the "Stygian council" of Milton's rebel angels (*PL,* II.50–506). The influence of the example is extensive: it shapes the overall configuration as well as the details of the debate. Equally extensive are its consequences for the reader.

The apothecaries gather for their consult in Apothecaries' Hall, a "beautiful edifice" of which the Company was vastly proud as a token of its growing eminence.[10] But for Garth, this reminder of the lesson of Milton's Pandaemonium (*PL,* I.693–97) is only a grandly "dreadful Shambles" (*Dispensary,* III.130; *shambles:* a table for selling meat; a slaughterhouse) that stands near London's own "*Stygian* poole":[11]

> Nigh where *Fleet-Ditch* descends in sable Streams,
> To wash his sooty *Naiads* in the *Thames*;
> There stands a Structure on a rising Hill,
> Where *Tyro*'s take their Freedom out to kill.
>   (III.126–29)

There, the apothecaries settle on the "design" (II.127, III.145, IV.100), which recalls the "bold design" of Milton's rebel angels. The apothecaries decide "The Faculty of *Warwick-Lane*... to Undermine" (II.177–78); the rebel angels resolve in lieu of storming heaven "to confound the race / Of mankind" (*PL,* II.382–83). Both consults end with a hollow roar,[12] and both have the same temporary success. The apothecaries do, by "all the Fiends that in low Darkness reign," cause the Dispensary to

---

9. The very fact that the apothecaries engage in a "consult" is damning. The "consult" had been one of the features of Galenical practice that had attracted most polemical and public notice. By the last quarter of the century, the practice had waned significantly, but the "consulting physician" was a stock satiric butt.

10. John Nourthouck, *A New History of London* (1773, 621; cited in Ellis, III.115n).

11. Ben Jonson, "On the Famous Voyage" (1616, 121). Pope uses the Fleet-as-Styx figure in *The Dunciad* (A II.313–16). For a useful review, see Rogers (141–66).

12. The apothecaries' consult is ended by a roar "from below" (III.303–10) that recalls the "murmur" of approval that Mammon meets in hell (*PL,* 2.284–86). In Jonson's "Voyage" such roars are the common stuff of the Fleet (91–98).

"fall" (III.49, 52) by corrupting the Apothecaries Physicians through the agency of a "little worm," the younger Ascarides.[13]

Each of Garth's three apothecaries adopts the role and the argument of one of Milton's rebel angels.[14] Diasenna, who knows and loves the appeal of "Int'rest," casts himself in the role of Mammon. Mammon plays on the "fear / Of thunder and the sword of Michael" and suggests the rebels "might rise / By policy... In emulation opposite to heaven" (*PL*, II.293–98). Diasenna, fearing that "from gath'ring Clouds Destruction pours" (III.152), counsels "Emulation" (III.150) of the College's baser side and argues for "influencing Art" (III.179) and the power of gold to sway.

Diasenna's respondent, Colocynthis, recalls Milton's Moloch. He denounces fear (*PL*, II.82; *Dispensary*, III.224–25), crying "let those / Contrive who need" (*PL*, II.52–53). So long as "Millions... stand in arms" (*PL*, II.55), Colocynthis-Moloch is for open war:

> We'll raise our num'rous Cohorts, and oppose
> The feeble Forces of our pigmy Foes;
> Legions of Quacks shall join us on the Place,
> From Great *Kirleus* down to *Doctor Case*.
> (*Dispensary*, III.240–43)

The consult is carried by the elder Askaris, who follows his original, Beëlzebub:

> Then let us, to the Field before we move,
> Know, if the Gods our Enterprize approve.
> (III.277–78)

Askaris-Beëlzebub's "easier enterprise" (*PL*, II.345) also involves "policy": "to learn... where [lies] their weakness" and to "[s]educe them to

---

13. Although Garth's sense of decorum does not allow him quite the freedoms Milton takes in the "intestine war" in heaven (*PL*, 5–6, esp. 6.469ff.), this is his most intestinal passage: Diasenna is a powerful cathartic or "purge," once known as the "Holy Powder" (Culpeper, 1642, 154); Colocynthis, or coloquintida, is another cathartic; ascarides are defined by Dr. Johnson as "Little worms in the rectum, so called from their continual troublesome motion, causing an intolerable itching."

14. Ellis remarks that Garth casts "Diasenna, Colocynthis, and the elder Ascarides, respectively, in the roles of Belial, Moloch, and Mammon" (III.125n), but as this discussion shows, Garth's figures correspond to Mammon, Moloch, and Beëlzebub. That Garth chose not to include Belial may result from the contradiction between the political role Garth assigns to his apothecaries and the sharply Royalist cast of Milton's Belial (see C. Hill, 1977, 407–8).

our party, that their God / May prove their foe" (*PL*, II.354–57, 368–69). Thus Askaris would seek those physicians who know Apollo not as the light of learning (science) but only as the gleam of gold (trade).

This design is fulfilled at the consult of the Apothecaries Physicians in Covent Garden. There, the younger Askaris seduces the willing Mirmillo, who "seal'd th' Engagement with a Kiss" (IV.78). It is not the apothecaries themselves who become rebels, following Colocynthis to answer "Honour's Call" (III.253), but Mirmillo, Querpo, and the other Apothecaries Physicians. Thus, while Askaris plies them with wily and lugubrious flattery, the Apothecaries Physicians make themselves dupes to the "influencing Art" of "policy." Led to the vanguard of the battle, these physicians are in turn made agents of corruption when the rebel Apothecaries Physicians tempt even the loyal Collegiate physicians into unseemly and dangerous violence, "all Order lost" (V.265).

Like the concentric design of the narrative, this extensive imitation of Milton limits any local play in values. There can be no doubt that we are to judge harshly the apothecaries and their devilish counsel. Here, too, the reader is offered a contained experience of peril. But where the narrative structure invites a wholly pretended threat, here Garth follows Milton in giving the fullest possible play to the power and appeal of the rebel. Like Milton's rebels, Garth's apothecaries do succeed in the poem and have in fact already succeeded with every phase of their designs to corrupt. Sloth, the presiding machine, succeeds in his scheme "[t]o blast [the College's] Hopes, and baffle their Designs" (I.202). Horoscope succeeds in executing Envy's charge: "The Faculty of *Warwick-Lane* Design . . . to Undermine" (II.178–79). The elder Askaris succeeds in finding those "Members of the Faculty . . . Who Int'rest prudently to Oaths prefer" (III.297–98). The younger Askaris, agent of his brother's scheme, succeeds when he exhorts the gathered Apothecaries Physicians to "Arm" (IV.97). And Querpo succeeds in turning both sides from talk to violence: "exert your Arm and kill" (V.192). Against all of this success, Garth can pose no promise of a savior already come as can Milton, no prophecy of a glorious future already past as can Virgil. Garth can only confront the violence with talk, conjuring up the shade of Harvey to repeat the arguments that had failed in Garth's *Harveian Oration* and to send the reader from violence to talk, to the succor of Nassau and his agent Somers: "Haste and the matchless *Atticus* Address" (VI.334).

Just as the personal experience of each of Milton's readers lends power to the threat represented in Satan, so the collective experience of social and political upheaval made powerful the threat represented in the apothecaries and their corrupted physicians. It is true, though not as Colocynthis means it, that "to Annihilate / Shews no less wond'rous Pow'r than to Create" (III.239–40), for like the civil disobeyer the Apothecaries Physicians have the power to put the established order of the College in an impossible double bind. To ignore them is to give them room to operate, to allow them to advance their cause in ever more daring, more scandalous actions. But to respond in kind is to become one of a kind with them, and so to lose the very ground of one's establishment. Thus *The Dispensary*'s talk is a response *not* in kind. It is a response of a kind that is the exclusive preserve, or so the story goes, of the gentleman—the kind for whom establishment, the power to create, is only proper, due. However harsh or crude or personal its satire, *The Dispensary* is the response of urbanity, wit, civility, and reason to a provocation that threatens to release the most unseemly passions. The temptation represented by the apothecaries and their physicians is the temptation to be no better than they.

A question remains about the nature of this temptation and its agents. By recapitulating the mock-tragedy of Milton's rebels, Garth's rebels mark themselves—but mark themselves *as what*? As evil and dangerous, no doubt; certainly as blameworthy. Were Garth not an atheist and a materialist, it would be impossible not to jump to the conclusion that the Miltonic connection gives an obvious cosmological and religious significance to the social disorder of the apothecaries. Social order, the argument would go, is both a part and an emblem of God's great Design, and to subvert it through pride or greed is to challenge the authority of the Creator. But if there is a threat to religion in *The Dispensary*, it comes from Garth himself: the order he defends is one decidedly more material than not. That the apothecaries are devils is relevant. Garth is not above exploiting his Christian readers' responses to the association between Milton's devils and his apothecaries. But the more relevant point of connection is simply that they are all rebels: Garth lost no opportunity to show that the conflict he portrays is a civil war among rival factions in the College; that it is fought in the interests of the apothecaries; that the goals of the combatants are gold, prestige, and power; that the fable is an allegory of civil violence; and that the moral concerns the fragility of civil order.

By systematically ignoring any religious reading of the devil-apothecaries and steadfastly pursuing a social one, Garth forces us to find a social diagnosis for the disease that sets the restless apothecaries on their work of corruption. Even though Garth's mock-epic aligns itself against the early modern acceptance of interests as morally and socially neutral determinants of behavior, it nevertheless accepts interests as primitives of social explanation. So it cannot fall back on that old standard, pride, to supply the key to the portraits. As a sin against God, identifiable and knowable as a disease of the soul, pride is a moral primitive. It will do nicely as a fully intelligible, all-purpose explanation of behavior. As a social phenomenon, however, pride is not so easy to capture. It is intermingled with too many desires—for wealth, power, prestige, and any number of displaced satisfactions. Pride can still name a motive; but the social diagnostician knows full well that to say "Pride!" is by no means to have explained the etiology of the disease. The primitive elements in Augustan moral psychology are self-interest and benevolence, the two competing forces of desire. In *The Dispensary* as in *The Rape of the Lock* and the *Dunciad*s, pride is the almost universal vice, but its manifestations are so various that each figure's characteristic vice gives pride an entirely new face—each finding a new expression of self-interest.[15] Here, as Garth's caricatured but talking portraits display their pride and the different ways in which that pride is grounded in self-interest, they display the diagnosis of their disease. How Garth develops this social diagnosis and captures it in the form of his portraits will be the subject of the next chapter, which examines Garth's portraiture in its fullest realization, the portrait of the chief villain, Horoscope.

---

15. Pope does retain some traces of pride as a primitive of moral psychology, but only in matters intellectual. The pride of the final *Dunciad*'s "gloomy Clerk" (B IV.459) and the "reas'-ning Pride" of *An Essay on Man* (I.123) approach the simple pride of Milton's Satan. But it is not much in evidence elsewhere.

"Dishonourable Confederacies"

7

The Apothecaries you say, would deserve the name of a Company of Dunces.
—*[Robert Recorde]*, A Detection of Some Faults

Garth's chief villain and the centerpiece of his diagnosis of the troubles in the College of Physicians is Horoscope. Horoscope is one Dr. Francis Bernard. If that name rings no bells, then my readers share something with many of Garth's original readers. Bernard's relative obscurity was one of the central challenges Garth faced in portraying Bernard and almost all his major persons. Indeed, the obscurity of the originals of the persons is a defining characteristic of most mock-epic, an initial fact from which so much else follows. To understand what follows from that obscurity, we must first understand in what it consists. For though Bernard and Garth's other persons are now almost wholly unknown and were then known only in medical circles, they were also eminent.[1]

At his death (on 9 February 1698), Francis Bernard was the senior of two physicians to one of London's major hospitals, St. Bartholomew's, a post he had held for some twenty years.[2] He had served as physician-in-ordinary to James II. He had a hand, early in his career, in formulating the first St. Bartholomew's pharmacopoeia, a document that remained the basis for St. Bartholomew's practice for more than two hundred

---

1. One of the College's major public-relations difficulties was that the Apothecaries Physicians included many of its most eminent members (socially, scientifically, and professionally).
2. The best source on the life of Francis Bernard is Moore (1918). Moore also wrote the *Dictionary of National Biography* entry on Francis and his brother Charles, but the information in the *History* is later and more comprehensive.

years.[3] He had collected a library remarkable for its size and variety, which was evidently a working library, and which included what "was reputed to be the largest collection of books on physic ever made in England."[4] Bernard died, according to one biographer, "a man of learning, well versed in literary history" (Munk, 418), and, according to another, "a man of intelligent interests and generous nature" (Moore, 518).

So Bernard and the others were certainly not obscure in the way we have conventionally spoken of the obscurity of Pope's dunces—as low characters unknown to all the world and "too mean even for Ridicule" (TE, V.321). But then neither were very many of the dunces.[5] The key to this obscurity is also given us by Pope: these are persons who act in ways that have what our authors see as profound public consequences, but who do so in the dark. Theirs is the obscurity of Milton's "darkness visible," the obscurity of consults, of cunning, of secret politics and hypocrisy—of "secret calumny or the arrow flying in the dark" (TE, V.320).

For Pope as for Garth, what is crucial is the public aspect of these obscure villainies: "[S]ince the danger is common to all, the concern ought to be so" (TE, V.319). Equally crucial is that these villainies be brought to light: "[T]here is no publick punishment left, but what a good writer inflicts" (TE, V.320). Far more important than the purported personal obscurity of Garth's villains is the obscurity of their public, institutional actions. The public knew only the widely publicized paper warfare in which *none* of Garth's central persons took part. Their actions were more private, more Collegial, and so more dangerous. In writing the poem, Garth is "going public" after years of increasingly public—yet still institutional—actions had failed. Thus Garth is reluctant "to persuade Mankind to enter into [The College's] Quarrels" (A5v), not because these are matters too parochial, but because to get tied up in the quarrel as a matter particular to the College is to miss the pervading public consequences (and motives) that for Garth are the heart of the matter.

---

3. Moore, relying on the work of Church (1884–86), insists that Bernard's original remained the basis for most subsequent editions (712). Bernard may have been responsible for other innovations: the earliest patient records of medications and other treatments are those of Bernard, now at the British Museum (720).

4. *DNB*. Book collecting "became almost a required pursuit of the physician" (O'Mally, 1972, 156), and Bernard's was one of the earliest and most distinguished collections, including a copy of Harvey's *Excercitationes de Generatione Animalum* presented to Bernard by Harvey himself (Mitchell, 1907; cited in Moore, 518).

5. The myth of duncely obscurity is an unexplored area in Pope criticism (see Damrosch, 123–25).

I have already discussed how Garth, and Pope after him, made these general, public consequences the central thematic of the design of the action. What the portraits add is Garth's diagnosis of the illness threatening the body politic, an illness that finds its etiology in personal failures and personal corruption. This personal diagnosis rescues Garth's analysis of the health of the body politic from what must otherwise seem great naïveté—Harvey's feeble prescription, the narrow institutional conservatism, the failure to recognize that an under-served public will find avenues to meet its needs. This diagnosis also aligns the analysis squarely with those conservative thinkers who sought to answer social theories grounded chiefly in economics. Garth's answer finds its depth in the complexity of his conception of personal virtue and the richness of his conception of interest.

This richness is already evident in the portraits of the apothecaries in consult, where exposure through self-disclosure is the order of the day. As these obscure persons publicize and bring to light their own dark actions, they show us how persons of influence can command the interests of others, how personal interests can both form and serve corporate interests, even how corporate interests can conform to and serve larger, less recognizable forces. But the full scope of Garth's diagnosis of the corruptions of interest is unfolded only in the portrait of his chief villain, Horoscope, who in his velvet "Chair of State" is the very picture of the apothecary as Satan.

The Truth about a Person

So tendentious a portraiture naturally raises questions about its accuracy. Had he lived, Bernard might have insisted that he, like Cibber, sit for a public portrait. And like Cibber, he might have had a case. In any event, others stood in his stead. Bernard's biographer defends him this way:

> Bernard is called Horoscope in Garth's "Dispensary." His notebooks show that he took interest in astrology, and had considered nativities, but Garth has exaggerated his fancies in this direction, and has also unjustly represented him as mercenary. The history of his work at St. Bartholomew's, and those of his letters which have been preserved, show him to have been a man of intelligent interests and generous nature. The untidy state of his library is perhaps accurately described. (Moore, 512–13)

Other knowledgeable readers, such as the noted medical historian and biographer of Garth, Sir William Osler, have expressed surprise that Bernard would be marked as Garth's chief villain. No doubt Garth's knowledgeable contemporaries were equally surprised: "I'm sorry Dr. Bernard couldn't be spared. But I think Horoscope and Mirmillo touch not much Dr. Bernard and Gibbons, because very little particular."[6]

The portrait of Horoscope is, of course, filled with particulars. But, I take it, this contemporary reader's point is that the portrait is not particular *to Bernard*, that the portrait is generalized—if not to the point of an "example" that must be "applied," then at least to the point of a type. As a result, the portrait's effects are supposed to be lessened; it "touch[es] not much Dr. Bernard" because it is not personal, not by Cibber's correspondence test a likeness. Moore, too, thinks the portrait is not like, but he takes a personal approach: features are "exaggerated," "unjustly misrepresented," "perhaps accurately described." So too does his defense of Bernard take a distinctly personal form: the records "show him to have been a man of intelligent interests and a generous nature."

Moore is certainly right to see that Horoscope is a personal affront to Bernard, personally taken and personally meant. But he misses the point of the portrait. Our contemporary witness is right that this portrait is not merely personal. But his claim that it "touch[es] not much" is, it seems, wishful thinking, more consolation than serious claim. Another, still better informed, contemporary brings us closer to a productive answer. In his copy of the 1706 edition, Pope identified Horoscope as "Dr. Bernard formerly an Apothecary." Ellis correctly notes that this "provides the necessary clue" to Garth's choice of Bernard as his chief villain. It is also the clue to Bernard's portrait.

Bernard was indeed "formerly an Apothecary"—just the kind of apothecary that had most troubled the College in recent years. Apprenticed in 1654 to the Master of Apothecaries, a Mr. Lorimer, Bernard was elected apothecary to St. Bartholomew's on 22 May 1661. By 1665 he was so respected that when the hospital's two physicians fled the plague, Bernard was selected to assume their practice and stand "in the said doctor's stead." (Moore, 326). On 23 December of that year, as part of the rewards "for work in late contagious times," the hospital gover-

---

6. Bodl. MS, Tanner 21, f. 90; cited in Ellis, II.90n. Cook concludes that Horoscope "is portrayed less as a particular person than as the epitome of a greedy quack," citing as evidence "the uncertainly as to his original" (81). The only such uncertainly came from Garth, who declined to name the recently deceased Bernard when the poem was first released.

nors voted "£25 to Francis Bernard the apothecary, who ministered to the sick, while the two doctors... absented themselves" (Moore, 326-27).

Though Moore is surprised and distressed that doctors would desert their patients, Bernard was not the only apothecary to begin openly to prescribe and practice medicine during the plague year. Collegiate physicians fled London in great numbers, so that the established system of care (inadequate for normal times) could not hope to meet the demand. Thus apothecaries, already the chief source of routine medical care for the poorest, began to practice more extensively and more openly—even, as in Bernard's case, with official sanction. In the year that Nedham's *Medela Medicinae* opened the direct campaign against it, the College disgraced itself in all eyes, not only providing the apothecaries a public-relations bonanza but also opening a new stage in the apothecaries' challenge to the College's authority. And there, serving bravely and advancing himself was Francis Bernard, apothecary.

Bernard's advancement came in 1678, when Francis Bernard, apothecary, became Dr. Bernard. Between 1665 and 1678 Bernard served with distinction as apothecary to St. Bartholomew's, and we can be sure that the additional authority he gained in the plague year was never wholly surrendered. On 6 February 1678 he was created M.D. by the archbishop of Canterbury,[7] and on 20 November 1678, he was unanimously elected assistant physician.[8] His election was aided by "a recommendary letter from the King," and "his great learning was a further qualification for the post." But "there can be no doubt that his constancy in his duty as apothecary to the hospital during the plague led to this result" (Moore, 512). Other advancements followed. In 1680 he was elected an honorary fellow of the College of Physicians (a minor position, automatically conferred); in 1687 he became a fellow of the College when the charter of James II forced the College to expand its ranks

---

7. I can find no details about the circumstances of his advancement. Though it was relatively unusual for apothecaries to become doctors (see Matthews, 1967, 116), it was perhaps not so extraordinary for an apothecary of Bernard's standing and political connections.

8. His opponent was Dr. Nathaniel Hodges (Moore, 512), who played a prominent role as "Dr. Heath" in Defoe's *Journal of the Plague Year* (1722) and whose death in 1688 "a prisoner, for debt, in Ludgate" was said to have moved Dr. Johnson to tears (G. Hill, 1897, II.90). Dr. Hodges was a formidable opponent. The year after the plague, he responded to the growing attacks on the College in *Vindici Medicinae et Medicorum, an Apology for the Profession and Professors of Physic* (1666). Later he wrote *Loimologia sive Pestis nuperae apud Populum Londinensem grassantis narratio* (1672), in which he attacked unlicensed practitioners as "wicked imposters" whose "medicines were more fatal than the plague, and added to the numbers of the dead."

and include many physicians it otherwise would not; he was appointed physician-in-ordinary to James II; and he was elected physician to St. Bartholomew's, the post once held by Sir William Harvey, Garth's Anchises.

Dr. Bernard was just the kind of apothecary the College had most to fear. By exploiting the College's institutional weaknesses and the personal failings of its members, by skillful behind-the-scenes politics, by luck and cunning, by learning and intelligence, and by extraordinary application, Bernard found an irregular path to power and position, prestige and wealth. In the judgment of history, "He was the most remarkable man who held the office of apothecary to St. Bartholomew's" (Moore, 711). In the judgment of St. Bartholomew's trustees, he was fit to be successor to Garth's idol, Harvey. Those facts must have burned at Garth, who as a staunch Whig and Williamite wouldn't have liked any better the role James II played in Bernard's advancement.

Were Bernard's story as exceptional as he seems to have been, there would be no threat. But Bernard's career paralleled and exemplified the rise in the fortunes of the Company of Apothecaries and the decline in the power of the College. As an example to his kind, Bernard could not be more dangerous. Moreover, even after his change in station Bernard remained loyal to his origins. He had been among the more politically active members of the Company of Apothecaries, and his efforts in its behalf continued after he entered the College. Considering his record of pro-Company, anti-College activities,[9] it is hard to take figuratively Garth's characterization of Bernard as a spy and saboteur.

So this is a portrait of a doctor, formerly and still an apothecary:

---

9. In his first year as a fellow, Bernard was fined as a member of the "opposition"; in 1693 he complained because he was publicly listed as a member of the College; in 1695 he refused to sign a bond "to stand by the officers of the College" and "[t]ranscribed with his own hand" a list of those who did sign and of those who had subscribed to the Dispensary, which lists he "delivered ... for the Use and Service of the Company of Apothecaries"; in 1696 he walked out, with "indecent and rude Carriage," on an extraordinary meeting of the College; in 1697 he joined William Gibbons (Mirmillo), George Howe (Querpo), and Sir Richard Blackmore (a Bard) in a petition to the visitors of the College opposing the recently revived anti-apothecary statutes; and he four times refused to subscribe to the Dispensary (Ellis, II.90n). Perhaps most important, when in 1695 Garth and John Bateman (Celsus) were appointed to oppose in Parliament a bill to release the Company of Apothecaries from all parish duties (an important sign of privilege, already conferred upon the College), Bernard was part of the apothecaries' party successfully led by Sir William Williams (Vagellius), who argued that the state should recognize the need for the apothecaries' medical practice among the poor who were neglected by the College.

> Long has he been of that amphibious Fry,
> Bold to Prescribe, and busie to Apply.
> (II.118–19)

Moore, missing the point of contention, claims that Garth exaggerates Bernard's interest in astrology, adding that Bernard was a man of "intelligent interests." If to select one particular of a person's character and make it definitive is to exaggerate, then Garth exaggerates. But as a diagnosis, as a display of Bernard's actions and motives, the displacement in the portrait of Horoscope could not be more incisive. For it is not just astrology that characterizes Horoscope-Bernard. Garth centers Horoscope around a group of related, archetypal apothecarial traits, themselves centered on the antiscientific, astrological mysteries of the horoscope:

> The Sage, in Velvet Chair, here lolls at Ease,
> To promise future Health for present Fees.
> Then, as from *Tripod,* solemn Shams reveals,
> And what the Stars know nothing of, foretels.
> (II. 134–37)

These prognostications and "solemn Shams" bear a strong relation to Horoscope's more conventional apothecarial practice: his remedies are all, astrological or not, "dull Frauds" and "senseless Mysteries" (II.160, 161).[10] Like the Mountebanks at nearby Smithfield, Horoscope knows and employs the power of show. Thus he sees his patients in a "shop" replete with "Foreign Trinkets, and Domestic Toys" (II.121), including Bernard's renowned library:

> Globes stand by Globes, Volumes on Volumes lye,
> And Planetary Schemes amuse the Eye.
> (II.132–33)[11]

---

10. Bernard's portrait also makes persistent, though somewhat submerged reference to alchemy, most prominently in the altar scene (III.72–125). The apothecaries' challenge to the College had been closely tied to the chemical medicine and Paracelsism, "a curious blend of the occult *and* the experimental approaches to nature" (Debus, 1966, 10; also see Yeats, 1964). Garth's representation implicitly denies that alchemists "search into Nature," seeing only the original emphasis on mysteries that are "senseless," on gold rather than health (II.107, 135), and on their original ties with black magic (II.75–78).

11. Critics have noted that Horoscope's shop gives "a realistic picture" (Sena, 1974b, 646) and closely parallels that in *Romeo and Juliet* (Schneider, 1964).

From the Mountebanks Bernard also learned the financial power of mass marketing and crowd psychology: Envy finds him "environ'd by the Crowd" of "the gazing Vulgar," "The num'rous Shoals / Of such as pay to be reputed Fools" (II.163, 120, 130–31).[12] These vulgar fools seek cures that are unfailingly unnatural—just the sort offered in profusion at Smithfield (II.138–59). Accordingly, the magus-astrologer works against rather than with nature and dabbles in areas beyond the doctor's proper ken, most notably the law:

> Some, by what means they may redress the Wrong,
> When Fathers the Possession keep too long.
> And some would know the Issue of their Cause,
> And whether Gold can solder up its Flaws.
>   (II.142–45)

We cannot be absolutely certain about each detail in Garth's portrait, but many, probably most, are accurate. As physician to St. Bartholomew's, Bernard would have conducted an extensive, conventional, and successful medical practice. Moore defends Bernard as a man of "intelligent interests": Garth the exposer represents not the public face of the eminent physician but the private practice of the apothecary turned doctor who will not relinquish his origins. Here is one at least who heeds Envy's call: "Be what thou shou'dst, by thinking what thou wast" (II.177). Horoscope does not *believe* his "senseless Mysteries." Unlike science's natural mystery, which "shuns the gross Access of vulgar Eyes" (I.23), Bernard's are "*dull* Frauds" that any fool, once informed, could see through:

> If they should once unmask our Mystery,
> Each Nurse, ere long, wou'd be as learn'd as We;
> Our Art expos'd to ev'ry Vulgar Eye,
> And none, in Complaisance to us, wou'd dye.
>   (II.182–85)

Horoscope is not stupid, only cunning. Garth's Bernard is a learned man of "intelligent interests," but one who also has too many of the

---

12. The Mountebanks' marketing skills were conventionally described in fishing images. Garth calls the apothecaries those "unto whom all is fish that comes to their Net" (*HO*, 18). Also see Thompson (1929, 80). Sena notes the portrait's focus on "The miraculous effects of money" (1986, 52), but he ignores the connection to Bernard.

wrong interests, and so betrays that learning and intelligence. If Garth has contempt for Bernard's actions, he expresses full respect for his skill, a skill Garth had experienced firsthand when they faced each other before Parliament.

> 'Tis true, thou ever wast esteem'd by me
> The great *Alcides* of our *Company.*
> When we with Noble Scorn resolv'd to ease
> Our selves from all Parochial Offices;
> And to our Wealthier Patients left the Care,
> And draggl'd Dignity of Scavenger:
> Such Zeal in that Affair thou didst express,
> Nought cou'd be equal, but the great Success.
> (II.168–75)

Like his counterpart Satan, Bernard is an adversary worthy of respect, admirable in all particulars, save one.

Class Portraits

Bernard's pride puts him in a class with Satan, but is his the satanic pride that serves as a moral primitive of Christian thinking? We have already seen a number of ways in which Bernard's pride is made a social as much as a moral issue. But it might be possible to remain within the traditional Christian analysis and see those social failures as expressions of the prior moral failure. What settles the issue is interest and its role in the portrait. The most serious charge made in the portrait has prompted the most serious charge against it: has Garth "unjustly represented [Bernard] as mercenary"? This is a difficult question, partly because this is the one trait that all of Garth's villains share. Is there something special about Bernard's way of being mercenary?

Putting aside, for the moment, the leitmotif of gold and fees, we can see that Garth's charge against Bernard is not in itself a simple one. Until the last major revision in 1714, that charge read:

> This *Wight* all Mercenary Projects tries,
> And knows, that to be Rich is to be Wise.
> By useful Observations he can tell

> The Sacred Charms that in true Sterling dwell;
> How Gold makes a *Patrician* of a Slave,
> A Dwarf an *Atlas,* a *Thersites* brave.
> It cancels all Defects, and in their Place
> Finds Sense in *Brownlow,* Charms in Lady *Grace.*
> It guides the Fancy, and directs the Mind;
> No Bankrupt ever found a Fair One kind.
>   So truly *Horoscope* its Virtues knows,
> To this bright Idol 'tis alone, he bows;
> And fancies that a Thousand Pound supplies
> The want of Twenty thousand Qualities.
>   (1699, II.93–106)

Although it is easy enough to see how this could be taken as merely a personal charge (it *is* a personal charge), the generalization should be clear. It's not that *Horoscope* is mercenary (though he is) but that he understands the "springs of action" in others. He understands how *others* are moved by mercenary considerations and how those motives can be tapped. Like other astrologers, Horoscope finds his most "useful Observations" not in the heavens but in humanity. In the 1714 revision, Garth suppresses the sense of Horoscope's personal mercenary interests (removing the word *mercenary* altogether) and highlights the generality of the description. The opening line becomes,

> This Visionarie various Projects tries,

and the closing couplet,

> And fancies such bright Heraldry can prove,
> The vile *Plebeian* but the third from *Jove.*
>   (II.104, 116–17)

It remains true that "To this lov'd Idol 'tis, alone, he bows" (II.115). He bows to it not as his only personal love but as his special tool, the object of his special understanding. Horoscope bows to this Idol alone because he knows that he is not alone in bowing before it.

So Bernard, like all Apothecaries Physicians, is mercenary, but in a social, public sense. On the one hand, the Apothecaries Physicians are as a class mercenary because they crave wealth. On the other, they are as a class mercenary because they "fancy" that gold's "bright Heraldry can prove, / The vile *Plebeian* but the third from *Jove.*" This is, of course, a travesty, a confusion of show for true worth, and a perversion of the true and original sources of authority and value. This is Shaftesbury's account of how economic thought had obscured any understanding of natural virtue:

> Men have not been contented to show the natural advantages of honesty and virtue. They have rather lessened these, the better, as they thought, to advance another foundation. They have made virtue so mercenary a thing, and have talked so much of its rewards, that one can hardly tell what there is in it, after all, which can be worth rewarding.[13]

The Apothecaries Physicians know perfectly well what is worth rewarding: anything that serves their cause. And they know how to make their rewards work. Their "useful Observations" are, as their history has shown, "more than guess." With Sloth, Envy, Disease, and Discord, they share a view of human nature that is a cynical, self-serving reflection of the conservative Augustan account of appetite and self-interest, a view strongly supported by the evidence at hand. This is the version in Garth's earliest poetic model:

> men like Ants
> Toyle to prevent imaginarie wants;
> Yet all in vaine, increasing with their store,
> Their vast desires, but make their wants the more.
> As food to unsound bodies, though it please
> The Appetite, feeds only the disease;
> (*Cooper's Hill,* A 30–34)

This is Garth's version:

> True Man, reply'd the Elf; by Choice diseas'd,
> Ever contriving Pain, and never pleas'd.
> A present Good they slight, an absent chuse,
> And what they have, for what they have not, lose.

---

13. *Characteristics,* I.66. Shaftesbury grounded his private interests on the passions (I.252), only one of which was avarice; thus the mercenary rewards of virtue might be any source of personal gratification.

> False Prospects all their true Delights destroy,
> Resolv'd to want, yet lab'ring to enjoy.
> In restless Hurries thoughtlesly they live,
> At Substance oft unmov'd, for Shadows grieve.
> Children at Toys, as Men at Titles aim;
> And in effect both covet but the same.
> This *Philip's* Son prov'd in revolving Years
> And first for Rattles, then for Worlds shed Tears.
> (V.93–104)

The Apothecaries Physicians are mercenary because they know how to tap the mercenary impulses of others. They know that in their quest for prestige and power, nothing will serve them better than gold and gilding—to gain prestige by the transforming force of its "bright Heraldry" and to gain power by the corrupting force of its "Sacred Charms."

Garth's stress on the economic base of the quarrel demands an analysis of interest that escapes the bounds of simple virtues and vices. When Garth characterizes the Apothecaries Physicians as those "Whose Int'rest prudently to Oaths prefer" (III.298), that interest represents a rich, but not fully articulated notion. Garth and his fellow Collegians understood, if they did not always articulate, the relation between their position and the general economics of health care. Their licensing power was the power to monopolize the means of production. When it began to fail as a mechanism of control, the College turned to blatant, monopolistic economic attack. Though proffered under the guise of charity, the medical and pharmaceutical services of the Dispensary were intended to rob the apothecaries of their economic base by underselling them, offering free treatment and medicines at cost. The apothecaries, too, understood that their growing social position was directly tied to that economic base. They could see the Dispensary for the economic assault that it was: "[T]heir whole Design is, only to ruine the *Apothecaries* Trade" (Salmon, 1668, 30). Thus this "quarrel" within the medical establishment has some features of what might very loosely be called class struggle.[14] The dispute cannot be described simply in terms of socioeconomic classes—indeed, it is unclear to what degree social and political developments in seventeenth-century Britain can be

---

14. This and other disputes tinged with aspects of class-like struggle (such as the "quarrel" between ancients and moderns) have been called by the principals and by modern historians "quarrels." For the class aspects of the ancients and moderns, see Levine (1981).

described in those terms.[15] Nevertheless, Garth's diagnosis of the College's ills is so strongly class- (or "status-group") oriented that, even if we must make adjustments in the concept of a class, it seems we had better proceed in terms akin to those.

The chief adjustment is to recognize that Garth's language for speaking of such matters is not the language of class defined by socioeconomic interests but the language of class as "Kind":

> Asses and Owls, unseen their Kind betray,
> If these attempt to Hoot, or those to Bray.
> (V.69–70)

The traditional notion of class-as-kind has a powerful allure for someone with Garth's interests. Class-as-kind sits happily with Garth's obsessional returns to origins, the centerpiece of his diagnosis as well as of his representations. Class-as-kind offers, ready-made, a form of representation by kind or type in which the College's situation is readily generalized and his persons readily made examples. Moreover, class-as-kind bears a strong association with class-as-natural-kind. Not only do natural kinds fit dominant ontological assumptions, but extended to the social sphere they offer the ruling class a conception of social and institutional relations such that all social and economic distinctions derive from the nature of things, all privilege is natural right, and such Christian humanist conceptions as the great chain provide human and divine authority for the social system that embodies and serves their interests. Thus Shaftesbury, the philosopher of natural virtue, can by examining "the common nature or system of the kind ['or species']" show that "virtue and interest may be found at last to agree" (*Characteristics*, I.281, 244).

If Garth is to use the discourse of class-as-kind in a class-oriented diagnosis of the College's troubles, he must resist its conceptual associations. He must not fall back on a generality achieved through

---

15. There is much controversy on this issue. Some years ago, Lawrence Stone argued that class should be replaced by "status division," which centers on the great and pervasive distinction between gentlemen and non-gentlemen and which includes "semi-independent occupational hierarchies" (1966, 16–18). There were several variations on this theme: see Perkin (1969); Laslett (1971); Zagorin (1971); Stone (1972); Mingay (1976). Others argued that despite the uneasy fit, class analysis is nevertheless crucial: see C. Hill (1967); Neale (1981); and Wood (1983). Then Stone and Stone (1984) reverted to a class-based account (also see Cannon, 1984). McKeon advances a moderate, compromise account: "Class criteria gradually 'replace' status criteria: which is to say not that the regard for status is obliterated but that it is subsumed under ... financial income and occupational identity" (163). For a recent history, see Beckett (1986).

representation by types; and he cannot see privilege as merely given by some appointment. He must instead see it as earned by industry, talent, and responsible action (the essence of the ideology of the professional).[16] To do so, Garth must displace the notions central to class-as-kind in order to make place within that discourse to speak of the social and personal power of socioeconomic interests and of affiliations that are in some deep sense voluntary.

Consider, then, the passage in which Garth most fully articulates his account of class-as-kind. When Mirmillo, fearful on the eve of battle, thinks he should write rather than fight, Discord responds with a homily on the proper use of talents:

> All shou'd, reply'd the Hag, their Talent learn;
> The most attempting oft the least discern.
> Let *P*—— speak, and *V*——*k* write,
> Soft *Acon* court, and rough *Caecinna* fight:
> Such must succeed; but when th' Enervate aim
> Beyond their Force, they still contend for Shame.
> Had *C*—— printed nothing of his own,
> He had not been the *S*——*fold* o' the Town.
> Asses and Owls, unseen their Kind betray,
> If these attempt to Hoot, or those to Bray.
> Had *W*—— never aim'd in Verse to please,
> We had not rank'd him with our *Ogilbys*.
> Still Censures will on dull Pretenders fall,
> A *Codrus* shou'd expect a *Juvenal*.
> Ill Lines, but like ill Paintings, are allow'd,
> To set off, and to recommend the good.
> So *Diamonds* take a Lustre from their Foyle;
> And to a *B*——*ly* 'tis, we owe a *B*——*le.*
> (V.61–78)

Were we to take this as the pure discourse of class-as-kind, we might be tempted to read here a story of pride and place of the sort so many critics have found in *The Dunciad*: like Satan, the apothecaries are evil

---

16. Compare Adam Smith on the social position of the professional class: "We trust our health to the physician; our fortune and sometimes our life and reputation to the lawyer and attorney. Such confidence could not safely be reposed in people of a very mean or low condition. Their reward must be such, therefore, as may give them that rank in the society which so important a trust requires" (I.x.a).

and dangerous because their pride, manifested as ambition, leads them to aspire above their appointed station. But here the language of class-as-kind is destabilized. Talent is too volatile a center for class-as-(natural-) kind. Talent is just the stuff on which aspiring upstarts like Bernard thrive, the lever by which they displace the nice orders of classes and kinds. There is not here, or anywhere else in *The Dispensary*, the language of appointed station. Between asses and owls there is no natural hierarchy to be displaced.[17]

Discord's homily is a discourse of class-like distinctions. Not only does it end with the class-charged example of Bentley and Boyle,[18] but in the example of C[olbatch] and S[af]fold it begins with another story of an aspiring apothecary turned doctor.[19] This is language charged with "Party," with Garth's diagnosis of the social and economic roots of both distinctions and aspirations. Moreover, the object of our attention at this point in the poem is no aspirer, but Mirmillo, William Gibbons, doctor turned "Opifer" (IV.37).[20] Gibbons aspires below his station, and for easily recognizable economic motives. For him to take up his pen is for him to assume his proper instrument. For him to employ it other than to write prescriptions is for him to betray his talent and abandon his station—not natural or appointed station but something more like professional station.

In this poem, the civil world is constituted by reciprocal relations of rights and duties articulated into a network of institutionalized professions (status groups with some features of classes) whose bounds—like the ancient wall that separates and joins the Old Bailey and the College—have acquired through time some of the force of nature. This is a world, and a view of the world, that has a deep and not wholly easy claim on the doctor-poet who, in order to articulate and preserve its

---

17. The conventional version of this story is that of the ass disguised in a lion's skin who betrays himself by braying. Between asses and lions there is a natural hierarchy.

18. "Towards the close of the last Century, there arose a Dispute between these two Gentlemen, about the Epistles of *Phalaris*, which was maintain'd with a great deal of *Urbanity* and *good Manners* on one Side, and with equal *Sufficiency* and *Pedantry* on the other side" (*Compleat Key*, 8).

19. Colbatch "was first an Apothecary, now a foolish member of the Colledge" (MS Key). Saffold was "a celebrated Empirick, whose Bills were formerly set up in all Publick *Diuretick* Places in *London* and *Westminster*" (*Compleat Key*, 8). He, too, became a physician of sorts, being licensed by the Bishop of London on 4 September 1674. Saffold was an important figure in the succession of quacks: he took over the practice of the celebrated empiric, Lilly, and passed on to "Doctor Case" (*Dispensary*, III.243) the "mysterious appliances, that had been used by Lilly to impress those who sought his aid and power" (C. Thompson, 42–49).

20. The motto of the Apothecaries was *Opiferque Per Orbem Dicor*, "I am called helper throughout the world."

distinctions, takes up his pen in a novel and surprising way.[21] And it is precisely this world that Mirmillo, like the other habitués of Covent Garden, turns upside down.

In the unformed discourse of profession-as-kind, Mirmillo is the obverse that ratifies the norm he violates. In the discourse of class-as-(natural-) kind, Mirmillo is a travesty or scandal. The doctor turned "Opifer" is the unthinkable, liminal figure who has a pivotal role in the action, mediating between the apothecaries turned doctors and doctors desperately trying to keep their place. Mirmillo's kind not only corrupts the doctors into violence but also disrupts the stable, conventional language of class-as-kind. With such liminal, "amphibious" creatures, Garth can make room for a hybrid discourse that takes seriously the social and economic influences on talents. Envy ends her homily on talent by rallying Mirmillo to "join your true intrepid Friends":

> Consider well the Talent you possess,
> To strive to make it more would make it less;
> And recollect what Gratitude is due,
> To those whose Party you abandon now.
> To them you owe your odd Magnificence.
> (V.79–83)

Envy uses the language of benefits and gratitude cynically, with a distinct mercenary cast. Mirmillo does owe gratitude—to the College he is about to abandon, not to the apothecaries he is about to join. Here we see the kind of degeneration found in Dryden's later heroic dramas: "[T]he gloom of the later plays is caused largely by their characters' sense that gratefulness has declined from former days and that the court view of gratitude, 'so much for so much,' now prevails (*Cleomenes*, VIII.296)" (Wallace, 1980, 119). In *The Dispensary* the degeneration is more serious, for what "is due" for Mirmillo is openly a debt, the return due for a gratuity, a bribe. The apothecaries have by their referrals and kickbacks made Mirmillo rich, and Envy has come to collect what is due to that "Party." This hybrid discourse centers on a notion of "Party" that, like "mercenary" and "talent," accrues in Garth's treatment a broad diagnostic significance. The very idea of parties marks how "this Difference" has upset the society within the College. In professions as in politics, parties are the residue of the damage factionalism has done to

---

21. Garth was attacked on these grounds: "tho poetry is a very pretty accomplishment, yet a poet and a physician are vastly different" (*Bellum Medicinale*, 1701, 9).

the good order of society. Compare the terms of praise Garth bestows on his hero Harvey—"He excell'd in Civility towards his Fellows, in constancy toward his friends, in Justice towards all ... stood need to few, but was beneficial to very many" (*HO*, 14)—and it is clear that, had Mirmillo the resources to understand the language of Envy rightly (and not as Envy means it), he would not have earned the "odd Magnificence" Garth gives him in the poem.

Like so much else in *The Dispensary*, this concept of Party develops through associations. We come to understand party, class, as defined by a series of associations—associations of production, of institutional power, of prestige, of personal interest and loyalty, of *place*, in its largest sense. These associations display in the formal structure of the portrait the operations of interest, the *mechanism* of social disease. Party is the name given to those forces that draw allegiance away from its true centers—the College or the kingdom—to the eccentric deposits of private interest. Persons are the sites at which these forces have their effect. Each person is a nexus of reciprocal relations of rights and duties, a point in a network of relations articulated in terms of "Duty," "Trust," "Fraternity," "Confederacy," "Right," "Power," "Industry," "Business," "Enterprize," "Trade," and most of all cash. "If the *Satyr* may appear directed at any particular Person," explains Garth in his preface, "'tis at such only as are presum'd to be engag'd in Dishonourable Confederacies for mean and mercenary Ends" ([A5v]).

Each nexus is an individual, fully a *person* with as much personality as his importance to the action allows. Umbra is obsequious, Colocynthis rough, Colon's is a "Tinsel Talent," while Horoscope and Mirmillo are as fully realized as persons in Augustan satire ever are. But these persons can be represented successfully, accurately, and—given Garth's purposes—most tellingly in terms of what we can now reasonably call their class affiliations. Thus each portrait has two competing centers— the particular that individuates the person and stands for the personality and the nexus of affiliations that identifies the class.[22] And, almost naturally, as the portrait becomes fuller, what grows is not the representation of the particular but the representation of the affiliations.

---

22. In using class in this way, Garth is characteristically moderate and complex. McKeon shows how in "progressive narratives" the social strategy is "the replacement of all the outworn fictions of status orientation by the emergent criteria of class" (223), where class rather precisely equals wealth. Garth's narrative (and later Pope's) develops a notion of class that has many of the features of a status orientation (and that gives little credit to wealth), but which largely ignores questions of nobility or gentry. His is the ideology of the professional.

The Dispensary is then a gallery of portraits that are representations by class. It is, if you will, a class portrait. In *The Dispensary* Garth undertakes the project that Pope would later describe and execute in the *Dunciad*s: to repair the defects of the law and to mete out "the only publick punishment left." Garth prescribes and administers his own bitter pill to those whose "Constitution . . . was not to be cur'd without Poison" ([A5v]), to those who though "plac'd high with artful Skill" (I.13) still "Int'rest prudently to Oaths prefer" (III.298). He gives them, in the threat of his satire, an interest in remembering their place. And in the representation of the portraits he gives his guiltless readers a lesson in the role of interest in the good order of the society. Garth exposes not only the apothecaries and their physicians but also their mysteries, the means by which their dis-ease has done its work: affiliations made and held in the dark that are, to the detriment of the general health, in the very worst sense private. "Our Art," cries Horoscope, "expos'd to ev'ry Vulgar Eye" (II.184).

A Taxonomy of Dunces

8

*He's Blest who like a Dunce may Write
Or like a Fool may Speak.*
—*Edward Ward,* A Trip to Jamaica

*Thus Signs, when first they came in fashion
Denoted each Man's Occupation*
—*Ward,* "Delights of the Bottle"

There are portraits everywhere in *The Dunciad*s, in the verse, in the notes, in the index, testimonies, and other apparatus. The importance of the portraits is reflected in most of what has been written about the poem, as critics have "by sure attraction" (B IV.75) and by Pope's design been led to feel the fascination of the dunces' "might of gravitation" (B II.318). Pope's contemporaries, friend and foe alike, were obsessed with the portraits, their obsession fed by the cries of Pope's victims, who set the tone and the agenda for most early discussions of the poem. But they were by no means alone. Dr. Johnson attends to the portraits as much as to anything else in *The Dunciad,* and from him runs a steady line down to the last editors before this century: "Those who look beneath the surface will find in this Satire a very remarkable picture of human nature, exhibiting, as it does, the friendships, the hatreds, the sensibilities, the deceptions, no less than the art, of a great poet" (E-C, IV.v).

In this century, the portraits of the dunces have been no less influential, although the responses to them tend toward avoidance more than anything else. James Sutherland's Twickenham edition gives the figures in Pope's portraits extensive, though scattered attention, subjecting them to the simplest form of correspondence test and reviving the old questions about Pope's accuracy and fairness. Reuben Brower (1959), typically avoiding all non-literary particulars, can find no "learned reference and epic allusion" in the portraits and so only attacks and dismisses them. Benjamin Boyce (1962) finds little room for *The Dunciad*'s portrait in his study of Pope's character sketches. Maynard Mack (1969) gives sidelong attention to the portrait of Cibber in his masterly account of political innuendo in *The Dunciad*, but he too has his attention elsewhere. Jean Hagstrum (1972) has added perhaps the most productive, though general, commentary on Augustan portraiture.

Of those critics centrally concerned with *The Dunciad*, the one who most recognizes how much it is a gallery of portraits is John Sitter, who argues that *The Dunciad* is for that reason not a true mock-epic. Sitter notes, as do Boyce and Hagstrum, that Pope uses "physical detail as an emblem of abstract qualities or... complex and indicative circumstances" (77). In keeping with his interest in the "abstract qualities" of the poem, Sitter thinks of these portraits as emblematic or iconographic and so has little interest in the details of the portraits themselves. With respect to those details, Aubrey Williams has the most useful account, yet he gives little explicit attention to the portraits as portraits. He includes them in the general category of "local detail" and so never allows them to come to the fore of his attention. Perhaps the most suggestive, though necessarily limited account, is to be found in Howard Erskine-Hill's (1972) primer on the poem; and the best resource is the historical background of Rogers's (1972) chapter, "Life Studies."

Since so much of the attention to the portraits focused on Pope's motives and his supposed inaccuracies (the legacy of Pope's first critics, his victims), it did little to explain their poetics. An inquiry into that poetics must begin with the role Garth played as Pope's model. In his portraits of the dunces Pope has followed and much refined Garth's lead, making his the kind of representations by class found in *The Dispensary*. That relationship has already been anticipated in the fact that my earlier analysis of Garth's portraits was keyed to Pope's own definitions set forth in the letter he wrote for Cleland's signature. Each of Pope's elements is equally evident in the more complex portraits of *The Dunciad*: the double obscurity (of the mean and low and of the arrow flying in the dark); the emphasis on exposing to the view of all mankind what the principal most wants to keep private and obscure; the special value given to self-exposure; the key role of affiliation, whether avowed or secret, personal or professional; the simple primacy of classification of all sorts. All these are keys to Pope's portraits, which like Garth's are individualized by single particulars and generalized by virtue of what the figures share with their class.

We can see quickly how representation by class dominates *The Dunciad*'s portraits and provides easy explanations of even problem portraits such as that of Aaron Hill. Hill's case was singled out for special attention in Johnson's *Life*:

> Aaron Hill, who was represented as diving for the prize, expostulated with Pope in a manner so much superior to all mean solicitation, that Pope was reduced to sneak and shuffle, sometimes to deny, and sometimes to apologize; he first endeavours to wound and is then afraid to own that he meant a blow. (II.267)

Pope's lines read:

> Then * * try'd, but hardly snatch'd from sight,
> Instant buoys up, and rises into light;
> He bears no token of the sabler streams,
> And mounts far off, among the swans of Thames.
> (A II.283–86)

Forgetting all the dreary talk of Pope's sneaking and shuffling, what is noteworthy about the case of Hill is how Pope cannot make his lines mean what he wants. Pope wants this to be a moderate portrait, giving Hill little more than a slap on the wrist. But the significance of Pope's representation by class so influenced readers that Pope could not make the fine distinction he clearly intended.

The portrait of Hill is accompanied by a note explaining how the lines are meant:

> This is an instance of the Tenderness of our author.... Our Poet here gives him a Panegyric instead of a Satire, being edify'd beyond measure, at this only instance he ever met with in his life, of one who was much of a Poet, confessing himself in an Error: And has supprest his name, as thinking him capable of a second repentance. (A II.283n)

This note does report Pope's point fairly: Hill has tried to affiliate himself with Pope's enemies, but is too good to remain in their company. Pope intends this brief portrait as a warning, a counterpart to the successful portrait of Addison as Atticus, which to hear Pope tell it had achieved its admonitory goal (Spence, I.72). Pope's problem is that everything in the poem's design militates against such careful discriminations between dunces and would-be dunces. Elsewhere in his satire Pope can and does make such fine distinctions,[1] but since duncehood is entirely a relational concept, dunces do not have degrees, only places nearer or farther from their "Mighty Mother." Pope's point-field representations make all dunces equal and defy fine discrimination. So powerful is the effect and so dominant is the place of representation by class in the design of *The Dunciad*, that these lines cannot have the merely admonitory force Pope seems to want for them. In a war, all intermediate positions become uninhabitable; in a rigidly enforced class structure, all liminal figures are anathema.[2]

Although it is everywhere evident that *The Dunciad*'s portraits follow Garth's example, it does not go without saying that Pope's portraiture has the same or even very similar significance as Garth's. *The Dunciad* is not, for example, concerned with the rights and responsibilities of the professional, though the dunces are sometimes blamed because they write for money (as, of course, did Pope). Scriblerus is no obvious help. When he speaks of class in connection to the portraits, his talk seems nearer to class-as-kind than to Garth's social diagnosis (TE, V.52). This chapter will address the question of the form and significance of Pope's portraits, focusing on the case of a minor dunce, "publican and poet" Ned Ward, whose role grew with the poem. It will show how that portrait, like Garth's, explores the role of desire and self-interest in the career of one with a checkered relationship with the muse. The growth of that portrait reflects Pope's brand of social diagnosis, as Ward's distinguishing particular, his association with ale, grows in significance as a mark of the dunce. Like *The Dispensary*, *The Dunciad* is a gallery of portraits, differentiated by single features but together defining the class dunce in terms of its mechanism, its "causes creative."

---

1. For an excellent account of such discriminations in *An Epistle to Dr. Arbuthnot*, see Weinbrot (1982, 240–70).

2. As is evident when Pope responded to the hypocritical Hill (who demanded an explanation just after he once again attacked Pope anonymously): "[T]he *Dunciad* meant you a real Compliment"; "[E]ven that Note [was] a Commendation, and [I] should think myself not ill us'd *to have the same Words said of me*" (*Corr.*, III.165). Given the contextual pressure created by the poem, that explanation could not satisfy one disposed to be fair, much less someone filled with "self-importance and pomposity" *(DNB)*. Pope has been much blamed for his conduct toward Hill. A reasonable consideration of the facts and circumstances of their relations in 1731 would lead to a less simple conclusion.

A Dunce's Story

Edward Ward (1667–1731) presents the interesting case of an obscure dunce who made his own place in *The Dunciad.* A "very voluminous poet" (A I.200n), Ward was also a literary journalist in the mold of Defoe or Tom Brown and was as prolific of prose as of verse. Though his background now seems uncertain (Troyer, 1968, 3–5), he was "known" by his contemporaries to have been "of low extraction and irregular education."[3] Certainly his works were "low" and "irregular." They were also popular enough to promise Ward a career prosperous by Grub Street standards. Nevertheless, in 1712 "at the height of his success" (Troyer, 169), Ward despaired of making a living by his pen, decided "'tis better / To live by Malt, than starve by Meter" (*Hudibrastick Brewer,* 1713), and opened a public house. Thereafter Ward continued to write, but was more publican than poet.

Ward's story is recapitulated by the story of his place among the dunces, which moves from poetry to a public house. It begins with *Peri Bathous,* first in the contentious chapter 6, "Of the several Kinds of Geniuses in the *Profound,* and the Marks and Characters of each." There Pope's zoo ranges "E.W." among the frogs, who "can neither *walk* nor *fly,* but can *leap* and *bound* to admiration: They live generally in the *Bottom of a Ditch,* and make a *great Noise* whenever they thrust their *heads* above *Water.*" Ward's second appearance comes in chapter 9, "Of Imitation, and the Manner of Imitating," where "E. W———rd" is said to be the "Poetical Son of John Taylor, the Water-poet."

Pope seems not to have had a personal reason for including Ward in the *Bathous.* Ward had attacked Swift in *The Hudibrastick Brewer,* but that was too small and too old an injury. If we accept the prevailing view that Pope personalized the satire in the *Bathous* in order to goad replies from those he was already poised to counterattack in *The Dunciad* (TE, V.xvi), then we can assume from Ward's trivial role in the first *Dunciad* that he was included in the *Bathous* only to fill out the taxonomy.[4] The chronicler of the "Dunghill of the Universe" (*A Trip to Jamaica,* 1698,

---

3. Theophilus Cibber, *The Lives of the Poets* (1753, IV.293–94).
4. Pope's purely personal reasons for making someone a dunce have been exaggerated: "There is animus, certainly; but it is critical animus.... Many of the quoted authors [in *Peri Bathous*] could not be called his enemies at all except in the most general sense" (Steeves, 171). Mack (1984) adds evidence of how few names in *The Dunciad* "spring from personal pique or resentment or a wish to retaliate for injuries received" (99).

13) made an admirable frog, an especially apt companion to James Moore and Tom Durfey, "who has made so many Men Drink."[5]

Ward seems to have ignored Pope's attack in the *Bathous*, and his place in *The Dunciad* remained only the trivial one that Pope had already given him:

> thus glorious mount in fire
> Fair without spot; than greas'd by grocer's hands,
> Or shipp'd with W—— to ape and monkey lands
> Or wafting ginger, round the streets to go,
> And visit alehouse where ye first did grow.
> (E-C, 1728, I.187–92)[6]

This innocuous mention recognized that Ward was "the Plantation Author" (*Trip to Holland*, 1699): his first successful work was *A Trip to Jamaica*, and thereafter he enjoyed brisk sales in the colonies. It is perhaps the mildest thrust in the poem, but it was enough to prompt Ward to distinguish himself among his Grub Street brothers. On 12 December 1728 appeared *Durgen: Or, a Plain Satyr Upon A Pompous Satyrist*, which was anonymous but widely known to be Ward's. Henceforth Ward would be classed not among the frogs of the *Bathous* but among the asses and owls of *The Dunciad*.

Why Ward ignored the *Bathous* and responded only to Pope's second thrust is not clear. Why Ward was stung by the second thrust is. It was not the stock joke about poems as scrap paper, nor even that he was branded a dunce. What stung Ward was the pattern of association, nascent in the *Bathous*, dawning in *The Dunciad* of 1728, and (under Ward's blundering guidance) flourishing thereafter, between Ward and ale. Ale put Ward in the company of Durfey and made him the poetical son of John Taylor, who had also been brought by financial necessity to earning his bread as a taverner. Ale revived unwelcome memories of Ward's first literary success, *A Trip to Jamaica*, which was, like Tibbald's children, the progeny of an alehouse and financial distress. Ale carried the stigma of its own low origins and associations: it hit too close to home for him to keep his peace. He knew that an ale-

---

5. Pope to Henry Cromwell, 10 April 1710, *Corr.*, I.81. Pope was much irritated by the preoccupation of his Binfield neighbors with Thomas Durfey, and he would always associate Durfey with a dull, low, unlearned, pandering kind of poetic pleasure.

6. Jonathan Richardson records no difference between the first edition and the First Broglio MS (Mack, 1984, 103).

house was a step down in the world, making him of a kind that *he* had placed among such lowlife as "the apothecaries, the quacks, the pettifoggers, and the hypocritical, dissenting clergy" (*Journey to Hell*, 1700). Even when he responded not with chagrin but defiance—proclaimed in *The Hudibrastick Brewer, or a Preposterous Union between Malt and Meter* (1713)—that defiance was deeply laden with just the kind of class consciousness Pope would exploit against him.

By 1728 Ward's defiant strain had subsided. He had, in a measure, succeeded, and with success mellowed. He had risen above the alehouse and become the comfortable master of the genteel Bacchus Tavern, an establishment fine enough that Pope is said to have visited there (Troyer, 175). He continued to write at a slowed pace, even continued his "hudibrastick strain," but gone were the Oldhamesque vehemence of the earliest works and the personal attacks of *The Hudibrastick Brewer*. The last thing Ward's less-than-placid temperament could bear was to have his quiet success disrupted by having Pope publicly associate him once again with his beginnings in an alehouse.

So, discontented with his minor place among the owls of the first *Dunciad*, Ward produced *Durgen* [an undersized animal; a dwarf], "Amicably Inscrib'd, by the Author, to those Worthy and Ingenious Gentlemen misrepresented in a late invective Poem, call'd the *Dunciad*." Mild as responses to *The Dunciad* go, *Durgen* includes the usual protestations that Ward had never "published against" Pope ([A3v]) and the usual charges of Pope's misconduct. Beyond the imprudence of responding at all, Ward made two mistakes to set him above the crowd. First he defended John Ward ("As thick as eggs at W——d in Pillory," E-C, 1728, III.26), charging that Pope had been bribed to attack John by Katherine, duchess of Buckinghamshire. Second, Ward ended with a rallying cry to the "injur'd Brethren of the Quill":

> Proclaim him Rebel to *Apollo's* Crown,
> And make him run the Gantlet thro' the Town,
> That e'ery Brother, he has us'd with scorn,
> May deal the Bard an adequate return.
>
> (42)

With such braying Ward his kind revealed. He now fit to a *T* Cleland's recipe for inclusion as a dunce: having before and after *The Dunciad* stooped "to personal abuse, either of [Mr. Pope], or (what I think he could less forgive) of his friends," Ward proclaimed his relationship to Dulness and joined those who "print[ed] themselves his enemies." As a result, Ward was "put into the number of them" and, in the *Variorum*, given his place in the Grub Street race. When Pope replaced the original owl frontispiece with the ass frontispiece of the *Variorum*, among the books supporting the weight of the owl, was "Ward's Works."

This was just a foretaste of what Ward and everyone else would find inside. Like the other names, the passing mention of "W——" was spelled out in Book I. Pope added Ward to a part of Settle's vision, which had originally referred to an unnamed poet, younger than Cibber (E-C, 1728, III.129–34).[7] So doing, he restored the association of *Peri Bathous* between Ward and Durfey, the association that recalled for Pope the boorish, boozy ways of his Binfield neighbors:

> From the strong fate of drams if thou get free,
> Another Durfey, Ward! shall sing in thee.
> Thee shall each Ale-house, thee each Gill-house mourn,
> And answ'ring Gin-shops sowrer sighs return!
> (A III.135–40)

A little later, *Durgen* appears in Settle's apostrophe to the most promising dunces—sandwiched between another "low writer" who earned himself a place in the poem (A III.159n) and Pope's delicious, beery parody of Denham's Thames couplet:

> 'Silence, ye Wolves! while Ralph to Cynthia howls,
> And makes Night hideous—Answer him ye Owls!
> 'Sense, speech, and measure, living tongues and dead,
> Let all give way—and Durgen may be read.
> 'Flow Welsted, flow! like thine inspirer Beer,
> Tho' stale, not ripe; tho' thin, yet never clear;
> So, sweetly mawkish, and so smoothly dull;
> Heady, not strong, and foaming tho' not full.'
> (A III.159–66)

Readers found more in the *Variorum* than a revised text. The notes and other apparatus tar Ward as thoroughly and as often as possible.

---

7. The lines had probably been meant for Thomas Cooke, author of a *Battle of the Poets* (1725, 1729), and "the son of a *Muggletonian*, who kept a Publick-house at *Braintree* in *Essex*" (A I.130n).

Pope cites or mentions *Durgen* six times, making the most of it in the note to A III.26, "As thick as eggs at Ward in Pillory."[8] There Pope paraphrases both Ward's defense of his namesake ("he had no *Eggs* thrown at him; his *Merit* preserv'd him") and Ned's charge that Pope had been bribed to attack John. Having marked the two Wards as two of a kind and made explicit one ground for their association, Pope waited until the last revision of 1729 to make explicit the second ground: Ned Ward's place in the rather large company of dunces who had known the prominence of the pillory. Pope adds: "But it is evident this verse cou'd not be meant of him [John Ward]; it being notorious that no *Eggs* were thrown at that Gentleman: Perhaps therefore it might be intended of Mr. *Edward Ward* the Poet"—who had in 1706 himself stood in the pillory.[9]

Ward's secrets were out. In *Peri Bathous* the association of Ward and alehouses had been unspoken, resting quietly in Pope's largely private experience of Durfey as a drinking master to the country squires of Binfield and in the potential genealogical relationships between Ward and John Taylor. Even in the first *Dunciad* the association remained an unspoken consequence of the juxtaposition of the sole mention of Ward and the reference to an alehouse two lines later. In the *Variorum* Ward's association with ale is trumpeted with the rude force of Ward's own words and Pope's bulldog tenacity. Ward becomes the central figure giving shape to a satiric motif—"*Alehouse*, the Birth-place of many Poems" (TE, V.239)—that before had no explicit connection to Ward at all. Now, of the five mentions of Ward in the "Index of Things (including Authors)," two speak of alehouses. The association with John Taylor from *Peri Bathous* is made explicit: *"John Taylor* the Water Poet ... (like Mr. *Ward*) kept a Publick-house in *Long-Acre"* (II.323n). And in a long note (cross-referenced at III.138), Pope recounts Ward's story using the words of Giles Jacob's *Poetical Register:*

> He has of late Years kept a publick house in the City (but in a genteel way) and with his wit, humour, and good liquor (Ale) afforded his guests a pleasurable entertainment, especially those of the High-Church party.

---

8. See A I.220n, III.26n, III.162n; and TE, V.201n, 204n. In the list of attacks published after the first edition (TE, V.211), Pope lists *Durgen* as "By *Edw. Ward*, with a little of *James Moore*," once again renewing the associations among the frogs of *Peri Bathous*. Ward later denied that Moore had any role in *Durgen* (*Apollo's Maggot*, 35).

9. Sutherland has Ward "pilloried in 1705" (A III.26n). Troyer, quoting the *London Gazette*, places it in November 1706 (95).

Employing the kind of license that has so distressed his critics, Pope has taken a small liberty: *he* has spoken the parenthetical "Ale." Later, after Ward brayed ale again in *Apollo's Maggot in his Cups* (1729), Pope used Ward's words to correct, or rather to call yet more attention to *Pope's* word, "Ale."

> ERROUR II. Book I. Note on Verse 200. Edward Ward *has of late kept a publick House in the City.]* The said *Edward Ward* declares this to be a great Falsity; protesting, that "He selleth *Port*; neither is his publick House in the *City,* but in *Moor-Fields.*"

Still later, in 1735, this material was incorporated into the notes by adding a sentence that corrected the location of Ward's public house but mentions not at all its bill of fare.[10] Of course, by keeping only the topographical connection, Pope changes the point of Ward's protest and only perpetuates the slur: port raises Ward's social standing; Moorfields can only lower it.

With the mean and anonymous *Durgen,* Ward made public his affiliation with Dulness's "injur'd Brethren of the Quill." So Pope the signpost-dauber marked him for a dunce and, the unkindest cut of all, branded him ever after as a "publican and poet." With Ward to give it point and focus, the minor leitmotif of the alehouse gains a new, more central role in the poem. In the line of father Flecknoe, whose badge of office is "a mighty mug of potent ale" (121; see *Hudibras* I.i.639ff.), Ward, Tibbald, Cibber, Durfey, Welsted, all the dunces find their inspiration in ale. Ward merits his prominence because he pours out not only verse but also the spirits themselves. Ward becomes a minor but not inconsequential center in Dulness's planetary scheme and a source of her influence, circulating ale through her system. He supplies Dulness's "uncreating Word," one of whose particular manifestations is this material first cause of duncely song.

Why all the fuss about ale? From Pope's side it is the one centering particular around which he builds the portrait. Ward is the dunce-as-alehouse-keeper, who shares with others of Pope's worthies personal

---

10. In a perfect example of Pope's success at making history, this part of the exchange was incorporated into the *DNB* biography of Ward, in a form that preserves Pope's highlights but ignores Pope's shaping hand: "Ward professed great indignation at this account, and said that his house was not in the city but in Moorfields." For the lowness of Moorfields, see Rogers (1972, 44ff).

knowledge of and a deep respect for the eminence of the pillory, and who shares a penchant for the grotesque and a spying acquaintance with the mean particulars of life in the streets. But he is distinguished and characterized by his long-standing association with ale. From Ward's side, the pointedness of the particular that set him to braying is not that Ward is a taverner but that in the social hierarchy of public houses the alehouse is among the lowest, the natural (and actual) haunt of the distressed dunce. The alehouse is, to be sure, somewhat above the Gill-house and vile Gin-shop; but these are all of a kind—as, in Pope's characteristically sonorous image:

> "Thee shall each Ale-house, thee each Gill-house mourn,
> And answ'ring Gin-shops sowrer sighs return!"
> (A III.139–40)

The theme of the distressed poet, living in the streets from one alehouse to the next, had been a staple of Ward's poetic production and a fact of his life. But Ward had overcome his origins as a distressed, ale-inspired poet and an ale-purveying tradesman. He had risen, by dint of talent, luck, and application, both as a poet and a publican. By 1728 he was the picture of a satisfied, comfortable tradesman, keeping the genteel Bacchus Tavern and trading on his poetry to garner a bit of the aura of the gentleman poet and to make a lively story for his patrons. But in Pope's own spying chronicle of life in the streets, Pope the signpost-dauber would restore the original, putting Ward in his place, the spot marked by this one particular, the sign of his own ale.

A Portrait's Designs

In Pope's portrait of Ward, as in Garth's Miltonic portraits, we find ourselves tempted to roll out our well-hewn understanding of the Christian humanist implications in Augustan poetry and to see this portrait as punishment for one who defies and so mars God's grand design. This is what Aubrey Williams does in his now-classic account of *The Dunciad*.

> The cause of an attempt to transcend one's status, to shed one role for another, is "pride" or "presumption," while the effect is to bring confusion into God's ordered plan, to spoil the play of

life for the other actors.... In Pope's view the dunces should have been content with roles for which they were better fitted. Theobald, presumably, should have remained an attorney, Ned Ward a bar-tender, Blackmore a physician. (94–95).

This is factually wrong. Ward's preeminence as a dunce preceded his bartending: when Ward became a bartender in 1712, he was already a successful author and could rightly see himself in the same company as Steele and Swift, let alone the fledgling Pope. It is also hermeneutically misguided. The issue in Ward's bartending is not pride, but whether its low origins will mark him ever after, an issue that rests both on a theory of social mobility and on a social hierarchy of potables. Like his mentor Garth, and like Fielding and Johnson after him, Pope understood the social uses of such "ancient classical view[s]" as the great chain and the theater of the world. Which is not to deny the importance of Christian humanist themes in *The Dunciad*. But it is to deny the relevance of foregrounding them here. What Pope in this portrait foregrounds or thematizes is simply ale, and the body of associations that Pope constructs around ale are inescapably social: class associations, not classical ones.

By understanding in this way the portraits Pope creates for such dunces as Ward, we can see how they are of a piece with Garth's major portraits in *The Dispensary* in two key ways. First is the role of particulars. The 1728 portrait is a minimal one in which Ward is characterized by a single particular—his ties to the odd and exotic.[11] This particular is both accurate and telling. Ward's success began when distress led him to seek and exploit the exotic in *A Trip to Jamaica* and culminated when he found the exotic at home in *The London Spy*.[12] In the greater portrait that grew in 1729, Ward is still characterized by a single particular, but now that particular is ale. He thrusts himself forward to claim the then-open place of master of ale, taking on himself what had been in 1728 a relatively unfocused theme of ale as the duncical muse

---

11. For *The Dunciad*'s interest in the exotic and grotesque, see Erskine-Hill (1962, 1972), Tanner (1965), and Jones (1968). For Scriblerian interest in the grotesque, see Lund (1978).

12. *A Trip to Jamaica* is a noxious sixteen-page account of the island and its inhabitants in the manner of Oldham. An anonymous imitator says that "the *Plantation Author... besbits* his own Nest" (*Trip to Holland*, 1699). Another imitator notes Ward's "Monsters of Foreign Growth" (*Trip to Ireland*, 1699). The exotic character of *The London Spy* is grounded in Ward's having found an audience among those for whom London is itself exotic, and in seeking out the odd, the unusual, the grotesque, as Swift complained in "A Proposal for Correcting, Improving, and Ascertaining the English Tongue" (1712).

and making for it a central and definitive place in the *Variorum*. Here is the truth of how the "[p]oem was not made for these Authors, but these Authors for the Poem" (TE, V.205).

Although the 1729 portrait centers on ale, it is still ultimately concerned with poetry. Ale serves first as a symptom of Ward's original and therefore proper social status, and second as an instance of the kind of material first cause that drives the engine of duncical poetic production. This association between ale and poetry was Ward's creation, not Pope's. Ward fell into his first literary success, *A Trip to Jamaica*, because of ale. Drunk and distressed by seven years of literary failure, Ward inadvertently shipped off to the West Indies. When his nasty account of that trip brought unexpected success, he smugly proclaimed it the product of an empty gut and a brain overcome by *"Derby-Ale"* (*Trip*, 5–6): "I made in a Month or two, as much Noise in the Town, as if this Seven Years I had scribled Drolls to Bartholomew-Fair, and had been the Renown'd Author of Whittington-Cat or Bateman."[13] When even this heady flush of this Smithfield success faded, Ward turned from consuming to purveying ale—thus, in Pope's duncical mythology, inspiring still other Smithfield productions. Who, Pope has every right to ask, is "Apollo's maggot in his cups"?

Thus Ward's crime is his *poetic* transgressions. His own words justify his place of punishment in *The Dunciad*:

> The Condition of an *Author*, is much like that of a *Strumpet*.... That the unhappy circumstances of a Narrow Fortune, hath forc'd us to do that for our Subsistance, which we are much asham'd of.
>
> The chiefest and most commendable Talent, admir'd in either, is the knack of Pleasing....
>
> The only difference between us is, in this particular, wherein the *Jilt* has the Advantage, We do our Business First, and stand to the Courtesie of our Benefactors to Reward us After; whilst the other, for her Security, makes her Rider pay for his *Journey*, before he mounts the *Saddle*. (*Trip*, 3)

If this is what poetry has come to in the hands of such as Ward, then Pope is indeed a "Rebel to *Apollo's* Crown" and will punish all the

---

13. "Preface" to *The Poet's Ramble after Riches* (1691, 1698), Ward's first unsuccessful poem, reissued after *A Trip to Jamaica*.

"Brethren of the Quill" who have made the poet's calling a whoring, pandering trade.

A second definitive feature of Pope's portrait of Ward recapitulates the structures of Garth's major portraits: Pope tars Ward with his own brush. In the treatise of Scriblerus (and later of Aristarchus), in the "Testimonies of Authors," in the various indices, errata, etc., and especially in the notes, Pope gives voice to all his dunces in order to give an air of authority to his indictment: "Out of thine own Mouth will I judge thee, wicked Scribbler!" (TE, V.21). This is the poetic purpose of those "appendages"—in part to identify, but also to animate the portraits and to lend them the authority of the authentic duncical voice. Pope's technique adds a brilliant, cunning refinement on Garth's example: by building the voice of his first resisting readers into the poem, he subordinates even their resistance to his poem's designs. When Pope speaks for his dunces, he usually does speak out of their own mouths, often using the very words that Pope himself has prompted them to say. If the dunces were made for the poem, Pope himself had a hand in that making.

The more important dunces speak in the poem itself. But Ward's is a mini-portrait that grew under the pressure of his braying, and Ward speaks his mind chiefly in the notes. The note on John Ward the forger (A III.26) has Ned Ward speak with Curll in defense of the "Merit" of "a *brave Suffer, a gallant Prisoner* expos'd to the view of all mankind!"[14] When Pope speaks in his own voice, he adds only the essential facts about Ward. Later, in the final revision of 1729, Pope would show his shaping hand, acknowledging that it was he who threw the eggs at Ward. Pope could have hoped for no better result of his egg-throwing than that the dunces would rush to defend one of their kind, exposing themselves and their values "to the view of all mankind."

In the biographical note on Ned, Pope again quotes one dunce (Giles Jacob) on another (Ned Ward). As we have seen, Pope takes a hand, inserting the offending *ale* that would ever more be Ward's signpost. In his own voice Pope supplies only the one fact essential to the plain sense of the poetic text: "Great numbers of his works are yearly sold into the Plantations." Later, in the 1729 "Errata," he adds Ward's authoritative correction, which after Pope's sharp selection was in 1735 in-

---

14. Curll's defense of John Ward came with typical dispatch: *A Compleat Key* appeared in less than a month, bound with the second edition (1728d). Curll first denied Ward's guilt (16); then in the second edition of the *Key* he blamed Pope for "writ[ing] a Satire, to please a certain Duchess" (16). Also see the *Curliad* (1729). John Ward would continue to hold a significant place in Pope's gallery of evils (Morris, 184–86).

corporated into the note: "Ward in a Book call'd *Apollo's Maggot*, declar'd this account to be a great Falsity, protesting that his publick house was not in the City, but in Moorfields."

This pattern is repeated throughout the poem. When in the apparatus Pope speaks in his own voice, he usually sticks to the fact that makes the poetic line intelligible and is usually accurate to the best of his knowledge.[15] There is, to be sure, a certain selectivity. But that follows what we can now see as a fully intelligible pattern, one that values the truth of the telling detail more than completeness. Otherwise, whenever Pope can so manage his text and his dunces, explicit attacks on a dunce come from the mouth of a dunce. If no good outside candidate can be found, the attack comes through the mouth of Pope's housedunces Scriblerus and (later) Bentley. But it is nothing short of remarkable that Pope is so consistently able to use the dunces' words, often words that Pope has prompted them to speak.

By so speaking for and through his duncely victims, Pope aims at a kind of authority in speaking about them that is, in the last analysis, absolute. This, it seems, is the more interesting sense in which the world-as-theater analogy opens the poem to us. The poem was from the very start a stage, an animated portrait gallery and poetic substitute for the pillory, on which the dunces were paraded to display and to expose themselves to the public punishment that only a good writer can inflict. From the first conception of *The Dunciad* and the first appearance of the stage-setting *Peri Bathous*, distinctions among the stage within the poem, Pope's staging in the world, and any independent world "outside" the poem were at best over-nice. When Pope added Book IV's sessions-piece—with its theatrical sources,[16] with Pope's new chief dunce a stage-manager cum playwright cum actor cum puppet of Walpole, with Dulness sending her progeny out to act in the world, and with the poetic prophesy that ended the *Variorum* transformed into a description of actual events—he only made more explicit and more pointed what had always been central to his poetic designs.

---

15. Pope's standards as an editor or scholar have exasperated many critics—as evidenced in Sutherland's dismissive catchphrase, "Pope's usual paraphrase." Modern scholars have not attended carefully to Pope's actual practice, and so have failed to distinguish intentional, significant alterations from accidental ones. Useful in this context is Steeves's account of Pope's practice in *Peri Bathous* when he wants to be accurate—which is not very different from those of other poet-scholars of his time (Dr. Johnson, for example) (172).

16. See Sherburn (1944).

The Poet's Designs

Even after we understand *The Dunciad*'s poetic design and its consequences, there will remain for some the sticky matter of Pope's sharp selections and, worse, his alterations of the facts—Ned Ward's ale, John Ward's eggs, Defoe's lopped ears. On this issue, many will find it hard not to stand with Cibber and his correspondence test. Yet Pope does have a rationale, if not an excuse. In the sharp selections, Pope follows a consistent principle of parsimony in keeping with the general design of his portraiture. In any representation, one or two particulars must stand for the whole. When it comes to Pope's additions or alterations, we find something very much akin to this principle of parsimony. When Pope falsifies a portrait (which happens less than we have been led to believe),[17] he adds or alters a single particular already charged as a sign for some body of social and moral values that serve to judge and place the figure in the portrait. Since in Pope's view the verdict on his persons is already in, adding the appropriate particular is the most minor adjustment. It amounts to little more than tidying up.

The Dunciad's portraits update the catalogue Pope had begun in the *Bathous*, transporting it from a beast fable to a mock-epic fable: "Of the several Kinds of Geniuses in the *Profound*, and the Marks and Characters of each." In the paradigmatic cases such as Ward's eggs or Defoe's ears, the "false" particular is independently charged as a mark, brand, or signpost for a class or kind. Since there is "no publick punishment left" for those whose villainy has remained secret or who have escaped the full force of the law's public scorn, Pope will on his stage throw the eggs at Ward or cut off Defoe's ears.[18] Since proper judgment is precisely what is at stake and in question, these small matters have loomed larger than it would seem they ought—they have, in short, become mock-epic.

In so marking his victims, Pope is not acting, as so many have assumed, only as an advocate presenting his case before the court of public opinion. There is advocacy in such parts as the "Testimonies of Authors," whose watchword is, "Be it as to the judicious reader shall seem good" (TE, V.39), but that advocacy pales before the more pervasive, domineering figure of angry justice. The rhetorical action of *The*

---

17. Rogers corrects several imputations that Pope falsified portraits (1972, 276–336).
18. According to the Second Broglio MS, Pope had at some point substituted "Dauntless" for "Ear-less" (Mack, 1984, 140). Clearly this, like Ward's eggs or Cibber's brazen brothers (see Chapter 9), is a purposeful alteration that reflects a conscious rationale.

Dunciad's design is less persuasion of the judicious than excoriation of those who know no shame. Pope seeks explicitly to remedy a culture that has lost the ability to enforce proper values through public shame and whose institutions for policing those values—either by emulation (the throne) or by deterrence (the pillory)—have decayed from within. If Smithfield and Westminster are the two horrifically complementary seats of Dulness, then the throne and the pillory are her furniture. And the degree to which they are indistinguishable means to preeminence indicates the enormity of the authority Pope claims for himself, first as prophet to and then, in the final *Dunciad,* as the sole surviving voice of Western culture. In response to this role, the relevant questions are less of the form 'Is this a fair copy?' than 'Is this a just punishment?' Judge with me, Pope says to his twentieth-century readers. We are the posterity on whom Pope relies to pass the judgments and throw the eggs his fellows would not. Pope was too smart, as Dr. Johnson recognized, "to have been ever of the opinion that the dread of his satire would countervail the love of power or money" (*Life,* II.284). The game is punishment, and Pope's designs are on us.

In some measure Pope has succeeded in his designs on posterity. Readers have happily perpetuated the myth of duncely obscurity, so that every biography of a dunce must confront the fact that Pope's mark will not fade. Too many of us have been willing to think badly of the dunces without evidence. It has too long been too easy to speak, for example, of someone like Ward as merely braying, as this chapter has repeatedly, unfairly done. Part of the measure of Pope's achievement as a satirist is his ability to make us enjoy the pleasures of his satire, suffused as it is with the exquisite cruelty known only to a connoisseur of insult and invective. At the same time, we chafe at the sentences Pope would have us pronounce, not so much because he was wrong about the dunces,[19] as because he was wrong about us. Who now will stand with Pope for guilt by association, for the absolute authority of social origins, for wholesale blame by class, for the priority of kind over person? So uncomfortable is the role cast for us that those willing to repeat Pope's sentences have also preferred to deny his persons their humanity, to see them chiefly as mere types and abstract them out of existence in order to mitigate our role as instruments of Pope's judgments. It was one thing, in a time when we saw ourselves driven by an unknown and

---

19. There is an important tradition in Pope criticism that worries that Pope and the "Tory Satirists" were wrong about history. For two illustrious examples, see Warton, *Essay,* II.344ff., and Mack (1969, 229ff).

unsettling social dynamic, to celebrate Pope as the poet of order. It is another to have to see how Pope has cast himself as the poet of law and order.

In a time when even postmodernism begins to seem old hat, such claims to authority ask to be debunked. It's bad enough that Garth set himself up as the spokesman for establishment; Pope stood up for the whole of Western culture, stood as one who, in the happy phrase Mack borrows, is compelled to "carry the culture." Nowadays, such presumption is hard to bear. While we struggle to come to terms with the diversity in our own society, it is often hard to have patience with Pope's efforts to limit the diversity in his essentially monocultural, mono-ethnic society.

Pope grounds his claim to authority on the myth of an innate, natural aristocracy of poetry, best articulated in Swift's mock-epic, *The Battle of the Books*. In this set piece contributed to the ancients-and-moderns controversy, the fable is simple and stark: the Ancients and their modern allies must defend their primogeniture on Parnassus against those Moderns who, believing "the right of possession [lies] in common," would level "the highest summit of Parnassus" which they were prevented from occupying "by [their] own unhappy weight, and tendency toward [their] center." In such "a strange confusion of place," Swift's fable literalizes his deeply social understanding of all such differences and provides a paradigm case of mock-epic. While epic was the genre of statecraft and state founding, whose great classical examples celebrated the hegemony, first of Greek, then of Greco-Roman civilization, mock-epic was the genre of state-preserving.

In *MacFlecknoe*, *The Dispensary*, *The Battle of the Books*, the several *Dunciad*s—even, in a way, in *The Rape of the Lock*— what is at stake is preserving established, ancestral rights. In *The Dispensary*, the risk had been to the College of Physicians: the "trading Tribe" that is a "Scandal of great *Paean's* Art" (II.204) deals only in drugs, nativities, and hocus-pocus. In *The Dunciad*, the trade is in words and ideas, and the scandal is to the greatest of Apollo's arts. The dunces are poet-tradesmen, purveyors of false culture who strumpet-like pander to the public's pleasures, and the state whose preservation is at issue is that inherited Greco-Roman civilization.

One way to think about such an inheritance is as a tradition, a link with the past, a source of identity and genius to which the individual with talent can surrender and so grow in value. Critics have liked to think of Pope's work in these terms, as Pope unquestionably did. Another way to think about such an inheritance is as a patrimony, a ground of production—of power (moral, cultural authority) and of wealth (due praise, influence, readers)—that must be defended when its value is threatened by new means of production that rest on no inheritance but on mere labor and a talent for pleasing. Pope thought of his inheritance in this way as well. If this social and economic conception is more evident in *The Dunciad* than elsewhere in his poetry, that is easily explained by the nature of its genre. Clearly Garth had thought of his patrimony from Linacre and Harvey as an estate, and saw a threat in the mass purveyors of health care whose many innovations in merchandising that care made the physician's inheritance irrelevant. In the same way, Curll's literary sweatshops, the weekly political press fueled by party money, even the individual recycling projects of a Theobald or Cibber, all represented means of literary production (and of marketing) that made the poet's classical inheritance irrelevant or, worse, a "specialty" for the carriage trade.

In this circumstance, where dunces were no more "ashamed to assume the same Titles with the greatest Genius, than their good Brother in the Fable was of braying in the Lion's Skin," a hybrid figure like Fielding could joke that his learned "introductory Chapters... [were] a Kind of Mark or Stamp" that "secured [him] from the Imitation of those who are utterly incapable of any Degree of Reflection, and whose Learning is not equal to an Essay" (*Tom Jones,* IX.1). Where Fielding could find in the need for such trademarks a source of new literary life for the epic, Pope could find only the darkness of a decayed and dying culture. Of course, that culture is our culture, and it did survive—as much as anything through the agency of dunces and journeymen authors like Fielding or Johnson. What did not survive—until twentieth-century critics revived it—was the myth of a dominant, uniform, continuous, aristocratic civilization. It could not survive because the social facts had outstripped the ability of the myth to contain them—because a Walpole was not only a successful but an effective minister and a Cibber was inevitably "admitted to as good a company" as Pope. Pope's oft-vaunted, much-valued independence of the "great Patricians" is the result of sharp trading in the myth itself. There would have been no independent life in the best Roman manner had not Pope shrewdly turned his talent for versifying a translation and a few years of his and others' hard labor into the solid estate at Twickenham:

> "Gay dies un-pension'd with a hundred Friends,
> Hibernian Politicks, O Swift, thy doom,
> And Pope's, translating three whole years with Broome."
> (A III.326–28)

Pope may have been in thrall of a myth, but he could see what was what. Like his dunces, Pope was a tradesman—but one who, in the best tradition of the eighteenth-century merchant, did his best to use his wealth to outlive that original fact. No small part of Squire Pope's moral authority was grounded in the estate he did not inherit but earned.[20] Thus what Pope could abide least of all was that the dunces somehow failed to see his difference from them. Ned Ward sealed his fate forever when he placed Pope among the Grub Street race, one among the "Brethren of the Quill."

20. See Mack (1969, 233).

A Succession of Monarchs

9

Col[ley]:   *A little longer silent sit,*
            I han't quite done your Picture yet:
Saw[ney]: *Thine's Sign-post Dawbing—Col. 'Faith, (that's true,*
            It would not else resemble you).
                    —Sawney [*Pope*] and Colley, A Poetical Dialogue

What, then, of Cibber's bill of complaint against Pope? The contradiction with which we began these discussions of portraiture still stands. On the one hand, we adopt Cibber's correspondence test and say with him that his portrait in *The Dunciad* is not a fair copy. On the other, we all (including the original himself) say that Cibber is the very picture of a dunce. It would be a mistake to underestimate the claim that Cibber's correspondence test has on us. It looms over accounts of *The Dunciad* as a shadow on the poem and Pope's character, something either to be enforced, combated, or explained away. It would also be a mistake to underestimate how deeply readers have felt Cibber's rightness for the role of King Dunce. When they apply the correspondence test, dunce defenders invariably find candidates worthier of defense than Cibber, and few critics after Cibber have lamented his displacement of Theobald.

There are, of course, any number of standards by which one might judge Cibber's portrait, but the standard of simple correspondence has the force of all of our normative, "default" conceptions grounded in basic neuromuscular routines and supported by folk beliefs. Think of the conventional scene envisioned in this chapter's epigraph: the painter positioned with canvas and subject adjacent in his field of vision, as he looks from one to another making the two visual correlates as like as possible. That we know this is a naïve view does not lessen its force, as is evidenced by the equally standard pictorial joke in which the painter stares intently at the subject while the canvas bears a modernist, "nonrepresentational" image. Against the appeal of this view stands the long record of our ambivalence between the unfairness and the rightness of Cibber's portrait, which suggests that we might be using some standard other than simple correspondence.

One such standard is found in the universalizing, metaphor-based poetics of the mid-century, which denies that the portraits are representational and so understands the mock-epic as "a consciously contrived hoax" (A. Williams, 60), making Pope the modernist painter of our joke. Another is the poetics of representation by class, that blend of Augustan caricature and early modern taxonomy in which persons are represented in terms of both a nexus of associations that define a social class (though not an economic class) and a single, identifying characteristic. In representation by class we have a way of thinking about these portraits grounded in Pope's practice rather than in the howls of his victims. With such a tool, we might make better sense of our responses, although applying such a standard to the case of Colley Cibber is a complicated business.

The difficulty with Pope's portrait of Cibber as dunce is that the portrait has a history that we find hard to ignore. One of the chief items in Cibber's bill of complaint is that the portrait once belonged to another. Blaming his new eminence on Warburton, Cibber complains:

> The bare Change of one Name for another is his whole Expence of Thought about it! The Materials, and Furniture of the Character, even to the same Books, in his study (which he knew would never be look'd into) stand just in their old Places! The Clouds, the Mists, the Fogs, and same Vapours of Dullness (let them never so much obscure the Likeness) will serve for any Mortal he has a mind to wrap in them! (*Another Occasional Letter,* 29)

With his special knack for asking the right question, Cibber sets us the task of deciding whether the particulars of his portrait will in fact "serve for any Mortal [Pope] has a mind to wrap in them." If we decide, contra Cibber, that the nexus of associations in his portrait defines a class smaller than all mortals, there remains the question of how specifically that class and this portrait suits King Col. But since the history of the portrait is part of what is at issue, we must pause a moment over the king Cibber displaced and ask first how well the class and its picture suits him.

A Succession of Monarchs

Dunce the First

It has been a truth widely repeated that Lewis Theobald was always less suited than King Colley to stand at the head of the dunces. This is, of course, an *interested* truth. Those who repeated it have been persons of great learning and scholarly attention to detail. It is only natural that they should be uneasy with Pope's attack on the "index-learning" of a Theobald, a person of dignified character and superb scholarly achievement, if not of great poetic talent. Many have believed that Theobald's only crime was besting Pope as an editor, so that Pope's resentful ego entirely beclouded his judgment. Indeed, some have thought Pope created the entire poem only to have a vehicle large enough to support his anger at Theobald, only so that the better poet could get even with the better editor. Better that King Dunce be renowned for his brazen stupidity and not his scholarship. It is hard enough to deal with the roles Pope assigns to Scriblerus and the great Aristarch without having a King Theobald to contend with as well.

It is true, of course, that in hindsight Cibber is the better king. It is also true that in the case of Theobald Pope's anger had gotten the best of his judgment. But it will not do to find Theobald less suited than Cibber because we see something of ourselves in Theobald and believe Pope to be wrong about the value of "Index-learning." For in this respect, at least, Theobald is the perfect dunce. Pope was "wrong" about much that he saw as epitomizing duncery. He could not see the scientific revolution that lay behind the seemingly foolish virtuosos, that they as much as Newton were indicia of what was new and valuable in science. He could not see that genuine artistic value could be packaged in such popular forms as the opera. He could not see the forces of social progress that fueled the social and economic changes he bemoaned. He could not see that, whatever its excesses, Walpole's rough-and-ready politics is one hallmark of the modern practice of participatory democracy. And he could not see the advance in knowledge and understanding made possible by the kind of index-learning represented in a Theobald, a Bentley, or even a Dr. Johnson (who reports Pope as saying, "he would allow the publisher of a Dictionary to know the meaning of a single word, but not of two words put together" [*Lives,* II.296]). Dulness's sons may be a motley crew, but their duncehood will not yield to our attempt to pick and choose among its parts. If we hope to find Theobald less suited to the throne than Cibber, we must find a reason *within* the logic of Pope's family portrait of dunces.

The portrait of Theobald in the first *Dunciad* so closely follows the pattern of representation by class that its configuration can almost be read directly off the page. The single particular that centers this portrait is Theobald's "Index-learning" (A I.233), that "low industry"[1] that "turns no student pale, / Yet holds the Eel of science by the Tail" (A I.233–34). This particular is exemplified in the "suff'ring brotherhood" of Theobald's library (A I.115–33), in his sacrificial altar founded on "A folio Common-place" (A, I.135–42), and in the account of his critical practice that Pope makes him speak:

> There, thy good Scholiasts with unweary'd pains
> Make Horace flat, and humble Maro's strains;
> Here studious I unlucky moderns save,
> Nor sleeps one error in its father's grave,
> Old puns restore, lost blunders nicely seek,
> And crucify poor Shakespeare once a week.
> For thee I dim these eyes, and stuff this head,
> With all such reading as was never read;
> For thee supplying, in the worst of days,
> Notes to dull books, and prologues to dull plays;
> For thee explain a thing till all men doubt it,
> And write about it, Goddess, and about it;
> So spins the silkworm small its slender store,
> And labours, 'till it clouds itself all o'er.
>   (A I.159–72)

How Theobald serves the cause of Dulness, not only a leader but a creator of dunces, can be seen in Swift's prescription for creating modern wits:

> Either first, to serve [books] as some Men do *Lords*, learn their *Titles* exactly, and then brag of their Acquaintance. Or, Secondly, which is indeed the choicer, the profounder, and politer Method, to get a thorough Insight into the *Index*.... For, the Arts are all in a *flying March*, and therefore more easily subdued by attacking them in the *Rear*.... What remains therefore, but that our last Recourse must be had to large *Indexes*, and little *Compendiums*....

---

1. Mallet, *On Verbal Criticism*; quoted by Pope at A I.164n.

> By these Methods, in a few Weeks, there starts up many a writer, capable of managing the profoundest, and most universal Subjects. For, what tho' his *Head* be empty, provided his *Common-place-Book* be full. (*Tale of a Tub*, VII)

This picture doubly suits Theobald's products, since he endeavors to fulfill both roles, providing index-stuffed poetry as well as his "large *Indexes* and little *Compendiums*":

> Not that my quill to Critiques was confin'd,
> My Verse gave ampler lessons to mankind;
> So gravest precepts may successless prove,
> But sad examples never fail to move.
> (A I.173–76)

In addition to his individuating trait, Theobald's portrait also displays his membership in the class. It is filled out with those particulars that he shares with all his brother dunces. Chief among them is his affinity for the grotesque and monstrous, for all that collects, confuses, mingles, and otherwise blurs distinctions:

> In each she marks her image full exprest,
> But chief, in Theobald's monster-breeding breast;
> Sees Gods with Daemons in strange league ingage,
> And earth, and heav'n, and hell her battles wage.
> (A I.105–8)

Theobald thus bears the usual attractions for and to Dulness. He is "supperless" (A I.109) and writes for money. He finds his inspiration variously in distress (A I.181) and in ale ("And visit alehouse where ye first did grow" [A I.202]). He conjoins both pride and envy: "The proud Parnassian sneer, / The conscious simper, and the jealous leer, / Mix on his look" (A II.5–7). He can sleep like the best of dunces: "Him close she curtain'd round with vapors blue" (A III.3). And he dreams the dreams of a dunce, "Which only heads, refin'd from reason, know" (A III.6).

In the portrait of Theobald we find a now-familiar figure, the representative of his class who shares with others of his class its distinctive features but who is individuated by a single, though here richly significant, particular. As with Garth's Horoscope, Theobald's individuating particular is both the mark of the chief dunce and the central, defining feature that unites the class. Horoscope's particular was the cynical cunning of a man of learning and intelligence who embraces the dull frauds of the astrologer-alchemist-mountebank because they please and gull the crowd. Theobald's particular is the dogged persistence of a man of learning and intelligence who brings to poetry only the detail-bound attorney's skills better suited to catching errors than ideas. This is a picture of one who endeavours not only to encrust but positively to supplant the works of genius with the fruits of his low industry, thus beclouding at once the public memory and the public judgment. Like Horoscope, Theobald is in his literary dealings "an unlicenc'd & presumptuous Mercenary."[2]

Theobald's is, of course, a narrative portrait, and his story follows the mock-epic pattern. Our hero first appears at a moment of crisis. Hungry, blocked, despairing, Theobald has been brought to a decision very much like that faced by Ward in 1712: he wonders whether he has neglected his "lawful calling" (TE, V.15) by misusing his "gray-goose-weapon." He sees no good choices, but Dulness intervenes to lift him above his despair and confirm him in his present course. Notice how this recalls Mirmillo's moment of decision in *The Dispensary*. Three courses of action lie before Theobald. He can return his pen to its original and proper use, "Take up th' Attorney's (once my better) Guide" (A I.190), where his index-learning and word-catching will stand him in good stead—just as Mirmillo can return his pen to its original and proper use, writing prescriptions. He offers to turn his pen to political controversy, "And save the state by cackling to the Tories" (A I.192)—just as Mirmillo offers to turn his to medical controversy. And he is led by Dulness to assail good sense and good literature—just as Mirmillo is led by Askaris to assail the College. Here, as in *The Dispensary*, Theobald takes the worst of his three courses, and Pope takes pains to point out that in doing so Theobald neglects and betrays not only his original—true, lawful—calling, but also his talent and profession.[3] Theobald has become a Politician of Parnassus.

At this point Theobald seems a most suitable candidate for king of dunces. He exhibits a respectable sample of shared duncely features. His

---

2. Pope to the Earl of Oxford, 16 October 1729, writing of Theobald's handling of Wycherley's posthumous works (*Corr*, III.59).

3. When Pope first introduces Theobald, he notes that he "was bred an Attorney, and Son to an Attorney" and repeats a Dennis insult: "who from an under-spur-leather to the Law, is become an under-strapper to the Play-house' " (A I.106n). Other reminders occur at A I.190n and 250n. Also see *Epigrams from the Grub-Street Journal*, 1730–31, II ("On Mr. M———re's Going to Law with Mr. Gilliver Inscrib'd to Attorney Tibbald") and V ("On the Candidates for the Laurel").

poetry is true heir to the spirit of Bartholomew Fair. His criticism is, by Pope's lights, trivial, obsessed with minutiae, always beside the point. And his individuating trait does seem an appropriate center—at least in 1728—for the busy minions of Dulness. In this light, if Cibber seems the better candidate, it must be by dint of the perfection of his gleeful impenetrability, not because Theobald is unsuited for the job.

There is, however, one feature of the pattern of mock-epic portraiture that is not so well exhibited in Theobald: the social connection. On the economic side, Theobald stands strong. England's Augustan poets were the first to see literary production become fully assimilated into the processes of commodity exchange, where books are no more than objects. This gave new meaning to the Horatian formula, *dulce et utile*, and new anxiety to the role of author. It is an anxiety that Theobald, echoing Dryden (*MacFlecknoe*, 98–101) and ultimately Horace, voices:

> 'Adieu my children! better thus expire
> Un-stall'd, unsold; thus glorious mount in fire
> Fair without spot; than greas'd by grocer's hands,
> Or shipp'd with Ward to ape and monkey lands
> Or wafting ginger, round the streets to go,
> And visit alehouse where ye first did grow.'
> (A I.197–202)

To be doomed to trade as mere object or commodity is its own kind of hell, and Theobald no more than Pope wants his progeny to be martyrs to commerce, marked by its odor. But this is precisely the kind of objectifying that Pope takes to be the essential feature of Theobald's treatment of the progeny of others.[4] As a poet-editor, Theobald is an especially troublesome figure for Pope. His kind of editing, which is of course our kind of editing, only furthers the process of making the poem a product of labor and an object of commerce—not a happy prospect for a poet forced into editing and long years of translating with Broome. So, on the economic side, Theobald presents an important opportunity for Pope once again to mark off his difference from a dunce who too much resembles him.

---

4. Not only was "hapless Shakespeare ... sore" (B I.133) from Theobald's lawyer talents, so was Pope. Pope's poetry had from the first suffered from the kind of legalistic literalism practiced by so many critics, and especially his nemesis Dennis.

At the same time, Theobald does not represent the kind of dangerous mixture of high and low that had been essential in mock-epic portraiture. True, Pope tries to mark index-learning as a low industry and reminds us that Theobald is a mercenary, a pen for hire; but Pope offers very little to make Theobald show himself sufficiently low in the relevant sense. Theobald was born to and brought up as an attorney, and that helps to mark him as one who has abandoned his talent and abused his professional skills. But Pope has no decisive facts of Theobald's life and affiliations to fix Theobald's connection to the Grub Street race. The best Pope can do is the lowness of Theobald's Smithfield muse, which may not be enough. Where Francis Bernard presented Garth with a hero who could be tied to the "Legions of Quacks," Theobald was not up to the role.

There is another problem with Theobald: he is not important enough for the job. Though he is editor of Shakespeare, and Pope considered his candidates carefully, Theobald has not brought himself high enough to bear the weight of the charges he must stand for, especially as Pope's account of a culture in decline grows and deepens through the many revisions. Theobald's trait, his index-learning, is an appropriate center of duncehood. And as the Augustan fascination with particulars grows into the Enlightenment love of the encyclopedia and dictionary, index-learning might bear the weight Pope needs to give it. But it seems a bit much to say of Theobald, the person,

> As man's maeanders to the vital spring
> Roll all their tydes, then back their circles bring;
> Or whirligigs, twirl'd round by skilful swain,
> Suck the thread in, then yield it out again:
> All nonsense thus, of old or modern date,
> Shall in thee centre, from thee circulate.
>   (A III.47–52)

The imagination is not fired by the image of Theobald leading through the streets a mass of mean dunces. It is hard to be repulsed by the image of Theobald prating away in the rooms of St. James's. Thus, the only reason to believe that Theobald is unsuitable for his post grows out of the *social* dynamic of Pope's portrait gallery. Even so, the demands of mock-epic were clear: Pope had to use the best hero he could find. If no candidate was perfectly suitable in all respects, that was enough to make a poet wish to have persons made for his poem.

Dunce the Second

It is striking how the change of hero has troubled readers of *The Dunciad*. That troubled response is in no small part a tribute to Cibber's skills as a propagandist, for despite all of Pope's efforts Cibber was the one who was able to establish the nature of their relationship. He made his contemporaries and ours judge not only Pope's quarrel with him but even Pope's finest poem in purely personal terms. Pope, however, was always clear that in his mind as in his poem the key issues were not personal but social. And in this respect, Cibber is everything that Theobald is not. As Pope says in the second Bentlean note added to the opening of *The Dunciad in Four Books*,

> It appears as plainly from the *Apostrophe* to the *Great* in the third verse, that Tibbald could not be the person, who was never an Author in fashion, or caressed by the Great; whereas this single characteristic is sufficient to point out the true Hero; who above all other Poets of his time, was the *Peculiar Delight* and *Chosen Companion* of the Nobility of England; and wrote, as he himself tells us, certain of his Works at the *earnest Desire of Persons of Quality.* (TE, V.268–69)

In virtue of "this single characteristic," Cibber is so much better suited to bear the social burden of leading the dunces that it is almost possible to credit the account of his ascendancy given in "Ricardus Aristarchus of the Hero of the Poem":

> For no sooner had the fourth book laid open the high and swelling scene, but he recognized his own heroic Acts: And when he came to the words,
> Soft on her lap her Laureat son reclines,
> (though *Laureat* imply no more than *one crowned with laurel*, as befitteth any Associate or Consort in Empire) he ROAR'D (like a Lion) and VINDICATED HIS RIGHT OF FAME. (TE, V.260–61)[5]

Although this is only clever casuistry, there is a sense in which Cibber, like so many dunces before him, has been prompted by Pope's master puppetry to claim and so make for himself his place in the poem. When

---

5. This account, probably contributed by Warburton (TE, V.xxxvii; E–C, IV.226), accords with that in the "Advertisement to the Reader," which was signed "W.W." but written by Pope (TE, V. 251).

Pope structures his portrait of the new king, he gives Cibber the "single characteristic" Cibber asked to be known for, his impudence: "Pert and dull at least you might have allowed me" (TE, V.261) King Coll. is above all a climber—"Pert," "brisk," "brazen" (B I.112, 194, 219).[6] The index-learning that had been the center of the portrait is, in the new configuration, submerged as one of the several *shared* duncical traits that Cibber represents and is represented by. The attack on index-learning remains prominent in the poem—indeed, as we shall shortly see, in some ways it competes with Cibber's pertness as a source of Dulness. But that duncical trait is now centered in the figure of Richard Bentley, the great Aristarch. Otherwise the portrait of *The Dunciad in Four Books* seems made for Cibber.

One reason the portrait can be reworked for a new hero is that much of it is given over to depicting the nexus of associations that define the class dunce. If Cibber does have the better claim to the throne, then a portrait of the chief dunce ought to suit him all the more. While the "Gothic Vatican" (A I.125) of Theobald's library might be said to loom overlarge when associated with Cibber, such a judgment cannot help but be colored by our knowledge of its history.

If the particulars that mark the character of the chief dunce suit Cibber, so should that character's story. Theobald's story is of the attorney turned critic and poet. When he asks, should he "[t]ake up th' Attorney's (once my better) Guide?" (A I.190), the answer is a clear and resounding yes. Theobald's choices include among them the answer to his crisis, which, through the intercession of Dulness, he unfortunately misses. When Cibber asks should he "[t]ake up the Bible, once my better guide?" (B I.200), the question has that special mock-epic edge. Of course Cibber should, could do no better than take up the Bible he has long ago forsaken. But when the question is Cibber's lawful calling, the prospect of this swearing, gaming, whoring son of Dulness toting a Bible is at once ludicrous and blasphemous. Cibber's original calling—his father intended him for the clergy[7]—is one for which he is so ill-suited that the scandal would have been far greater, though perhaps less socially damaging, had he accepted his father's mold. With the horror of Cibberian "Sermons and Pastoral Letters" (B I.200n) before us, Pope is

---

6. For Cibber's pertness, see *Peri Bathous* (64–65). For his briskness, see his *Apology* (244).

7. The following is Pope's own comment, as usual allowing the victim to condemn himself. "Hear his own words: '... who knows but that purer fountain might have washed my Imperfections into a capacity of writing, instead of Plays and annual *Odes*, Sermons and *Pastoral Letters?' Apology for his Life*, chap. iii [p. 39]" (B I.200n).

able to pursue in *The Dunciad in Four Books* a religious thematic that is *not* centered on the figure of "the world as theater with each player his assigned role." Centered on the figure of Cibber as the "Antichrist of wit" (B II.16) and so agent of Dulness's "uncreating word" (B IV.654),[8] this theme grows with the poem: "In its final form, in other words, *The Dunciad* records the triumph of a philosophical system that Pope, together with the Christian humanist tradition, regarded as the type and paradigm of atheistical thought down through the centuries" (Battestin, 113). The greater religious focus in the final *Dunciad* is made possible because Cibber is so much the better hero for the poem's dominant social thematic.

Though the specter of a Cibberian clergy serves Pope's purposes quite nicely, it presents Cibber no real choice. Neither do the other courses of action Cibber sees before him—to join the "vent'rous Heroes" (gamesters) or "Party to embrace" (B I.201, 205). What action then remains for Cibber?—none. A Cibber need only be: "What then remains? Ourself." King to Smithfield, jester to the Court, puppet to Walpole, and agent of Dulness's insensate action in the world,

> Still, still remain
> Cibberian forehead, and Cibberian brain.
> This brazen Brightness, to the 'Squire so dear:
> This polish'd Hardness, that reflects the Peer;
> (B I.217–20)

This pertness, this "Monumental Brass" (B II.313), is the single particular that centers and individuates Cibber's portrait. Cibber made this focus easy for Pope by displaying at length the full dimension and all the features of his pertness, in his self-satisfied *Apology for the Life of Colley Cibber* (1740) and in his response to *The New Dunciad*, in which he "VINDICATED HIS RIGHT OF FAME," *A Letter to Mr. Pope* (1742). More than with any other dunce, Pope is able to make Cibber expose himself with his own words.

Happily for Pope, Cibber's self-portrait only confirms and retouches his existing public image. As early as 1729 the notable features of Cibber's pertness had been delineated by Bolingbroke's *Craftsman*:

---

8. Both quoted phrases were present in the earliest versions (see A I.12, III.340), but the theme is present in these versions more *in potentia* than in fact. In *The Dunciad in Four Books* Pope greatly increased the number and seriousness of the biblical allusions, especially in Cibber's book, Book I.

I have, said I, young Kinsman, a great Regard for Mr. *Cibber's* Performances as an *Actor.* In some Parts he does mighty well; as in the *Buffoon,* the *Coxcomb,* the *Pert,* the *Impudent,* the *Gamester.* He tops the Part of the Sharper. He is *felonious* within, or out of the reach of the *Law;* with a becoming and a natural Grace.... The Part of *Brazen* seems likewise to be naturally design'd for Him; but in *Gibbet* he is all Perfection. He plunders with an Air adroit, genteel, and intrepid. There is a Gallantry and a Frankness in his Behaviour, even to the People, whom he injures.[9]

Pope, however, isolates the feature that unites and, in a measure, produces the various manifestations of this pertness. Cibber's pertness encompasses—is—in its most blatant, even militant form the essential trait of all dunces and all mock-epic villains: this pertness runs roughshod over all categories and distinctions, natural, social, and religious. Since duncehood is first and foremost a relation, Cibber's pert disregard for distinctions makes him the perfect son of Dulness, ready to embrace all. Like Belinda, whose eyes "shine on all alike" (*Rape,* II.14), Cibber's "sev'nfold Face" reflects and reflects on all alike.

Knowing no distinction, this pertness knows no shame. This is the galling, perfectly Cibberian trait that gives the portrait its sharpest edges. If the only public punishment left for such as Cibber is the punishment that a good writer inflicts, there is no punishment at all for one who cannot feel the shame that is the writer's only weapon. Theobald at least had the decency to deny and defend, not proclaim his faults. At the end of Book I of *The Dunciad in Four Books,* Dulness voices her hope for a king of dunces whom she can "Curtain" and thus "Shade him from Light, and cover him from Law" (B I.314). This is just exactly what Cibber's brazen visage does for him. Unlike Homer's heroes "sheath'd in Brazen Arms" (*Iliad,* 2.517), who must don their armor, Cibber's is a permanent fixture. Such "brazen Brightness"—that reflects all nonsense, that is proof against all shame, and that thrusts itself forward at every opportunity—is "Monumental Brass" indeed.[10]

9. *Craftsman,* 7 June 1729; quoted in Mack (1969, 159). This portrait is, of course, a thinly disguised allegory of Walpole's management of the state; but all of the details were then and for years later taken as characteristic of Cibber.

10. This passage also has significant political implications. Dulness wishes for a "Monarch all our own" (B I.311), political as well as literary. Cibber was widely associated with that other monumental brass, Walpole, who ever since he had protected those responsible for the South Sea Bubble had been known as the "screen."

Thus the primary, centering image of Cibber's pertness is his surpassing brass, his utter shamelessness. The image is introduced, characteristically, by a topographical association, that between Cibber and his "brazen, brainless brothers," the statues of "Raving Madness" and "Melancholy" that stood over the gates of Bedlam as signposts to the realm of Madness. They were the other legacy of Caius-Gabriel Cibber, the poet's father. Pope gives this initial appearance of the image a characteristically Popean emphasis: he falsifies a telling detail, substituting instead one that more aptly signifies the nature of the association. The statues were of stone, not brass, a fact that Pope knew when he used the image and that he knew would be discovered by his enemies: "[N]o matter if the Criticks dispute about it."[11] So Pope used the telling but altered particular, waited for Cibber to raise a ruckus about it, and then in a note (B II.3n) used Cibber's own words to emphasize what Pope had already made central to the truth about Cibber. Thereafter, *brass, bronze,* and *brazen* are used seven times in the poem (B I. 219, II.10, 254, 313, III.104, 199, IV.365). More important, brass becomes the focus of a large group of related images (the impudent forehead, the bland reflecting face, the thrusting and presumptuous social climber, the mad and brainless blockhead, the small change passed from hand to hand, etc.)[12] which document at the level of the image what the portraits also document, how all Dulness "[s]hall in thee centre, from thee circulate" (B III.60).

Succession

Cibber's pertness is Dulness in action: Cibber is her agent and his brazen brotherhood her executive branch. As such, brass has displaced from its central role Dulness's other face, that represented by the weighty Theobald. But Dulness's weightier face is by no means removed from the poem entirely. The two chief manifestations of Dulness are "Firm Impudence, or Stupefaction mild ... Cibberian forehead, or

---

11. Pope to William Bowyer, 13 November [1742], *Corr.,* IV.426. Pope had been warned by his printer, William Bowyer, in late 1742 that the statues were not brass (see B II.3n). I see no good reason to assume that Pope had used the epithet by mistake.

12. There was not, at the time, a systematic distinction made between *brass* and *bronze. Brass* was common slang for money, especially small change. Also, "Friar Bacon's brazen-head" was the "usual sign" of fortune-tellers and astrologers (Defoe, *Journal,* 30).

Cimmerian gloom" (B IV.530–32). The two chief causes of Dulness are a blithe Cibberian disregard for all distinction, detail, standards and an earnest Scriblerian obsession with minute distinction, excessive detail, irrelevant standards. In the *Variorum*, Theobald's weight of learning overwhelms Cibberian brass. In the four-book *Dunciad*, where both faces of Dulness are fully revealed, the dialectic of impudence and stupefaction reigns supreme. Cibber's "Brothers at Bedlam" are "not *Brazen*, but *Blocks*," yet this in "no way lessened the Relationship" (B II.3n). Brass and stone, brazen and brainless, forehead and blockhead; these pairs that exclude all sense are essential to Pope's anatomy of Dulness. It extends, in Dulness's planetary circles, from the two chief persons, Theobald and Cibber, to the least of Dulness's children:

> Fast by, like Niobe (her children gone)
> Sits Mother Osborne, stupify'd to stone!
> And Monumental Brass this record bears,
> 'These are,—ah no! these were, the Gazetteers!'
> (B II.311–14)

Just as the two manifestations of Dulness are two faces of the same coin, so the two causes of Dulness are two expressions of the same force. Since cause—agency—is the central issue of all mock-epic, both aspects of Dulness's motive force are represented in all of the *Dunciads*. In the *Variorum*, the relationship between the two expressions of the force of Dulness is less explicitly delineated. In *The Dunciad in Four Books*, the relationship is made evident in the relationship between the two texts themselves.

It is only appropriate that a textual relation be central to Pope's explication of the force of Dulness. Of all Pope's self-conscious texts, *The Dunciad* is the one that most fully insists on its own textuality (Kinsley, 1971). As Scriblerus and his cohorts explain, analyze, preface, index, and quibble line by line, readers cannot avoid the fact and the history of the text they are reading. *The Dunciad's* genre, its literary subject matter and persons, its scholarly notes, its anthology of "Testimonies of Authors," its complex publication history, all make it more than anything a text among texts. Thus when Cibber claims prominence of place in *The New Dunciad* and dethrones Theobald in *The Dunciad in Four Books*, the textual succession, revision, and replacement defines the relationship between the two motive forces of Dulness. Succession was the key to the poem's fable; it allowed Pope to craft a union between the poem's literary subject and the mock-epic concern with statecraft and civic virtue. Succession had always been a key to the mock-epic, in Pope, Swift, Dryden.[13] Succession had even been key in those aspects of the Virgilian model to which the mock-epic was drawn. Now, in *The Dunciad in Four Books,* succession defines and unites the poles of Dulness and, in doing so, gives new point and focus to the civil concern. Now we see that, just as Swift had prescribed in *A Tale of a Tub,* the labor of the weighty, stone stupidity of a Theobald produces the blithe, brazen impudence of a Cibber. Brass will inevitably gain the ascendancy over stone.

This succession is the proper context for assessing the relation between the two heroes. It makes as little sense to blame Pope for making Cibber succeed Theobald as to praise him for finally finding the proper hero for his poem. Theobald is *twice* succeeded in the final *Dunciad*— once by Cibber as the King of Dunces and again by "kingly" Bentley (B IV.207) as the poem's chief pedant. If we look back from the 1743 poem to the 1728 poem, it is evident that these successions *and the original choice* are more than apt. Since the *Variorum* gives precedence to the stone weight of Dulness over its brazen impudence, Theobald—or even Bentley—was in every respect better suited to the role of King Log (see Parnell, *Battle of the Frogs and Mice,* 1717). Between Theobald and Bentley the choice was in 1728 equally clear. Bentley was the elder and, as Master of Trinity College, Cambridge, socially the more eminent of the two pedants. However, Theobald had the better claim, first because of his hubris in besting Pope, but also because Bentley had no single work to compare with Theobald's Shakespeare.

The question of their claims was addressed in Pope's portrait of a "Word-catcher" in "Fragment of a Satire" (1727). There Pope acknowledges Bentley's temporal precedence, "From slashing B——y down to pidling *Tibbalds*" (14), but focuses the portrait on Theobald because he "may some Notice claim, / Wrapt round and sanctify'd with *Shakespear's Name*" (17–18). For that Theobald is granted pride of place in *The Dunciad*—and, just to keep matters clear, Bentley receives only scant attention. But after his surpassingly duncely 1732 edition of *Paradise Lost,* Bentley's claim was equal or even superior to Theobald's, a fact reflected in Pope's revisions of the "Fragment of a Satire" when in 1735 he

---

13. For an account of succession in *MacFlecknoe,* see Seidel.

inserted them into *An Epistle to Dr. Arbuthnot* (163–68). By 1742, when the first *Dunciad's* copyright had run and Pope was free to make substantial revisions, Pope had changed, the principals had changed, and, most important, Pope's diagnosis of the state of the nation had changed. The weighty attraction of Dulness had done its work, making way for dullness's monumental brass.

Theobald is not, however, fully banished from the poem. Indeed, Cibber's new, bad eminence redounds fully to Theobald's discredit. Critics have liked to speak of the duncical literary productions as *signs* of Britain's cultural decline. What the *Variorum* argued and the final *Dunciad* made clearer is that they are for Pope not just signs but *causes* of that decline. The final *Dunciad* gives Theobald's weighty labor the full credit of its effect: Britain's cultural decline is itself a duncical literary product. Thus Theobald retains his place in the final *Dunciad*, though the significance of that place has changed. He retains a minor presence in the verse (B I.133, 286), gains a new place among the poem's annotators, and reappears in Book IV's treatise on "Modern Education" (B IV.501n)[14] in the person of his successor pedant, Bentley. Most of all, he stands, in the poem's intertextual relation to its former selves, as "Dunce the first" (B I.16). This is no small presence. Pope transfers the full force of the original portrait of Theobald by neatly attributing to Bentley Theobald's index-learning,[15] and goes it one better by centering the portrait on Bentley's yet more microscopic "Fragments," his "something yet more great than Letter" (B IV.230, 216).[16] Thus the new scion of index-learning remains as a complement and even a competitor to Theobald's successor king. He, more than the recumbent Cibber, presides over the poem's final ceremonies—a fact that gives further evidence for Pope's account of Cibber claiming his own place. In *The New Dunciad*, Bentley is the more dominant figure.

Yet even there the weighty pedant is displaced. When Bentley appears in Book IV, he is chased away by the more active minions of Dulness, who are explicitly identified in a note with "Forwardness or Pertness":

---

14. Much of Book IV seems to be an adaptation of material originally intended for a companion piece to the *Essay on Man* that Pope sometimes called his "Essay on Education." See Sutherland (TE, V.xxx–xxxi).

15. Never one to lose a good line, Pope adapts two of the key parts of the original to the new portrait. Compare A I.159–64 with B IV.211–16, and A I.165–72 with B IV.249–54.

16. Pope also has Bentley participate in the ongoing disputes about spelling and pronunciation in the classical languages. See B IV.220n, 222n. In fact, Bentley's digamma was the "greatest innovation in Homeric scholarship" by "the Newton of European philological and literary studies" (Brink, 76, 3).

> In flow'd at once a gay embroider'd race,
> And titt'ring push'd the Pedants off the place:
> (B IV.275–76)[17]

Thus Bentley's appearance recapitulates the course of Dulness's progress: the labor of dull learning produces, or is at least the breeding ground of swarms of forward, active dunces. Throughout the final *Dunciad*, when Theobald is now John the Baptist to Cibber's Antichrist, now a sham and imposter usurping Cibber's rightful place, we are reminded not only that "Dunce the second reigns like Dunce the first" (B I.6), but why this is so.

More important, we are reminded why, given the signification of Pope's portraiture, Dunce the second now has the better claim. When Cibber prays to Dulness, he asks,

> Did the dead Letter unsuccessful prove?
> The brisk Example never fail'd to move.
> (B I.193–94)

This repeats a verse of Theobald's prayer to Dulness, transforming it from a mere commonplace into an archetypal Cibberian boast with typical Popean textual richness. Theobald had given preference to his verse over his criticism because, according to the cliché, though "gravest precepts" may have no effect, "sad examples never fail to move" (A I.175–76). Ostensibly Cibber is only one-upping Theobald along the same lines. For Theobald, it was his verse that "gave ampler lessons to mankind" (A I.174); for Cibber, even the far more active stage is too "confin'd." His "Life gave ampler lessons to mankind" (B I.191–92). Thus the "dead Letter" is abortive, uncreative duncical poetry: the letter that "killeth" while "the spirit giveth life" (2 Corinthians 3:6). Here is also a sidelong glance at the dead letter by which Cibber earned his role as an example—Cibber's *Letter to Mr. Pope*, with its explicit concern for the efficacy and accuracy of Pope's lettered portraiture. But the "dead Letter" displaced by Cibber's example is also, perhaps primarily, the dead letter of index-learning, the dead letter of "all such reading as was never read" (A I.166; B IV.250), the dead letter that is Bentley-Theobald's trademark.

---

17. In the original version of Book IV, *The New Dunciad*, this passage included the couplet, later moved to Book I, which first names Cibber's trait: "Dulness delighted ey'd the lively Dunce, / Remembr'ing she herself was Pertness once."

Theobald's "sad example" did not "unsuccessful prove," did not "fail to move." The flood of duncical paper after the dunces' first family portrait was proof enough of Theobald's success in moving readers to emulation, sparking them to the essential duncical action, writing and publishing nonsense. But such motion is too tame, such examples too static for Cibber's brand of duncery. Theobald's example did not *move*—about town, into positions of power and prestige, in the best circles, bearing the Smithfield muses to the ears of kings. From its first conception, the examples of *The Dunciad* have not been examples that inculcate precepts, that move (spark emulation and application); they have been examples that *move* ("act, and be, a Coxcomb with success" [B I.110]). That movement recapitulates the generic movement from epic to mock-epic—from giving examples to making examples—and is recapitulated in the succession of Dulness's heroes. Theobald's "sad example" must make way for the "brisk Example" who claimed his place as the "more considerable Hero" (TE, V.215) and the more efficacious of the motive forces of Dulness.

As the greater, more considerable hero and as the representative of the active arm of Dulness, Cibber opens a wider and more fertile path to Pope's political thematic, which, like the religious thematic, is more developed in *The Dunciad in Four Books*. The key factor is picked out by Aristarchus-Bentley, whose overriding passion for textual purity makes him positively enraged that his own surrogate had been mistaken for the true hero: "Tibbald... was never an Author in fashion, or caressed by the Great; whereas... the true Hero... was the *Peculiar Delight* and *Chosen Companion* of the Nobility of England; and wrote, as he himself tells us, certain of his Works at the *earnest Desire* of *Persons of Quality.*" Pertness is shamelessness, pertness is blindness to distinction, pertness is impudence, and pertness is also social climbing.

Theobald's is not the only laurel Cibber succeeds to. When the "Fool of Quality," Pope's old nemesis Lord Hervey, joined those who in the "promis'd land... sleep among the dull of ancient days" (B II.292–94), Pope was able to have Cibber assume his destined place as fool at court:

> Thou Cibber! thou, his Laurel shalt support,
> Folly, my son, has still a Friend at Court.
> Lift up your gates, ye Princes, see him come!
> Sound, sound ye Viols, be the Cat-call dumb!
> (B I.299–302)

These lines introduce perhaps the most explicit political satire in any of the *Dunciad*s. Sutherland notes that "Pope comes very near to a direct criticism of George II's reign," but Mack has amply shown that this culminates a sustained political critique that is necessarily conducted as an "exercise in innuendo" but which, given the "remarkable instrument of satiric communication [that] lay ready to his hand" (the "extensive vocabulary of disaffection"[18]), was anything but obscure.

Mack's account of the political dimension of *The Dunciad in Four Books* is too well argued and too well known to rehearse here. But it is good to remember the limits that Mack's purposes place on that discussion, which serves chiefly to establish Walpole and Pope as "Mighty Opposites," the somewhat overwrought title of his final chapter. There Mack detects in Pope's attachment to the epithet "brazen" an important relationship between Cibber and Walpole. Remarking on Pope's letter to his printer, Mack suggests, "There was more at stake in the term 'brazen,' it would seem, than a happy but mistaken epithet; and if I am right in supposing that what was at stake was an allusion to Robert Walpole, triggering a further allusion to Horatio Walpole in 'brainless,' this would account for the fact that in the surviving letter Bowyer, or someone, has cut at least one line of Pope's postscript away" (1969, 158). Although we have seen better reasons for Pope to keep and so emphasize the offending epithet, Mack is certainly right that this does also glance at the Walpoles and that this Walpole-Cibber connection is crucial to the poem. Add to this Mack's account of "the analogy, well-rooted by 1742–43, between the actor, gambler, and stage-manager who was patentee of Drury Lane and the 'actor'-'gambler'-'stage-manager' who for two decades seemed to have a permanent hold on St. James's and St. Stephens's" (158), and we cannot ignore the attraction of Mack's concluding suggestion that it must have been

> clear to almost everybody whose figure the laureate was surrogate for ... [and] that the poem's professed hero is a symptom not a cause.... The true hero of the poem, in other words, is Walpole, who, with the aid of a do-nothing foreign king and a queen whose name is Dulness but who is occasionally to be identified with Queen Caroline, has created the conditions that make it possible for Dulness to mount in Book IV a much solider and

---

18. Mack (1969, 136, 128); see Weinbrot (1982) on the "Persian" aspect of Pope's satires of the 1730s and 1740s.

more influential throne than the one she was seen on or near in Book I. (161–62)

But of course Walpole is not the true hero of the poem in any sense. He is no more the cause of Dulness's reign than is Cibber—or, more precisely, he is a symptom of that cause in just the way that Cibber is. Though we would be remiss to underestimate Walpole's qualifications as a true son of Dulness, Cibber makes the far better king, better even than George himself. Walpole shares with Cibber that essential pertness that links him with all that is coarse and vulgar, in a form distorted and fixed by wealth and power (see Plumb, II.245–50). And Walpole is the social climber nonpareil, this coarse, minor country squire who understood his world far better than Pope and who through cunning, talent, application, a stint in the Tower, and an utter lack of manners or morals made himself not only rich and "great" but the surrogate for the king. When we focus exclusively on the political satire that grew with the poem, Walpole seems to have been made for the poem. But Pope has in mind more than politics, and in this wider compass Cibber is unsurpassed. *The Dunciad* is, as we have seen all mock-epics to be, grounded in figures of substitution; but the substitutions of *The Dunciad* do not create surrogates. Like *The Dispensary, The Dunciad* offers a social diagnosis expressed in the figure of a field of forces, of myriad particulars all ranged round a common center in the galaxy of Dulness. In this compass, Walpole lacks the essential social pliancy of the "Sev'nfold Face," which gives Cibber such ready converse with the highest and the lowest and all between—an essential attribute in one "who brings / The Smithfield Muses to the ear of Kings." Cibber's is the story not of one who aspires above his appointed station but of one who aspires only to be a dunce, but for whom being a dunce is enough to open any door, even that of a king.

What Cibber brings to the political satire is his encompassing network of class affiliations with *all* species of duncery, especially in literature. The empire of Dulness does not begin with such as Walpole, though it does find an end there. It begins with the likes of Bentley and Busby, who prepare the "Boy-Senator" (B IV.147) to learn

> As much Estate, and Principle, and Wit,
> As Jansen, Fleetwood, Cibber shall think fit.
> (B IV.325–26)

Only *after* the public estate of learning, taste, and morals has been shaped by the education of the school and the town—that is, by literature—are they ripe for Walpole's touch.[19] Only after social relations and responsibilities have been disrupted and the institutions that instill and enforce those social relations have been enfeebled can the kind of economic relations on which Walpole depends come to the fore as a motive force, as the ground of social action. And like bad money, bad motives drive out the good:

> By this progression, the first men of a nation will become the pensioners of the last; and he who has talents, the most implicit tool to him who has none. The distemper will soon descend, not indeed to make a deposite below, and to remain there, but to pervade the whole body. (Bolingbroke, *Works*, II.394.)

The corruption "pervade[s] the whole" and what is lost is the superior power of "talents." What is lost in the apocalyptic catastrophe of *The Dunciad* is not a king or a minister, but literature: "all is Night" only when "*Art* after *Art* goes out" (A III.346, B IV.640). Literature is, for Pope, the chief support of culture. If we cannot reach to so grand a conception, then we feel the force of our distance from the values of *The Dunciad.*

In the interim between the reign of Theobald and that of Cibber, Dulness has progressed in the "influencing Art" that Garth's apothecaries had used to spur the progress of social contagion. When Pope added to the *Variorum* the compliment to Swift, he also added the picture of a brooding, breeding Dulness:

> Here pleas'd behold her mighty wings out-spread,
> To hatch a new Saturnian age of Lead.
>
> (A I.25–26)

By 1742, the new age had come to fruition and had produced an end yet worse than that predicted. Not only had the leaden age replaced the golden, but it had replaced it with a new-minted, yet more corrupting version of the original:

---

19. Like his political mentor, Bolingbroke, Pope believed that the one unshakable support of the "orders" of the state was the "spirit and character of the people," the sense of duty and civic virtue that a viable society must instill in its members (Bolingbroke, *Works*, II.393–94).

> Of dull and venal a new World to mold,
> And bring Saturnian days of Lead and Gold.
> (*The New Dunciad,* 15–16)

What those new days meant became clear when, enlivened by the exchange of kings, *The New Dunciad* was reunited with the old. In the *Variorum*'s age of lead,

> Heav'n had decreed to spare the Grubstreet-state.
> (A I.184)

Now, in the final *Dunciad,* Pope said outright what had been implicit—that Dulness would not be confined to the "Grubstreet-state"; that the danger was larger and elsewhere; that the range of reference and relevance was greater than was said and "more is meant than meets the ear":

> Heav'n [had] decreed to save the State.
> (B I.195)

Now Dulness had a king worthy to be a center, a point-source of her spreading contagion, of whom Pope could justly say,

> All nonsense thus, of old or modern date,
> Shall in thee centre, from thee circulate.
> (B III.59–60)

Joined to her new-minted, brassy gold, Dulness's lead has become more than the driving, steadying force of the dunce in state ("The wheels above urg'd by the load below" [A I.180; B I.184]); it has become a currency for the dull intellect:

> Nonsense precipitate, like running Lead,
> That slip'd thro' Cracks and Zig-zags of the Head.
> (B I.123–24)

With these twin currencies—lead and brass, stupidity and impudence—and with the newer of the two lending her corruption swifter wings, Dulness also has a worthy center of exchange. As successor to and improver of Hervey's role as fool at Court[20] and as brother to Walpole, Cibber can circulate in the best West End circles. Where Walpole's corrosive gold will touch but few hands and reach but few souls, Cibber's brass—his small change—passes through the hands of all. As successor to and improver of Settle's role as Laureate and as patentee of Drury Lane, Cibber can circulate in the best Grub Street circles. Where Bentley's sublimely weighty lead will meet but few eyes and will run in but few heads, Cibber's brass passes before the eyes of all. At home in Curll's literary sweatshops, in Smithfield's teeming, vulgar shows, in the carriage trade of Drury Lane, in the yet more refined show in St. James's, Cibber is Dulness's broker to the nation. He has circulated her influence everywhere around the kingdom and planted at its door her signpost—his brazen, sevenfold face.

---

20. Note how Cibber changes Hervey's position and how that change suits Pope's larger purposes. Predominantly in the Sporus portrait but also throughout Pope's poetry, Hervey is the man of birth and station so corrupted that his evil transmogrified him into a Satanic, poisonous reptile (see Weinbrot, 1982, 259–65). Cibber's evil, on the other hand, is the banal, not notably malevolent, and yet more dangerous evil of the perfect, self-satisfied fool such as has amused the crowds at Smithfield since earliest days.

Epilogue

"Speak, Goddess! since 'tis Thou that best can'st tell"
—The Dispensary

It is only appropriate that Pope's final mock-epic should end in apocalypse. Mock-epic is a genre of extremes. It asks us to take a long and large view of its subjects, as though we stood with Denham on Cooper's Hill to enjoy the distant sight that exposes the busy vanity of the city. Yet it also drags us closer to its subjects than many of us have liked, as though we were being shown the ropes, a kind of upper-crust *London Spy*. Mock-epic asks us to believe seriously that what's at stake is civilization itself, and yet it shows us individuals whose particular threat is small and who are, individually, something less than satanic, who can even be engaging. Mock-epic stands for the public interest and the common good, but it springs from the private struggles and frustrations of its creators, and it serves their personal interests. Perhaps, then, it should not be surprising that mock-epic has always provoked extreme responses—or at least did so until a comfortable home was found for it in "the professional Popean's Natchez-Augustan manor."[1] But the poems—and the world—resist all efforts to confine them to eternal truths and universal views. Though the poems might ask us to stand in the place of posterity, or might put Pope in the place of Virgil or put William Harvey in the place of Anchises, the nature of those places changes as the world changes, and the poets and their poems know it. What the poems argue, if anything, is that anyone who cannot see the need both for continuity in change and for the change itself sees with the eye of a dunce.

1. Kenner (1958). I owe the citation to Keener (1974, 5), who raises questions that remain important but who answers them in a way very different from mine.

As I earlier said of Garth, the mock-epic poet expects his reader to stand at the edge between figure and ground—discriminating in the face of complexity and able to change perspectives and figures as the occasion warrants. The mock-epic's values are not located in other lands, though they might come to us from there; its contest of values is here and now. The work of discrimination carries great demands, demands not only on our powers of observation but also on our knowledge. The work of recovering the mock-epic's background—literary, philosophical, ethical—has proved valuable and even necessary. Yet that effort cannot allow us to forget the work of recovering the poems' figures and their background. And neither recovery effort can be allowed to make us forget ourselves and our background. So there is one sense in which we can read the mock-epic as it asks us to. If our knowledge and powers of imagination are up to it, and if our ideas are sufficiently anchored in our own circumstances, then we might stand at the mock-epic's edge between figure and ground. If we can maintain so delicate a poise, then we too "can be pleased with the image, without being cozened by the fiction."

Yet our interest in this poetry extends beyond being pleased without moral deception. After the question of these poems' truth is the question of their design. On that score I stand squarely with my predecessors: these poems are a "corrective to a too narrow idea of poetry."[2] In the twentieth century as in the eighteenth, criticism has undertaken to understand poetry in terms of what it is not, to make it special by defining it against a gray, factual norm. The poetic is what is not referential, not subordinated to plain fact, not merely scientific. Even today, postmodern heirs to the midcentury poetic are eager to think of poetry as a special case of the "rhetorical" powers of language, in terms of its need always to escape reference, truth, the norm. In its pursuit of a rhetoric of truth telling, the mock-epic presents a challenge to compartmentalized views of poetry. This study pursues and confirms that challenge, showing the degree to which history, this poetry's truth-telling capacities, reaches deep into *all* the poems' structures. It offers a view of poetry—and of truth—that is anything but narrow. The point is not so much that the mock-epic's truth of class/category/prototype anticipates our best contemporary semantics, which it does, but that the mock-epic's effort to see and say the truth produced a form of truth/history/science that stood as a living alternative to the simple, gray truth of correspondence.

2. Edwards (1971, 304).

Bibliography

Ackerman, Steven. 1979. "The 'Infant Atoms' of Garth's *Dispensary.*" *MLR* 74:513–23.
Appleby, Joyce O. 1978. *Economic Thought and Ideology in Seventeenth-Century England.* Princeton: Princeton University Press.
Austin, J. L. 1962. *How to Do Things with Words.* 2d ed., 1975. J. O. Urmson and M. Sbisa, eds. Cambridge, Mass.: Harvard University Press.
Ayloffe, William. 1707. "Preface." In *The Poetical Works of the Honourable Sir Charles Sedley, Baronet.* London.
Babington, Anthony. 1971. *The English Bastille: A History of Newgate Gaol and Prison Conditions in Britain 1188–1902.* London: Macdonald and Co.
Battestin, Martin. 1974. *The Providence of Wit: Aspects of Form in Augustan Literature and the Arts.* Oxford: Oxford University Press.
Beckett, J. V. 1986. *The Aristocracy in England 1660–1914.* Oxford: Oxford University Press.
Blackmore, Richard. 1716. *Essays upon Several Subjects.* 2d ed., rpt. 1971. New York: Garland Publishers.
Bond, Richmond P. 1932. *English Burlesque Poetry 1700–1750.* Cambridge, Mass.: Harvard University Press.
Boyce, Benjamin. 1947. *The Theophrastan Character in England to 1642.* Cambridge, Mass.: Harvard University Press.
———. 1962. *Character Sketches in Pope's Poems.* Durham, N.C.: Duke University Press.
Boys, Richard C. 1949. *Sir Richard Blackmore and the Wits: A Study of "Commendatory Verses on the Author of the Two Arthurs and the Satyr against Wit" (1700).* Rpt. 1969. New York: Octagon Books.
Brink, C. O. 1985. *English Classical Scholarship: Historical Reflections on Bentley, Porson, and Housman.* Cambridge: J. Clarke.
Brower, Reuben A. 1959. *Alexander Pope: the Poetry of Allusion.* Oxford: Clarendon Press.
Brown, Laura. 1985. *Alexander Pope.* Oxford: B. Blackwell.
Byrd, Max. 1974. *Visits to Bedlam: Madness and Literature in the Eighteenth Century.* Columbia: University of South Carolina Press.
———. 1978. *London Transformed: Images of the City in the Eighteenth Century.* New Haven: Yale University Press.
Cambridge, Richard Owen. 1751. *The Scribleriad: An Heroic Poem.* London.
Cannon, John. 1984. *Aristocratic Century: The Peerage of Eighteenth-Century England.* Cambridge: Cambridge University Press.
Caretta, Vincent. 1983. *The Snarling Muse: Verbal and Visual Political Satire from Pope to Churchill.* Philadelphia: University of Pennsylvania Press.
Chatman, Seymor. 1978. *Story and Discourse: Narrative Structure in Fiction and Film.* Ithaca: Cornell University Press.

Church, Sir William, M.D. 1884–86. "Our Hospital Pharmacopoeia and Apothecary Shop." *St. Bartholomew's Hospital Reports.* London.
Cibber, Colley. 1740. *An Apology for the Life of Colley Cibber.* Rpt. 1968. B. R. S. Fone, ed. Ann Arbor: University of Michigan Press.
———. 1742. *A Letter from Mr. Cibber, to Mr. Pope, Inquiring into the Motives that might induce him in his Satyrical Works, to be so frequently fond of Mr. Cibber's Name.* London.
———. 1744. *Another Occasional Letter From Mr. Cibber to Mr. Pope.* London.
[Cibber, Colley]. 1743. *The Egotist: Or, Colley upon Cibber.* London.
Cibber, Theophilus [Robert Shiels]. 1753. *The Lives of the Poets of Great Britain and Ireland.* London.
Clifford, James L. 1965. "The Eighteenth Century." *MLQ* 26:111–34
Cohen, Murray. 1977. *Sensible Words: Linguistic Practice in England, 1640–1789.* Baltimore: Johns Hopkins University Press.
Cohen, Ralph. 1967. "The Augustan Mode in English Poetry." *ECS* 1:3–32.
———. 1974. "On the Interrelations of Eighteenth-Century Literary Forms." In *New Approaches to Eighteenth-Century Literature.* Phillip Harth, ed. New York: Columbia University Press.
———. 1977. "Pope's Meanings and the Strategies of Interrelation." In *English Literature in the Age of Disguise.* Maximillian E. Novak, ed. Berkeley and Los Angeles: University of California Press.
Colomb, Gregory G. 1978. "The Argument of Values in the Augustan Mock-Epic." Dissertation, University of Virginia.
———. 1986. "Semiotic Study of Literary Works." In *Tracing Literary Theory.* Joseph Natoli, ed. Urbana: University of Illinois Press.
Cook, Richard I. 1980. *Sir Samuel Garth.* Boston: Twayne Publishers.
Culpeper, Nicholas. 1651. *A Physical Directory.* London.
Cumberland, Richard. 1672. *De Legibus Naturae.* Trans. John Maxwell under the title *A Treatise of the Laws of Nature*, 1720. London.
Curtis, Dennis E., and Judith Resnik. 1987. "Images of Justice." *Yale Law Journal* 96:1727–72.
Damrosch, Leopold, Jr. 1987. *The Imaginative World of Alexander Pope.* Berkeley and Los Angeles: University of California Press.
Davis, Lennard J. 1983. *Factual Fictions: The Origins of the English Novel.* New York: Columbia University Press.
Debus, Allen G. 1966. *The English Paracelsians.* New York: F. Watts.
Dennis, John. 1939. *The Critical Works of John Dennis, Volume I: 1692–1711.* Edward Niles Hooker, ed. Baltimore: Johns Hopkins University Press.
———. 1943. *The Critical Works of John Dennis, Volume II: 1711–1729.* Edward Niles Hooker, ed. Baltimore: Johns Hopkins University Press.
DePorte, Michael V. 1974. *Nightmares and Hobbyhorses: Swift, Sterne, and Augustan Ideas of Madness.* San Marino, Calif.: Huntington Library.
Desaguliers, J. T. 1728. *The Newtonian System of the World, the Best Model of Government.* London.
Doody, Margaret Anne. 1985. *The Daring Muse: Augustan Poetry Reconsidered.* Cambridge: Cambridge University Press.
Downie, J. A. 1979. *Robert Harley and the Press: Propaganda and Public Opinion in the Age of Swift and Defoe.* Cambridge: Cambridge University Press.
Drennon, Herbert. 1938. "James Thomson and John Norris." *PMLA* 53:1094–1101.
Eco, Umberto. 1979. *The Role of the Reader: Explorations in the Semiotics of Texts.* Bloomington: Indiana University Press.

Edwards, Thomas R. 1963. *This Dark Estate: A Reading of Pope.* Berkeley and Los Angeles: University of California Press.

———. 1971. "Visible Poetry: Pope and Modern Criticism." In *Twentieth-Century Literature in Retrospect.* Reuben A. Brower, ed. Cambridge, Mass.: Harvard University Press.

Ehrenpreis, Irvin. 1970. "The Style of Sound: The Literary Value of Pope's Versification." In *The Augustan Milieu: Essays Presented to Louis A. Landa.* Henry Knight Miller, Eric Rothstein, and G. S. Rousseau, eds. Oxford: Clarendon Press.

Elkin, Peter Kingsley. 1973. *The Augustan Defence of Satire.* Oxford: Clarendon Press.

Elliott, Robert C. 1960. *The Power of Satire: Magic, Ritual, Art.* Princeton: Princeton University Press.

Erskine-Hill, Howard. 1962. "The 'New World' of Pope's *Dunciad.*" Rpt. 1968, in *Essential Articles for the Study of Alexander Pope.* Maynard Mack, ed. Hamden, Conn.: Archon Books.

———. 1972. *Pope: The Dunciad.* London: Edward Arnold.

———. 1975. *The Social Milieu of Alexander Pope: Lives, Examples and the Poetic Response.* New Haven: Yale University Press.

Erwin, Daniel Timothy. 1984. "Some Augustan Designs: Intentional Structure in the Eighteenth-Century Text." Dissertation, University of Chicago.

Evans, Gareth. 1982. *The Varieties of Reference.* John McDowell, ed. Oxford: Clarendon Press.

Fabricant, Carole. 1979. "Binding and Dressing Nature's Loose Tresses: The Ideology of Augustan Landscape Design." *Studies in Eighteenth-Century Culture* 8:109–35.

———. 1982. *Swift's Landscape.* Baltimore: Johns Hopkins University Press.

Feinberg, Leonard. 1968. "Satire: The Inadequacy of Recent Definitions." *Genre* 1:31–37.

Foucault, Michel. 1961. *Madness and Civilization: A History of Insanity in the Age of Reason.* Trans. Richard Howard, 1965. New York: Pantheon Books.

Frege, Gottlob. 1892. "On Sense and Meaning." Rpt. 1952 in *Translations from the Philosophical Writings of Gottlob Frege.* Peter Geach and Max Black, eds. Oxford: Blackwell.

Gally, Henry. 1725. *The Moral Characters of Theophrastus. Translated from the Greek, with Notes. To Which is prefix'd A Critical Essay on* Characteristic Writings. London.

Garrison, James D. 1975. *Dryden and the Tradition of Panegyric.* Berkeley and Los Angeles: University of California Press.

Goodall, Charles. 1684. *The Royal College of Physicians of London Founded and Established by Law.* London.

Goodman, Nelson. 1976. *Languages of Art: An Approach to a Theory of Symbols.* Indianapolis: Hackett.

Gordon, I. R. F. 1976. *A Preface to Pope.* London: Longman.

Griffin, Dustin H. 1978. *Alexander Pope: The Poet in the Poems.* Princeton: Princeton University Press.

Guilhamet, Leon. 1987. *Satire and the Transformation of Genre.* Philadelphia: University of Pennsylvania Press.

Hagstrum, Jean. 1972. "Verbal and Visual Caricature in the Age of Dryden, Swift, and Pope." In *England in the Restoration and Early Eighteenth Century: Essays on Culture and Society*. H. T. Swedenberg, ed. Berkeley and Los Angeles: University of California Press.

Halliday, M. A. K. 1961. "Categories of the Theory of Grammar." *Word* 17:241–92.

Hatfield, Glenn. 1968. *Henry Fielding and the Language of Irony*. Chicago: University of Chicago Press.

Hesse, Mary B. 1961. *Fields and Forces: The Concept of Action at a Distance in the History of Physics*. New York: Nelson.

Hill, Christopher. 1967. "Review of *The World We Have Lost*." *History and Theory* 6:117–27.

———. 1977. *Milton and the English Revolution*. New York: Viking Press.

Hill, George Birkbeck. 1897. *Johnsonian Miscellanies*. Rpt. 1966. New York: Barnes & Noble.

Hirschman, Albert O. 1977. *The Passions and the Interests: Political Arguments for Capitalism before Its Triumph*. Princeton: Princeton University Press.

Hodges, Nathaniel. 1666. *Vindici Medicinae et Medicorum, an Apology for the Profession and Professors of Physic*. London.

———. 1672. *Loimologia sive Pestis nuperae apud Populum Londinensem grassantis narratio*. Trans. John Quincy, M.D., under the title *Loimologia: or, An Historical Account of the Plague in London in 1665: with precautionary Directions against the like Contagion*. 1720. London.

Hooper, W. Eden. 1935. *The History of Newgate and The Old Bailey*. London: Underwood Press.

Hughes, Peter. 1977. "Restructuring Literary History: Implications for the Eighteenth Century." *NLH* 8:257–78.

Hunter, J. Paul. 1975. *Occasional Form: Henry Fielding and the Chains of Circumstance*. Baltimore: Johns Hopkins University Press.

Irving, William Henry. 1928. *John Gay's London: Illustrated from the Poetry of the Time*. Cambridge, Mass.: Harvard University Press.

Jack, Ian. 1952. *Augustan Satire: Intention and Idiom in English Poetry*. Rpt. 1971. Oxford: Clarendon Press.

Jackson, James L. 1950. "Pope's *Rape of the Lock* Considered as a Five-Act Epic." *PMLA* 65:1283–87.

Jackson, Wallace. 1983. *Vision and Re-Vision in Alexander Pope*. Detroit: Wayne State University Press.

Jakobson, Roman. 1960. "Concluding Statement: Linguistics and Poetics." In *Style in Language*. Thomas A. Sebeok, ed. Cambridge, Mass.: MIT Press.

Jenyns, Soame. 1757. *A Free Inquiry into the Nature and Origin of Evil*. In *The Works of Soame Jenyns*. Rpt. 1969. Westmead, England: Gregg International Publishers.

Johnson, Samuel. 1757. "Review of *A Free Inquiry*." Rpt. 1810–11, in *The Works of Samuel Johnson*, vol. 6. London.

———. 1952. *Lives of the English Poets*. 2 vols. London: Oxford University Press.

Jones, Emrys. 1968. "Pope and Dulness." Rpt. 1980, in *Pope: Recent Essays by Several Hands*. Maynard Mack and James A. Winn, eds. Hamden, Conn.: Archon Books.

Keener, Frederick M. *An Essay on Pope*. New York: Columbia University Press.

Ker, W. P. 1900. *Essays of John Dryden*. 2 vols. Oxford: Clarendon Press.

Kernan, Alvin B. 1959. *The Cankered Muse: Satire of the English Renaissance*. New Haven: Yale University Press.

Kinsley, William. 1971. "*The Dunciad* as Mock-Book." *Huntington Library Quarterly* 35:29–47.

———. 1975. "Physico-demonology in Pope's 'Dunciad' IV, 71–90." *MLR* 70:20–31.

Knoche, Ulrich. 1949. *Roman Satire*. Trans. Edwin S. Ramage, 1975. Bloomington: Indiana University Press.

Korshin, Paul J. 1971. "The Intellectual Context of Swift's Flying Island." *Philological Quarterly* 50:630–46.

———. 1973. *From Concord to Dissent: Major Themes in English Poetic Theory 1640–1700*. Menston, Yorkshire: Scholar Press.

Kramnick, Issac. 1968. *Bolingbroke and His Circle: The Politics of Nostalgia in the Age of Walpole*. Cambridge, Mass.: Harvard University Press.

Krieger, Murray. 1961. "The 'Frail China Jar' and the Rude Hand of Chaos." Rpt. 1968, in *Essential Articles for the Study of Alexander Pope*. Maynard Mack, ed. Hamden, Conn.: Archon Books.

Kropf, C. R. 1974. "Libel and Satire in the Eighteenth Century." *ECS* 8:153–68.

Lakoff, George, and Mark Turner. 1989. *More than Cool Reason: A Field Guide to Poetic Metaphor*. Chicago: University of Chicago Press.

Land, Stephen K. 1974. *From Signs to Propositions: The Concept of Form in Eighteenth-Century Semantic Theory*. London: Longman.

———. 1986. *The Philosophy of Language in Britain: Major Theories from Hobbes to Thomas Reid*. New York: AMS Press.

Laslett, Peter. 1971. *The World We Have Lost*. 2d ed. London: Methuen.

Leicht, Wilhelm J., ed. 1905. *The Dispensary. Kritische Ausgabe*. Heidelberg: C. Winter's Universitätsbuchhandlung.

Levine, Joseph M. 1981. "Ancients and Moderns Reconsidered." *ECS* 15:72–89.

Lovejoy, Arthur. 1936. *The Great Chain of Being*. Rpt. 1960. New York: Harper & Row.

Lukács, Georg. 1971. *The Theory of the Novel*. Trans. Anna Bostock. Cambridge, Mass.: MIT Press.

Lund, Roger. 1978. "Metamorphosis and Mechanism." Dissertation, University of Virginia.

McKeon, Michael. 1987. *The Origins of the English Novel 1600–1740*. Baltimore: Johns Hopkins University Press.

McKillop, Alan Dougal. 1942. *The Background of Thomson's Seasons*. Minneapolis: University of Minnesota Press.

Mack, Maynard. 1951. "The Muse of Satire." *The Yale Review* 41:80–92.

———. 1969. *The Garden and the City: Retirement and Politics in the Later Poetry of Pope, 1731–1743*. Toronto: University of Toronto Press.

———. 1986. *Alexander Pope: A Life*. New York: Norton.

———, ed. 1984. *The Last and Greatest Art: Some Unpublished Poetical Manuscripts of Alexander Pope*. Newark: University of Delaware Press.

Matthews, Leslie G. 1967. *The Royal Apothecaries*. London: Wellcome Historical Medical Library.

Meyers, Milton L. 1983. *The Soul of Modern Economic Man: Ideas of Self-Interest, Thomas Hobbes to Adam Smith*. Chicago: University of Chicago Press.

Miller, Henry Knight. 1972. "The 'Whig Interpretation' of Literary History." *ECS* 6:60–84.

Miner, Earl. 1967. *Dryden's Poetry*. Bloomington: Indiana University Press.

Mingay, G. E. 1976. *The Gentry: The Rise and Fall of a Ruling Class*. London: Longman.

Moore, Norman. 1918. *The History of St. Bartholomew's Hospital*. London: C. A. Pearson.

Morris, David B. 1984. *Alexander Pope: The Genius of Sense*. Cambridge, Mass.: Harvard University Press.

Murrin, Michael. 1969. *The Veil of Allegory*. Chicago: University of Chicago.

Neale, R. S. 1981. *Class in English History.* Oxford: Blackwell.
Nedham, Marchamont. 1665. *Medela Medicinae.* London.
Nicolson, Marjorie, and G. S. Rousseau. 1968. *"This Long Disease, My Life": Alexander Pope and the Sciences.* Princeton: Princeton University Press.
Norris, John. 1688. *The Theory and Regulation of Love: A Moral Essay.* Oxford.
Nussbaum, Felicity, and Laura Brown, eds. 1987. *The New Eighteenth Century: Theory • Politics • English Literature.* New York: Methuen.
O Hehir, Brendan. 1969. *Expans'd Hieroglyphicks: A Critical Edition of Sir John Denham's* Cooper's Hill. Berkeley and Los Angeles: University of California Press.
O'Mally, C. D. 1972. "The English Physician in the Earlier Eighteenth Century." In *England in the Restoration and Early Eighteenth Century: Essays on Culture and Society.* H. T. Swedenberg, ed. Berkeley and Los Angeles: University of California Press.
Oden, Richard L., ed. 1977. *Dryden and Shadwell: The Literary Controversy and Mac Flecknoe (1668–1679).* Delmar, N.Y.: Scholars' Facsimiles and Reprints.
Oldham, John. 1686. *The Works of John Oldham.* Rpt. 1979. Ken Robinson, ed. Delmar, N.Y.: Scholars' Facsimiles & Reprints.
Paulson, Ronald. 1967. *Satire and the Novel in Eighteenth-Century England.* New Haven: Yale University Press.
———, ed. 1971. *Satire: Modern Essays in Criticism.* Englewood Cliffs, N.J.: Prentice-Hall.
Paxton, Peter. 1703. *Civil Polity, A Treatise Concerning the Nature of Government.* London.
Perkin, Harold. 1969. *The Origins of Modern English Society, 1780–1880.* London: Routledge and Kegan Paul.
Phillips, Steven R. 1969. "Sir Samuel Garth, *The Dispensary* (1699): An Old Spelling Edition with Introduction and Historical Notes." Dissertation, University of Rochester.
Plumb, J. H. 1956, 1960. *Sir Robert Walpole.* 2 vols. London: Cresset Press.
Pollak, Ellen. 1985. *The Poetics of Sexual Myth: Gender and Ideology in the Verse of Swift and Pope.* Chicago: University of Chicago Press.
Pound, Ezra. 1918. "Marianne Moore and Mina Loy." Rpt. 1973, in *Selected Prose 1909–1965.* William Cookson, ed. London: Faber and Faber.
Price, Martin. 1964. *To the Palace of Wisdom: Studies in Order and Energy from Dryden to Blake.* Carbondale: Southern Illinois University Press.
Putnam, Hilary. 1981. *Reason, Truth, and History.* Cambridge: Cambridge University Press.
de Quincey, Thomas. 1890. *The Collected Writings of Thomas de Quincey.* David Masson, ed. Edinburgh.
Quinlan, Maurice J. 1967. "Swift's Use of Literalization as a Rhetorical Device." *PMLA* 82:516–21.
Rapin, René. 1674. *Reflections on Aristotle's Treatise of Poesey.* Trans. Thomas Rhymer. London.
Reynolds, Richard. 1975. "Libels and Satires! Lawless Things Indeed!" *ECS* 8:475–77.
Richetti, John J. 1969. *Popular Fiction Before Richardson: Narrative Patterns, 1700–1739.* Oxford: Clarendon Press.
———. 1983. *Philosophical Writing: Locke, Berkeley, Hume.* Cambridge, Mass.: Harvard University Press.
Roberts, Philip E. 1966. "A Critical Edition of Garth's *Dispensary.*" Dissertation, University of Edinburgh.

Rochester [Thomas Alcock and John Wilmont]. 1677. *The Famous Pathologist or The Noble Mountebank*. Rpt. 1961. Vivian de Sola Pinto, ed. Nottingham, England: University of Nottingham.

Rogers, Pat. 1972. *Grub Street: Studies in a Subculture*. London: Methuen.

———. 1985. *Eighteenth-Century Encounters: Studies in Literature and Society in the Age of Walpole*. Brighton, Sussex: Harvester Press.

The Roll of the Royal College of Physicians of London. 1878. 2d ed. Compiled by William Munk. London.

Rothstein, Eric. 1981. *Restoration and Eighteenth-Century Poetry 1660–1780*. Boston: Routledge and Kegan Paul.

Russo, John Paul. 1972. *Alexander Pope: Tradition and Identity*. Cambridge, Mass.: Harvard University Press.

Salmon, William. 1668. *A Rebuke to the Authors of a Blew-Book*. London.

Schneider, Duane B. 1964. "Dr. Garth and Shakespeare: A Borrowing." *English Language Notes* 1:200–202.

Seidel, Michael. 1979. *Satiric Inheritance, Rabelais to Sterne*. Princeton: Princeton University Press.

Sena, John F. 1974a. "The Letters of Samuel Garth." *Bulletin of the New York Public Library* 78:69–94.

———. 1974b. "Samuel Garth's *The Dispensary*." *Texas Studies in Literature and Language* 15:639–48.

———. 1986. *The Best-Natured Man: Sir Samuel Garth Physician and Poet*. New York: AMS Press.

Shaftesbury. 1711. *Characteristics of Men, Manners, Opinions, Times*. Rpt. 1964. John M Robertson, ed. New York: Bobbs-Merrill.

Shankman, Steven. 1983. *Pope's Iliad: Homer in the Age of Passion*. Princeton: Princeton University Press.

Sherburn, George. 1944. "*The Dunciad*, Book IV." *University of Texas Studies in English* 174–90.

Siebert, Donald T., Jr. 1976. "Cibber and Satan: *The Dunciad* and Civilization." *ECS* 10:203–21.

Simmonds, Andrew. 1977. "The Blindfold of Justice." *ABA Journal* 63:1164.

Sitter, John E. 1971. *The Poetry of Pope's "Dunciad"*. Minneapolis: University of Minnesota Press.

Spacks, Patricia Meyer. 1971. *An Argument of Images: The Poetry of Alexander Pope*. Cambridge, Mass.: Harvard University Press.

Spence, Joseph. 1964. *Anecdotes, Observations and Characters of Books and Men*. Samuel Weller Singer, ed. Carbondale: Southern Illinois University Press.

Spingarn, J. E. 1957. *Critical Essays of the Seventeenth Century*. Bloomington: Indiana University Press.

Spitzer, Leo. 1944–45. *Classical and Christian Ideas of World Harmony: Prolegomena to an Interpretation of the Word "Stimmung."* Rpt. 1963. Anna Granville Hatcher, ed. Baltimore: Johns Hopkins University Press.

Steeves, Edna Leake, ed. 1952. *Pope, The Art of Sinking: A Critical Edition*. New York: Russell & Russell.

Stone, Lawrence. 1966. "Social Mobility in England, 1500–1700." *Past and Present* 33:16–55.

———. 1972. *The Causes of the English Revolution, 1529–1642*. New York: Harper & Row.

———, and Jeanne C. Fawtier Stone. 1984. *An Open Elite? England 1540–1880*. Oxford: Clarendon Press.

Swedenberg, H. T. 1944. *The Theory of the Epic in England 1650–1800*. Berkeley and Los Angeles: University of California Press.
Swift, Jonathan. 1953. *Political Tracts, 1713–1719*. Herbert Davis and Irvin Ehrenpreis, eds. Oxford: Blackwell.
Tanner, Tony. 1965. "Reason and Grotesque: Pope's *Dunciad*." Rpt. 1968, in *Essential Articles for the Study of Alexander Pope*. Maynard Mack, ed. Hamden, Conn.: Archon Books.
Thompson, Charles. 1929. *The Quacks of Old London*. Philadelphia: J. B. Lippincott.
Thompson, E. P. 1975. *Whigs and Hunters: The Origin of the Black Act*. New York: Pantheon Books.
Thornbury, George Walter. 1897. *Old and New London: A Narrative of Its History, Its People and Its Places*. London: Cassell & Company.
Tillotson, Geoffrey. 1938. *On the Poetry of Pope*. 2d ed., 1950. Oxford: Clarendon Press.
A Transcript of the Registers of the Company of Stationers of London. 1876. Edward Arber, ed. London.
Trapp, Joseph. 1744. *The Works of Virgil*. In *Lectures on Poetry Read in the Schools of Natural Philosophy at Oxford*. Rpt. 1970. New York: Garland Publishers.
Troyer, Howard William. 1968. *Ned Ward of Grub Street: A Study of Sub-Literary London in the Eighteenth Century*. London: Frank Cass & Co.
Viner, Jacob. 1972. *The Role of Providence in the Social Order: An Essay in Intellectual History*. Princeton: Princeton University Press.
Volosinov, V. N. 1973. *Marxism and the Philosophy of Language*. Trans. Ladislav Matejka and I. R. Titunik. New York: Seminar Press.
Wallace, John M. 1974. " 'Examples are Best Precepts': Readers and Meanings in Seventeenth-Century Poetry." *Critical Inquiry* 1:273–90.
——— . 1980. "John Dryden's Plays and the Conception of a Heroic Society." In *Culture and Politics: From Puritanism to the Enlightenment*. Perez Zagorin, ed. Berkeley and Los Angeles: University of California Press.
Ward, Edward. 1698. *A Trip to Jamaica*. London.
——— . 1700. *Journey to Hell*. London.
——— . 1713. *The Hudibrastick Brewer, or a Preposterous Union between Malt and Meter*. London.
——— . 1729. *Durgen: Or, a Plain Satyr Upon A Pompous Satyrist*. London.
——— . 1729. *Apollo's Maggot in his Cups: or, the Whimsical Creation of a Little Satyrical Poet*. London.
Warton, Joseph. 1756. *An Essay on the Writings and Genius of Pope*. Rpt. 1974. New York: Garland Publishers.
Watt, Ian. 1957. *The Rise of the Novel: Studies in Defoe, Richardson and Fielding*. Berkeley and Los Angeles: University of California Press.
Webb, Sidney, and Beatrice Webb. 1922. *English Prisons Under Local Government*. London: Longmans, Green, and Co.
Weinbrot, Howard. 1978. *Augustus Caesar in Augustan England*. Princeton: Princeton University Press.
——— . 1982. *Alexander Pope and the Tradition of Formal Verse Satire*. Princeton: Princeton University Press.
White, Douglas H. 1970. *Pope and the Context of Controversy: The Manipulation of Ideas in* An Essay on Man. Chicago: University of Chicago Press.
Wilding, Michael. 1969. "Allusion and Innuendo in *Mac Flecknoe*." *EC* 19:355–70.
Williams, Aubrey L. 1955. *Pope's* Dunciad: *A Study of Its Meaning*. Rpt. 1968. Hamden, Conn.: Archon Books.

Williams, Joseph M. Forthcoming. " 'O, when degree is shak'd': Sixteenth Century Anticipations of Some Modern Attitudes toward Usage." In *Essays In Historical Sociolinguistics.* Charles T. Scott, ed. Oxford: Oxford University Press.
Wood, Neal. 1983. *The Politics of Locke's Philosophy.* Berkeley and Los Angeles: University of California Press.
Yeats, Francis A. 1964. *Giordano Bruno and the Hermetic Tradition.* Chicago: University of Chicago Press.
Youngren, William. 1968. "Generality, Science and Poetic Language in the Restoration." *ELH* 35:158–87.
———. 1982. "Addison and the Birth of Eighteenth-Century Aesthetics." *Modern Philology* 79:267–83.
Zagorin, Perez. 1971. *The Court and the Country: The Beginnings of the English Revolution.* New York: Atheneum.
Zwicker, Steven N. 1972. *Dryden's Political Poetry: The Typology of King and Nation.* Providence: Brown University Press.

Index

accessory ideas, 39–42, 121
Achilles, 24
Ackerman, Steven, 84 n. 10
action, 1, 3, 4–15, 21–22, 25, 28–30, 33–34, 44, 91, 110, 112, 119, 129–36, 138, 151, 154, 160–61, 188, 193
  eloquence of, 132
Addison, Joseph, 5, 6 n. 8, 39–40, 62–63, 81, 85, 126, 166
advice to a painter poem, 4, 51 n. 18, 65
Aesop, 5
affect, 6, 19–21, 25, 30, 33, 39, 52, 64, 66–68, 82, 95, 136
affiliation, xvii, xx n. 15, 102, 131, 158, 161–62, 164–65, 190, 202
Alcock, Thomas, 107 n. 14
ale, 94, 115, 166, 168–76, 178, 187

allegiance, xv, 75 n. 27, 101, 137
allegory, 1, 4–8, 16, 20–22, 30, 59, 76, 119, 143
ancients and moderns, xv, 27, 40–42, 73, 77, 156 n. 14, 180, 204
anxiety, 11, 27–28, 35, 101, 139, 143, 189
Apollo, 99, 135, 137–38, 142, 169, 180
apothecaries, 11, 25, 29–30, 54, 70, 90, 99–102, 116, 119, 134, 136–43, 145, 147–51, 156, 158–60, 162, 169, 191, 203
Apothecaries Hall, 55
Apothecaries Physicians, 11, 22, 54, 74, 75 n. 27, 101–4, 107–8, 116, 131–32, 135, 137–43, 145 n. 1, 154, 156
Apothecaries, Society of, 11, 22–23, 25, 137, 140, 150, 153
Appleby, Joyce O., 82

application, 30, 36, 40, 66, 95, 148
argument, 3, 5, 7, 20–21, 23, 25, 29–30, 43, 102, 129–30, 142
aristocracy, xvii, 53, 106–7, 115, 180–81, 191, 200, 202
Aristotle, xviii, 5–6, 61, 66, 84, 89 n. 14, 133
Arnold, Matthew, xiv, xix
astrology, 99, 147, 151–54, 188
atheism, 84, 85, 90, 143
atomism, 84 n. 10, 85
Atterbury, Francis (Urim), 130, 134
Austin, J. L., 14
Ayloffe, William, 23 n. 23, 64 n. 13

Babington, Anthony, 52 n. 20, 115 n. 23
Bateman, John (Celcus), 22 n. 22, 150
Battestin, Martin, xvi n. 9, 21 n. 20, 100 n. 4, 127 n. 13, 193
battle, 9–16, 22–23, 27, 33–34, 42, 48, 69, 98, 103, 132, 142, 158
Beckett, J. V., 157 n. 15
Bedlam (Bethlehem Hospital), 37, 56–57, 114 n. 20, 195
Belinda. *See* Fermor, Arabella
benefits, 75, 86, 102, 160–61
Bentley, Richard, 159, 177, 185, 187, 191–92, 197–99, 202, 205
Berkeley, George, 41 n. 8, 81
Bernard, Francis (Horoscope), 55, 60 n. 4, 75 n. 27, 90–91, 99, 102, 104, 106 n. 13, 116, 119, 134, 139, 142, 144–62, 190
Blackmore, Richard, 2, 27, 40, 62, 92, 110, 112, 114–15, 150 n. 9, 174
  Prince Arthur, 4–5, 61
  Satire against Wit, 60 n. 1, 96
Boileau-Despréaux, Nicolas, xi, 4, 9, 16–19, 29, 37, 45–46, 97
Bolingbroke, Lord, 81, 84, 86, 193, 203
Bond, Richmond P., 17 n. 17
Boyce, Benjamin, 164
Boys, Richard C., 97
Brant, Sebastian, 50 n. 18
brass, 38, 56, 120, 185, 193–98, 201–5
Brink, C. O., 198 n. 16
Brower, Reuben A., 164
Brown, Laura, xiii–iv, xv n. 6, 88 n. 13, 108 n. 15
Brown, Tom, 59, 96–97, 167

Bunyan, John, 20 n. 21
burlesque, xviii n. 10, 1, 16–17
Butler, Samuel, 17, 64, 74 n. 26
Byrd, Max, 43 n. 10, 57 n. 29

Cambridge, Richard Owen, xviii, 18–19
Cannon, John, 157 n. 15
Caretta, Vincent, 60 n. 2
caricature, xvi, 129, 134
Case, Doctor, 23, 72
cause, xvi, 7, 16, 84, 87, 90, 92, 94, 97, 133, 147, 166, 172, 175, 196, 198, 202
Celsus. *See* Bateman, John
characters. *See* persons
Charles I, King, 135
Chatman, Seymor, xviii n. 12
Chevy Chase, 6 n. 8, 62
Cheyne, George, 81 n. 4
Cibber, Colley, 3 n. 5, 8, 26, 92, 119–28, 147–48, 170, 172, 177–78, 181, 183, 185, 191–205
  Another Occasional Letter From Mr. Cibber to Mr. Pope, 184
  Apology for the Life of Colley Cibber, 120 n. 1, 122, 192–93
  brazen and brainless brothers, 38, 56, 119–20, 178 n. 18, 195–96
  Letter from Mr. Cibber, to Mr. Pope, 26, 120 n. 1, 122, 193
Cibber, Theophilus, 167 n. 3
circles, 54, 79, 88–94, 116, 138, 142, 172, 195–96, 202, 205
civic duty, xvii, 11–12, 69, 75–76, 82–84, 86, 115, 136–37, 159–62, 203 n. 19
civil war, 10, 28, 119, 132, 135–36, 138, 140, 142–43
class, xii, 12, 54, 72, 93 n. 18, 101 n. 5, 115–16, 128, 143, 153, 156–62, 164–66, 169, 174, 178, 184,
  as kind, 157–62, 166, 186–87, 192, 208
Clifford, James L., xiv n. 5
Cohen, Murray, 21, 39 n. 4
Cohen, Ralph, xiii n. 1, xiv, 2 n. 3, 14, 39 n. 5, 44 N. 14, 89
Colocynthis. *See* Gardiner, Thomas
commerce, 77, 86, 96, 105, 110, 123, 203–4
conservatism, xvii, 72, 80, 82–83
controversy, 12, 35, 63, 97
Cook, Richard I., xix n. 13–14, 10 n. 11

Index

Cooper, Gary, 126–27
correspondence theory, 39–40, 148, 163, 178, 183–84, 208
counterfeit, 35, 92, 102, 107, 121
Courthope, William John, xi, 28, 43, 99, 110, 163
Cover, Robert, 50 n. 16
Cowley, Abraham, 49 n. 15
criticism
   Augustan, xviii, 5, 18, 63, 66, 208
   historical, xii, xiv
   mid-century, xix, 18, 184, 208
   neoclassical, 3–4, 10, 119
   new, xii, xiv n. 4
   nineteenth-century, xix
Culpeper, Nicholas, 141 n. 13
culture, xv, xviii, 19–20, 26, 28, 34, 79, 87, 94, 100, 108, 114, 179–81, 190, 198, 203
Cumberland, Richard, 79, 83, 84
Curll, Edward, 3 n. 5, 43, 176, 205
Curtis, Dennis E., 50 n. 16–17
Cutler, Sir John, 69, 73–77

Damrosch, Leopold, Jr., xv, 146 n. 4
Davis, Lennard J., 9 n. 10, 64 n. 15
de Quincey, Thomas, 67
debate, 24, 132, 134, 139–40, 147
Debus, Allen G., 151 n. 10
Defoe, Daniel, 57 n. 30, 149 n. 8, 167, 178, 195 n. 12
Denham, John, 4, 71–72, 207
Dennis, John, 17–18, 106 n. 13
   Essay upon Publick Spirit, 64
   Reflections on Essay on Criticism, 126
   Remarks on Prince Arthur, 5, 7
   Sir John Edgar, 64–65
depiction, xvi, 29, 36–38, 42, 54, 75, 87, 120, 145, 192
DePorte, Michael V., 57 n. 29
Desaguliers, J. T., 84 n. 10
description, xvi, 1, 3–4, 15, 20–22, 29–30, 35, 37–38, 49, 56, 75, 89, 91, 99, 112, 119, 127, 177
design, 3, 9, 13, 29, 34, 37, 41, 43–44, 61, 67, 72–73, 77, 80, 82, 106, 122, 128, 139–40, 142–43, 147, 166, 173, 176–79, 208
   as intention, xvi, 4–5, 15, 18–19, 66, 98, 101, 156

as structure, xvi, 1, 4, 15, 116
desire, 1, 11, 13, 28, 75, 127, 137, 139, 143, 166, 207
diagnosis, xvi, 72, 79, 87, 102, 111, 116, 128, 143–45, 147, 151, 157, 159–60, 166, 198, 202
Diasenna. *See* Gelsthorp, Peter
disease, 43, 70, 87, 90, 139, 144, 161–62
Dispensary, 9–10, 29, 69, 102–3, 156
Doody, Margaret Anne, xviii n. 11, 2 n. 3, 110 n. 18
double perspective, xix, 52, 53, 54, 70–71, 76, 99, 135
Downie, J. A., 64 n. 15, 97 n. 2
Drennon, Herbert, 80 n. 1
Dryden, John, xi, xiv, 4, 13, 16–20, 27, 37, 39, 42 n. 8, 46, 51, 56, 60, 63–65, 82, 86, 115 n. 22, 124, 160
   "Apology for Heroic Poetry and Poetic License," 16, 19, 29 n. 27
   "Dedication to the Aeneis," 20 n. 19, 61–62
   "Discourse concerning the Original and Progress of Satire," 16–17, 45
   MacFlecknoe, xi, xv, 2, 4, 20, 29, 37, 45, 48–50, 60, 64, 65, 77, 97, 126, 180, 189, 197
   Medal, 121
   "Of Dramatic Poesy," 18
   Palamon and Arcite, 74
   "Parallel of Poetry and Painting," 1
   "To Mr. Lee," 120
Dulness, 7, 8, 13, 16, 21–22, 29, 59, 79, 90, 92–94, 110, 115–16, 166, 169, 177, 179, 185–89, 191–94, 196
dunce, xvi, xix, 13, 22, 26–27, 29–30, 59, 64, 79, 90–91, 93–94, 97, 108–10, 112–16, 119, 126, 145–46, 163–82
Durfey, Tom, 168, 170–72

Eco, Umberto, xx n. 15
economics, 2, 69, 82–83, 86–87, 96, 98, 100–101, 104, 147, 152, 156–61, 181, 184–85, 189, 203–4
Edwards, Thomas R., xiii n. 3, xiv n. 5, 208 n. 2
Ehrenpreis, Irvin, 108 n. 15
Elkin, Peter Kingsley, 59 n. 1
Elliott, Robert C., 59 n. 1

INDEX

Ellis, Frank H., 60 n. 2, 69, 71, 73, 76 n. 29, 103 n. 9, 105 n. 12, 130 n. 1, 131 n. 2, 137, 140 n. 10, 148, 150 n. 9
emblem, xiv, 164
epic, xii, xv, xvii–viii, 1–10, 13, 15–16, 18, 21 n. 20, 22 n. 22, 27, 33–34, 43, 45–46, 50, 61–62, 70, 87, 90, 94, 97, 111 n. 19, 114, 132, 136–37, 140, 180–81, 200
  breakdown, 44–46, 51, 70
Erskine-Hill, Howard, xiv, 60, 73 n. 24, 164, 174 n. 11
Erwin, Daniel Timothy, xvi n. 9
establishment, xvii, 2, 101, 125, 143, 180
Evans, Gareth, 40
example, xvi, 4–8, 21, 119, 199–200
experience, 30, 35, 37, 41–42, 44, 46, 61, 67–68
exposure, 139–40, 147–48, 152, 162, 164, 178, 193

fable, 1–8, 12–13, 15, 18, 20–21, 29–30, 83, 119, 143, 178, 180, 197
Fabricant, Carole, xv n. 6
faction (party), 10, 19, 59, 64, 143, 160–61, 181, 193
familial relations, 82–83, 86
feigned examples, 18, 20, 30
Feinberg, Leonard, 59 n. 1
Fermor, Arabella, 12, 22, 28–29, 67, 101, 194
fiction, xviii, 5, 7–10, 13, 15–30, 56 n. 27, 59, 67, 122–23, 128, 208
Fielding, Henry, 10, 21 n. 20, 174
  Amelia, 83 n. 6
  Jonathan Wild, 86
  Shamela, 122 n. 6
  Tom Jones, 44, 83 n. 6, 132, 136, 139, 181
  Tragedy of Tragedies, 121
  Vernoniad, 29
figural language, xiv, 15–30, 95, 98, 103, 121, 123
figure. *See* persons
figure/ground, xiv–vi, 25, 164, 174, 208
force of an utterance
  illocutionary, 14
  performative, 124
  perlocutionary, 14
  thematic, 14–15
Foucault, Michel, 57 n. 29

Frege, Gottlob, 40 n. 7

Gally, Henry, 122 n. 7, 133 n. 6
games, 9–10, 13, 22, 76, 92, 112
Gardiner, Thomas (Colocynthis), 23–25, 135–37, 141, 143, 161
Garrison, James D., 2 n. 2
Garth, Samuel, M.D., xvi, xix, 4, 7, 8, 10–16, 19, 22–29, 33–34, 40, 47–58, 60, 64–65, 68–77, 82, 89–90, 96–97, 101–9, 114, 125–26, 128, 145–62, 166, 176, 181, 187, 203, 208
  Dispensary, xi, xiii, xvii, xix, 8–12, 15–16, 18, 22–30, 33, 37, 47–58, 60, 62, 64, 68–77, 87, 90–91, 97, 101–9, 111, 113, 123, 145–62, 164, 174, 180, 188, 202, 207
  Harveian Oration, 23, 74–76, 86, 152 n.12
Gay, John, 21, 181
  Beggar's Opera, 54
  Trivia, 21, 86
Gelsthorp, Peter (Diasenna), 137–38, 141
generality, xvi, 5–7, 41, 94–95, 97, 104, 108, 111, 147–48, 154, 157, 165
genre, xi, xiii, xv–viii, 2, 4, 9, 14, 18, 33, 35, 37, 46–47, 60, 61, 65, 67–68, 76, 86–87, 95, 119, 127 n. 13, 180–81, 207
George II, King, 26, 201–2
Gibbons, William, M.D. (Mirmillo), 24, 75 n. 27, 102, 104–6, 108, 116, 138, 142, 148, 150 n. 9, 158–61, 188
Gold, William, (Umbra), 130–31, 161
Goodall, Charles, M.D. (Stentor), 10, 43
Goodman, Nelson, 44, 123 n. 9
Gordon, I. R. F., 114 n. 20
gravitation, 79, 116, 163, 196, 198
  moral, 79–94, 98
great chain of being, 87–88, 101–2, 108, 157, 174
Griffin, Dustin H., xiii n. 3, xiv, 109 n. 16, 122 n. 8
Guilhamet, Leon, 60 n. 2

hacks, 2, 30, 167–68
Hagstrum, Jean, 164
Halliday, M. A. K., 39 n. 6
Harvey, William, M.D., 22 n. 22., 28, 62, 75, 126, 139, 142, 146 n. 8, 147, 150, 161, 207
Hatfield, Glenn, 36 n. 1

Index

hero, 8, 9, 27–28, 97, 161, 191–94, 200–202
heroic, 11, 13, 16, 19, 28, 52, 62, 114, 136–37
Hervey, Lord, 120 n. 2, 200, 205
Hesse, Mary B., 83 n. 7, 84
Hill, Aaron, 165–66
Hill, Christopher, 141 n. 14, 157 n. 15
Hill, George Birkbeck, 149 n. 8
Hirschman, Albert O., 11 n. 12
history, xii, xiv, xvii, 6, 19, 27, 42, 66, 95, 196
Hobbes, Thomas, 83, 85
Hodges, Nathaniel, 149 n. 8
Homer, 9, 61–62, 112–13, 126
   Iliad, 5, 61, 113, 194
   Odyssey, 5, 113, 125
homicide, 11, 23–26, 30, 142
Horoscope. *See* Bernard, Francis
Howe, George (Querpo), 74, 130, 132, 142, 150 n. 9
Hughes, Peter, 44 n. 14
humanism, xii, xiv, 6, 27–28, 157, 173–74, 193
Hume, David, 80, 85
Hutcheson, Francis, 80–81

identification, xvii, 36, 38–39, 42, 50, 55–56, 58, 60–61, 63, 65–67, 124, 134, 184
identify, xvii, 38–39, 55, 58, 65–67, 69, 89, 101–7, 114–16, 127, 180
ideology, xvii, 2, 34, 62, 95, 100–101
imitation, 1, 19, 35
index-learning, 185–90, 192, 196, 198–99
inheritance, xv, 34, 36, 42, 98, 180–81, 189
interest, xvi, xvii, 2, 11–12, 50, 54, 61–62, 69, 96, 98, 103, 111, 128–29, 139, 142–44, 147–48, 151–58, 185, 208
   public, xvii, 75, 80, 83, 96, 98, 127, 137, 207
   self-, xvii, 2, 50, 72, 75, 77, 80–83, 96, 98–99, 122, 127, 137, 144, 147, 155, 161–62, 166, 207
Irving, William Henry, 43 n. 11

Jack, Ian, 36 n. 1
Jackson, James L., 12 n. 15
Jackson, Wallace, xiii n. 2
Jacob, Giles, 171, 176
Jakobson, Roman, 99

James II, King, 10, 145, 149–50
Jenyns, Soame, 101 n. 5
Johnson, Samuel, xix, 6 n. 8, 40, 61, 67, 69, 101 n. 5, 126 n. 11, 141 n. 13, 149 n. 8, 163, 165, 174, 177 n. 15, 179, 185
Jones, Emrys, xiii n. 2, 174 n. 11
journey, 10, 15, 22 n. 22
judgment, xii, xvi, 3–4, 16, 18, 29, 33–34, 36–37, 39–42, 44, 47, 50–51, 54, 57, 62, 66–67, 95, 97, 115–16, 119, 122, 124–25, 127, 134–38, 150, 176, 178–79, 185, 188, 192
Justice, 38, 47, 50–54, 62, 69
   blindfold of, 50–53
justice, 25, 27, 30, 53, 107, 122, 125, 139, 161, 178

Keener, Frederick M., 207 n. 1
Kernan, Alvin B., 59 n. 1
Kinsley, William, 81 n. 5, 84 n. 10
Knoche, Ulrich, 59 n. 1
knowledge, 30, 34, 37–44, 46–47, 49, 51, 61, 67–68, 73, 76–77, 85, 98, 101, 108–9, 115–16, 125, 134, 208
Korshin, Paul J., 59 n. 1, 60 n. 2, 64 n. 14, 84 n. 10
Kramnick, Isaac, 81 n. 5, 86
Krieger, Murray, 12
Kropf, C. R., 64 n. 15

lagniappe, xix
Lakoff, George, 23 n. 23, 100 n. 3
Land, Stephen K., 39, 41 n. 8
language, xvi, 18, 23–24, 34–35, 41, 61, 66, 87, 97, 139, 157, 160
   change, xvi, 34–40, 67
   of controversy, 22, 25–26
   of judgment, 29, 37, 57, 66–67
Laslett, Peter, 157 n. 15
laureate, 205
   counter-, 125
law, xvii, 10, 34, 50, 60–67, 91, 101, 111, 113–14, 124–27, 152, 180, 188, 192, 194
Le Bossu, René, 4–5
Levine, Joseph M., 156 n. 14
libel, 19, 63–64
literal language, 19, 21, 25
literalized metaphor, 21–30, 119
Locke, John, 30, 41, 83, 85, 115

INDEX

London, 34, 43, 47–58, 86, 103, 145, 149
  Barbican, 48–49, 56, 77
  City, xvii, 8, 23, 33–34, 71, 75 n. 27, 76, 92, 110–11, 177
  City Wall, 48, 50
  Covent Garden, 55, 104–6, 137, 142, 160
  Drury Lane, 43, 55, 105, 205
  Fleet Ditch, 29, 43, 92, 94, 112, 114, 116, 140
  Grub Street, 43, 56 n. 27, 115, 121, 170, 205
  Little Brittain, 55, 90, 104
  Moorfields, 43, 172, 177
  Rag-Fair, 43, 55–56
  Smithfield, 29, 90, 104, 106 n. 13, 151–52, 175, 179, 190, 193, 200, 205
  St. Mary's of the Strand, 92, 112, 116
Lovejoy, Arthur, 100
Lucretius, xvii
Lukács, Georg, 3 n. 4, 132 n. 5
Lund, Roger, 174 n. 11

machinery, 3 n. 5, 8, 11, 27, 68, 99, 101
  Discord, 11, 158–59
  Disease, 134,
  Envy, 11, 91, 152, 155, 160–61
  Fortune, 12
  Health, 12
  Sloth, 11, 142, 155
Mack, Maynard, xix, 14, 65 n. 16, 97 n. 2, 127 n. 13, 164, 167 n. 4, 178 n. 18, 179 n. 19, 180, 201
Mandeville, Bernard, 83
map, 37, 44, 98, 115
mark (brand, trademark), 36, 48, 51, 68, 72, 94, 96, 98, 100–101, 104, 114, 123, 140, 143, 148, 166–67, 178–81, 187, 189–90, 192
Marvell, Andrew, 4, 60, 121
Matthews, Leslie G., 149 n. 7
McKeon, Michael, 3 n. 4, 9 n .10, 22 n. 21, 72 n. 22, 157 n. 15, 161 n. 22
McKillop, Alan Dougal, 81 n. 5, 85, 100 n. 4, 108
mechanism, xvi, 79, 81 n. 5, 83, 84, 85, 87–90, 92, 161, 166
medicine, xvi–vii, 9, 23, 26 n. 25, 70, 73, 77, 97, 102–4, 108, 131, 145–46, 149, 151–52, 156

memory, 42, 108–9, 114, 188
metaphor, xiii–iv, 15, 17, 20–30, 67, 119, 184
metonomy, xvi, 12, 43 n. 12, 72, 90, 95, 103, 202
Meyers, Milton L., 82
militarism, 11, 27–28, 136–38, 141–42
Miller, Henry Knight, xiv n. 4
Milton, John, 3 n. 5, 4, 24, 27–29, 126, 132, 141–43, 146, 197
Miner, Earl, 68 n. 18
Mingay, G. E., 157 n. 15
Mirmillo. *See* Gibbons, William, M.D.
mock-heroic, xi, xv, xviii, 4, 8, 16, 18–20, 29, 46, 48–49, 51, 54, 70, 103–4, 121, 135
money, 11, 72, 75, 77, 110–11, 121, 147, 152–56, 160–61, 166, 179, 181, 187, 190, 195, 203–5
Moore, Norman, 145 n. 2, 146–52, 168
moral instruction, xvi, 1, 4–5, 7–8, 30, 61–62
Morris, David B., xiii–iv, 12 n. 15, 57 n. 29, 60, 65 n. 16, 125 n. 10, 176 n. 14
motive, xvii, 1, 82, 87, 92, 96, 116, 122–23, 131, 133, 136–37, 144, 146, 151, 154, 159, 164, 196, 199–200, 203
Motteux, Peter, 17, 20
mountebanks, 54, 57, 72, 102, 105–8, 151–52, 188
Murrin, Michael, 5 n. 7, 30

name-calling, 26, 36, 40, 68
names, 9 n. 9, 26, 35–77, 115, 122–24, 131
  place, 37, 48, 61
  proper, 36, 37, 41–42, 60–66
narrative, xvi, 2–3, 9–10, 20–25, 29–30, 44, 128, 132–34, 142, 188
Neale, R. S., 157 n. 15
Nedham, Marchamont, 84 n. 11
network of relations, xvi, 21, 37, 44, 57, 68, 98, 100, 161, 166, 192, 194, 202
Newton, Isaac, xvi–vii, 79–94, 185
Nicolson, Marjorie, 84 n. 9
Norris, John, 80 n. 1, 84 n. 8
not-far-from topos, 48, 69, 104
novel, xviii, 2, 3, 9
Nussbaum, Felicity, xiv

Index

Old Bailey, 37, 47–58, 69–70, 98, 102, 113–15
Oldham, John, 36, 60, 102 n. 6, 122, 169
origin, xx, 7, 25, 29, 35, 73, 97, 107, 139, 150, 152, 157, 173–75, 179, 188
Osler, William, M.D., 148

panegyric, 2, 62
Parliament, 10, 150 n. 9, 153
particulars, xi–xx, 3–5, 15, 30, 33–34, 37, 41–42, 44, 61, 65–66, 68, 77, 95–99, 103, 106, 108–16, 130, 137, 151, 164–65, 173–74, 178, 186–87, 190
   as specifying properties, 55, 90, 161, 184, 191–93, 195
passion, 5, 11, 24, 50, 155 n. 13
Paulson, Ronald, 3 n. 4, 59 n. 1
Paxton, Peter, 80
periphrasis, 38–40, 44, 47–48, 50, 57, 131
Perkin, Harold, 157 n. 15
person, xvi, 1, 8, 28–30, 37, 44, 55, 59–60, 64, 66–68, 112, 119–20, 122, 132, 134, 151, 161,
   obscurity of, 145–47, 164, 179
   self-defining character, 122, 124, 128–29, 147, 176
   Theophrastan character, 122–23, 129, 133
philosophy, 6, 39, 83, 85
   moral, 80, 82–83, 95
   natural, xvi, 79, 87, 116
physician, 11, 12, 22–25, 57, 62, 65, 70, 87, 102, 104, 116, 126, 130, 136, 142–43, 148–50, 152, 159–60, 162, 174, 181
Physicians, Royal College of, 4, 9–12, 22–25, 26 n. 25, 29, 35, 43, 48, 51, 56, 69, 72–76, 90, 96–99, 101, 103, 111, 116, 126, 137–38, 141–43, 145–50, 157, 161, 180
physico-theology, 81 n. 5, 82, 100
piety, xiii, 11, 48, 73–77, 99, 127
pillory, xiv, xvi–vii, 125, 127, 169, 171, 173, 179, 194
place, 12, 37–38, 42, 44, 48–49, 51, 55, 57, 61, 100, 105–6, 110, 116, 119, 129, 158, 160, 162, 166, 178, 198, 200
   schema of, 100–101, 108
plot, xvi n. 9, 10, 46
Plumb, J. H., 202

poems on affairs of state, 4
poetic justice, 18, 21 n. 20, 46, 139
poetic license, 15–22, 172
poetical relation, xvi, 9, 15–16, 22, 26
poetics, xi–iii, xvii–viii, xx n. 15, 14, 109, 164
   Augustan, 2
   mid-century, xiv–v
   mock-epic, xv, 60, 66, 99
   modernist, xii–iii
point of focus in a field of view, xvi–vii, 12–13, 28, 72, 87–96, 98, 103–16, 128, 202, 204
   attraction/repulsion, 87, 90–93, 116
   circulation, 93, 110, 116, 190, 195, 204–5
   expansion/spread, 54, 79, 88–92, 94, 116, 134, 204
polemic, 7, 15, 34
politics, xvii, 22, 27, 60, 62–63, 69, 72, 81 n. 5, 83, 86, 97, 100–101, 105–16, 128, 146, 150, 164, 188, 200–202
Pollak, Ellen, xv n. 6
Pope, Alexander, xi, xiii–v, xviii–ix, 1, 3, 8–9, 12–15, 17, 19, 25–29, 34, 60, 62, 67, 73, 79, 82, 93, 100, 146, 148, 163–205, 207
   Correspondence, 63 n. 11, 64, 65 n. 16, 119, 125, 188 n. 2
   Dunciad, xi, xiii, xv, xvii–ix, 3, 7–9, 13, 15–16, 18, 22, 26–30, 33, 36–37, 40, 43, 46, 55–57, 61, 63 n. 11, 67–68, 79, 87–88, 90, 92–94, 97, 108–16, 123–26, 128, 144, 163–205
   Dunciad in Four Books, 56, 65, 72, 84, 91–92, 97, 133, 191–92, 194, 196–98, 200–201, 204
   Dunciad Variorum, 56, 64–65, 76, 79, 91–92, 133, 170–71, 175, 177, 196–98, 203–4
   Epigrams from the Grub Street Journal, 188 n. 3
   Epilogue to the Satires, 59, 63, 125
   Epistle to Dr. Arbuthnot, 26, 63 n. 11, 65 n. 16, 126, 166, 198
   Essay on Criticism, 61, 126–27
   Essay on Man, 87–88, 90, 95, 116, 198 n. 14
   Imitations of Horace, 65
   New Dunciad, xvii, 59, 79, 91, 119–20, 133, 193, 196, 198

Odyssey, xviii n. 10, 17
Pastorals, 94
Peri Bathous, 167–68, 170–71, 177–78
Rape of the Lock, xi, xiii, xviii–ix, 8–9, 12–13, 18, 22, 28–30, 43, 62, 67–68, 133, 144, 180, 194
Temple of Fame, 89
Variorum notes and apparatus, 36–37, 61, 65, 68, 109, 128, 163, 170–71, 177, 196
Port-Royal masters, 39
portrait, 3 n. 5, 92, 109, 116, 119–205
    gallery, xvi, 125, 127, 162, 164, 166, 177, 190
Pound, Ezra, 115
precept, 3, 4–8, 59, 95, 199–200
Price, Martin, 36 n. 1
prisons
    Bridewell, 92, 112–115
    Fleet, 51, 113
    Newgate, 51, 54, 113
    Ludgate, 51, 113
profession, xvii, 101–2, 106–7, 135, 159–61, 164, 166, 190
progress, 12–13, 22–23, 73, 92, 110–11, 119, 203
propaganda, xiii, xv–vi, 12, 34–35, 57, 64, 69, 191
punishment, xvi, 4, 12–13, 25, 35–36, 43, 52, 60, 62, 67–68, 146, 162, 175, 177, 179, 194
Putnam, Hilary, 123 n. 9

quacks, 22–23, 30, 76, 93, 101–2, 106, 148 n. 6, 169, 190
Queen Anne, 27, 103 n. 8
Queen Caroline, 201
Querpo. *See* Howe, George
Quinlan, Maurice J., 29

Rapin, René, 133
reference, 21, 25, 30, 36, 39, 42, 49, 53–54, 57, 96–101, 103, 108, 111–13, 115, 123, 130–31, 204
referent, 18, 20, 50–51, 55, 123, 208
Renaissance, xvi, 5, 6, 18
representation, xii, xix, 15, 18, 29, 62, 67, 90, 95, 103, 121, 123, 178
    accuracy of, 16, 19, 147–48, 164, 169
    by class, 157–62, 165, 184, 186–87, 192
    forms of, xii, xvi, 6, 8, 18, 115, 157–58, 184
    object of. *See* referent
reputation, 61–65
Resnik, Judith, 50 n. 16–17
rhetoric, 16–19
Richardson, Samuel, 122
Richetti, John J., 9 n. 10, 39 n. 3
Rogers, Pat, xiv, 43, 48, 49 n. 15, 52 n. 21, 56 n. 27–28, 93, 99, 110, 112, 115 n. 23, 164, 178 n. 17
Rothstein, Eric, xviii n. 10, 43 n. 12, 68 n. 18
Rousseau, G. S., 84 n. 9
Russo, John Paul, 122 n. 8

Saint Bartholomew's Hospital, 104, 147–50, 152
Salmon, William, 156
Satan, 102, 132 n. 4, 142–43, 147, 153, 157, 207
satire, xi, xvi–ix, 2, 4, 7, 9, 13, 17, 19, 28–29, 36, 41, 49, 52, 59, 60, 62–64, 87, 103, 120, 122–24, 127, 162–63, 166, 171, 179, 201–2
    general, 66, 124
    particular, xvi, 18, 59, 60–61, 64–67, 143, 161, 167, 169
Schneider, Duane B., 151 n. 10
science, 34–35, 38–39, 70, 73, 77, 80, 84, 87–89, 95, 98–99, 108, 126, 138, 142, 151–52, 185
Scriblerus, 7, 8, 16, 166, 176–77, 185, 196
Seidel, Michael, 2 n. 2, 97 n. 1, 197 n. 13
semiotics, xii, xv–vi, 19, 38, 100, 121
Sena, John F., xix n. 14, 27 n. 26, 60 n. 3, 103 n. 8–9, 151 n. 10, 152 n. 12
senses, 24–25, 39
setting, xvii, 4, 37–38, 42, 44, 47–58, 68–77, 90, 98–99, 105, 109–10, 112, 116
Shadwell, Thomas, 29
Shaftesbury, 83, 155, 157
Shankman, Steven, xiii n. 3
Shelley, Percy Bysshe, 61
Sherburn, George, 177 n. 16
Sidney, Sir Philip, 6
Siebert, Donald T., Jr., xiii n. 2
signpost, 76, 120–28, 163, 172–73, 176, 178, 183, 205
Simmonds, Andrew, 50 n. 17, 51 n. 18
Sitter, John E., xviii, 2 n. 1, 3 n. 5, 27, 91 n. 16, 164

Index

Smith, Adam, 158 n. 16
social
  change, 34–37, 79, 142, 185, 207
  domination, xvii, 135, 139
  obligation, 79–94
  order, xvi, xvii, 12–13, 22, 28, 33–34, 38, 80–81, 83–84, 86, 88, 90, 100, 107, 115, 127, 135–37, 143, 157–62, 180
  theory, early modern, 11, 72, 80, 82–83, 122, 127, 143, 147, 155
Spacks, Patricia Meyer, xiii n. 3, 57 n. 29
Spence, Joseph, 166
Spenser, Edmund, 20–21
Spitzer, Leo, 100 n. 4
state, affairs of, xvi, 1–2, 27, 29, 33–34, 47–58, 61–63, 76–77, 105, 107–8, 132, 147, 180, 197, 207
Steeves, Edna Leake, 167 n. 4, 177 n. 15
Stentor. *See* Goodall, Charles
Sterne, Laurence, 10
Stone, Lawrence, 157 n. 15
succession, 2, 97, 183–205
suspension of belief/judgment, 47, 49, 51, 54–55, 70
Sutherland, George, 109, 163, 171 n. 9, 177 n. 15, 201
Swedenberg, H. T., 62 n. 8
Swift, Jonathan, 42, 55, 59, 64, 167, 174, 181, 186–87
  Battle of the Books, xi, xvii, 28–29, 97, 180
  City Shower, 86
  Political Tracts, 1713–1719, 63
  Tale of a Tub, 29, 109, 186, 197

talent, 158–60, 173, 180–81, 185, 189, 202–3
Tanner, Tony, 174 n. 11
Tassoni, xi, 9, 16–17, 45, 49
Tate, Nahum, 51 n. 18
taxonomy, xvi, 38, 116, 163–82, 184
Taylor, John, 167, 171
Theobald, Lewis, 8, 18, 63 n. 11, 92–93, 119, 126, 168, 172, 174, 181, 183–200, 203
Thompson, Charles, 152 n. 12, 159 n. 19
Thompson, E. P., 53 n. 23
Thomson, James, 38, 80–83, 89
Thornbury, George Walter, 74 n. 25
Tillotson, Geoffrey, 38, 43, 99, 103, 104
Tolstoy, Leo, 27

topography, 43, 69, 71, 98–99, 104, 109–10, 112, 130–31, 172, 195
trade, xvii, 111, 142, 156, 161, 173, 180–82, 188, 205
Trapp, Joseph, 33
tropes. *See* figural language
Troyer, Howard William, 167, 171 n. 8
truth, 16, 19, 21, 25–26, 29–30, 34, 36, 39–42, 44, 57–58, 61, 66–69, 76, 96, 123–25, 137–38, 207–8
Turner, Mark, 23 n. 23, 100 n. 3

Umbra. *See* Gold, William
Urim. *See* Atterbury, Francis

Vagellius. *See* Williams, William
values, xii–iii, xv, 6, 15, 25–26, 37, 40–46, 48, 51–52, 54, 57–58, 68, 72, 76, 85, 90, 96, 99–100, 104, 109–11, 114, 134–36, 138–40, 142, 155, 180, 203, 208
victim, xvi, 18, 26–27, 46, 60, 61, 63, 65, 82, 96, 115, 122, 133, 163–64, 184
Viner, Jacob, 100 n. 4
violence, 10–11, 13–15, 22–25, 28, 64, 99, 119, 137–38, 142–43, 160
Virgil, 4, 11, 17, 20, 40–41, 49, 74, 106, 111 n. 19, 125–26, 139, 142, 197, 207
Volosinov, V. N., 39 n. 6

Wallace, John M., 6–7, 30, 160
Waller, Edmund, 60
Walpole, Robert, 29, 177, 181, 185, 193, 194 n. 9–10, 201–3, 205
Warburton, William, 56 n. 28, 184
Ward, Edward, 163–82, 188
  Apollo's Maggot in his Cups, 171 n. 8, 172, 177
  Durgen, 168–72
  Hudibrastick Brewer, 167, 169
  Journey to Hell, 169
  London Spy, 174, 207
  "Poet's Ramble after Riches," 175 n. 13
  Trip to Jamaica, 167–68, 174–75
Ward, John, 176
warfare, 10–12, 23, 25, 27–29, 62
Warton, Joseph, xviii, 179 n. 19
Watt, Ian, 3 n. 4, 9 n. 10
Webb, Sidney and Beatrice, 114
Weinbrot, Howard, xv n. 7, 64 n. 11, 65 n. 16, 166 n. 1, 201 n. 18, 205 n. 20

228 INDEX

White, Douglas H., xiii n. 3, 81 n. 5
wholes/larger views, xiii, 15, 21, 37, 41, 43–44, 46–58, 68–77, 103, 116, 123, 138–39, 207
William, King, 27, 103 n. 8, 135–36, 142, 150
Williams, Aubrey L., 14–15, 42–43, 68 n. 18, 100 n. 4, 109, 112, 127 n. 13, 164, 173, 184
Williams, Joseph M., 36 n. 1
Williams, William (Vagellius), 130, 150 n. 9
Wilmont, John, Lord Rochester, 35, 106–7

wits, xvii, 97
words, 28–29, 36–37, 39–40, 42, 53, 132, 138, 180, 193
world-upside-down topos, 106, 135–38
Wycherley, William, 122 n. 5

Yeats, Francis A., 151 n. 10
Youngren, William, 6, 42 n. 9

Zagorin, Perez, 157 n. 15
Zwicker, Steven N., 64 n. 14

www.ingramcontent.com/pod-product-compliance
Lightning Source LLC
Chambersburg PA
CBHW032128010526
44111CB00033B/222